AFRICAN LABOR HISTORY

VOLUME 2

SAGE SERIES ON AFRICAN MODERNIZATION AND DEVELOPMENT

African Labor History

PETER C.W. GUTKIND,
ROBIN COHEN, and
JEAN COPANS
Editors

 SAGE PUBLICATIONS   Beverly Hills / London

For information address:

SAGE PUBLICATIONS, INC.
275 South Beverly Drive
Beverly Hills, California 90212

SAGE PUBLICATIONS LTD
28 Banner Street
London ECIY 8QE

Printed in the United States of America

Library of Congress Cataloging in Publication Data
Main entry under title:

African labor history.

(Sage series on African modernization and development; v. 2)
1. Labor and laboring classes- -Africa- -Addresses, essays, lectures.
I. Gutkind, Peter Claus Wolfgang. II. Cohen, Robin. III. Copans, Jean. IV. Series. HD8774.A36 331'.096 78-6635
ISBN 0-8039-1063-0
ISBN 0-8039-1064-9 pbk.

FIRST PRINTING

CONTENTS

INTRODUCTION

ROBIN COHEN
University of the West Indies

JEAN COPANS
Ecole des Hautes Etudes en Sciences Sociales

PETER C. W. GUTKIND
McGill University

AFRICAN LABOR AND COLONIAL CAPITALISM

"These people must submit to new laws of which the most imperious, as well as the most salutary, is assuredly the law of labor." Thus directed King Leopold of Belgium to his district commissioners in the Upper Congo on June 16, 1897 (Louis and Stengers, 1968:16). The horrifying depredations of the Belgians in the Congo in their pursuit of wild rubber and ivory was but one notorious case of the operations of colonial policy in Africa. All over the continent, the general laws of capitalist development were set in motion by the colonial powers. By this we do not mean simply that merchants and traders from Europe had reached the shores of Africa and begun an exchange of goods (for this process had been going on for centuries). Rather, with Maurice Dobb (Dobb, 1963:17) we look for the opening of the capitalist period when changes in the mode of production occurred—in particular when labor was directly subordinated to the particular modes of capitalist production. The precondition for this process was that the means of production—in Africa principally land—had to be stripped from the ownership and control of the husbandman, farmer, pastoralist, hunter, and gatherer. No longer were the fruits of the soil and the products of the forest to be theirs to dispose of as they saw fit.

7

King Leopold had decreed otherwise. By a stroke of the pen, the whole land surface of the Congo, with minor exceptions, was declared "ownerless" and "vacant," the property of the "Congo Free State." From 1891 to 1892 the Congolese, again with some small exceptions, were not permitted to collect economically exploitable primary products or to trade with European merchants. Instead, as E.D. Morel (Louis and Stengers, 1968:44) wrote: ". . . .

> The aboriginal citizens of this strange creation [the Congo State] were by law called upon to provide recruits for the army, workmen for the construction of important public works, transport of stores, building up of houses and prisons, cutting and maintenance of roads and bridges, up-keep of plantations and creation and repairs of resthouses. . . . They were compelled to labour, *with no legal limitation either in regard to time or quantity*, in the collection, coagulation and and transport of india-rubber for the profit of their governors.

At least three objections may be made to this description of the modus operandi of colonial capitalism. First, was not the Congo State a grotesque perversion of colonialism even by the standards of that notorious carve-up, the Berlin Agreement? Certainly, the Belgians were condemned by significant sections of European colonial, missionary, commercial, and paliamentary opinion (Cookey, 1968). Second, is it not the case that labor power was expropriated and surplus value accumulated even within domestic social formations? Who was it who serviced, built, and maintained the great states of the Western Sudan, the ancient Kingdom of the Kongo, and the monumental stone fortresses of Zimbabwe—now celebrated by the new Africanist historiography? Even within smaller scale, and more autarchic formations, did not descent groups take over the expropriating functions of social classes? Third, and most importantly, is it not the case that in most parts of Africa precapitalist modes of production, if not left undisturbed, were not rent asunder with the degree of finality, viciousness, and brutality witnessed in the Congo Free State?

Such objections to a totalizing demonology of colonial capitalism are both serious and, to a degree, valid; but they do not rebut the overall point that with the coming of the colonial powers, new relations of production, capitalist relations, were introduced on a hitherto unknown scale. More and more Africans were wrenched from their previous modes of production and reproduction and constrained to place their labor power at the disposal of alien forces of production. Yes, there were periodic bursts of outrage in Europe at the degree of compulsion that was deployed to secure this labor power, but Morel and his powerful supporters in the Congo Reform Movement,who included John Holt, the famous West African merchant and leading figure in the Liverpool Chamber of Commerce, were not by any means opposing capitalist penetration of the African continent. Rather, they represented a more progressive fraction of capital that wished to destroy trading monopolies and domaines privés much as an earlier generation of progressive capitalists had upheld "legitimate trade" as against the slave trade. "Commerce, blessed commerce," as Holt once wrote to Morel, "is the peacemaker, the establishment of the freedom and the rights of man" (Louis and Stengers, 1968:212). The protests directed against the Belgian administration, though sincerely motivated by humanitarian considerations, must therefore also be considered in light of intracapitalist competition and the involvement of other "national" capitals. British, French, and American capital owned a quarter of the shares in the Belgian companies, while the shipping line, Elder Dempster, Morel's former employer, transported the "red rubber" of the Congo to European capitals.

LABOR POLICIES: FRANCE, PORTUGAL, BRITAIN

The fact that colonial capitalism shared certain common features, whatever its national origins, can be seen in the labor policies of the European powers, who all made widespread use of forced labor. In Oubangi-Chari (French Equatorial Africa) the Belgian system was applied with rigor and enthusiasm and in complete disregard of liberal French colonial and capitalist opinion. The area was divided between concessionaires who claimed ownership of all products in their areas. African producers were thus not trading, but rather, according to the new legality, they were being paid wages by the companies. That these "wages" were often in tokens, redeemable only in the company stores, should not perhaps surprise us (Coquery-Vidrovitch, 1972). Even in the more beneficent areas of French control in West Africa, prestation, a labor tax which allowed the administration to compel all adult males to work for a number of days each year, was not abolished until 1946 (Davies, 1966:33-35). Though formally the term of required labor was short (eight to twelve days in French West Africa) and had been progressively reduced to this period, the regulations were more widely honored in their breach than in their observance. Moreover, as Echenberg convincingly argues in this volume, the French colonial armies acted not only in conventional terms, but also as reservoirs of cheap and disciplined wage labor:

> [S]oldiers in colonial French West Africa . . . constituted perhaps the largest single group of men in state employ in the entire French empire in Africa . . . . French colonialism often engaged African soldiers in a series of construction tasks such as the building of posts, barracks, and other infrastructure and in various labor tasks

required to maintain an occupation army of roughly 10,000 men posted permanently in the Colony . . . . After the [First World] War several thousand Africans were conscripted into the detested conscript labor brigades of the so-called "second portion" of the annual military draft. These units were turned over to private contractors for three-year stints under atrocious conditions on such projects as the Markala dam . . . or as maintenance laborers on the Dakar-Niger railway.

As Echenberg shows, it was not without coincidence that the "Tragedy at Thiaroye" befell soldiers who were at one and the same time workers in the uniform of France.

Let us turn next to the "overseas provinces" of Portugal which, so Salazar boasted, were to last for eternity. As was clearly established by successive observers and campaigners from H.W. Nevison (1906), William A. Cadbury (1910), Sir John Harris (1913), Edward Alsworth Ross (1925), to Basil Davidson (1955), where the Portuguese did not practice outright slavery (as in Principe and São Thomé), they used forced labor on an immense scale right until the nadir of their empire (Davidson, 1955: chapters 18-21). In the 1950s an estimated half-million contratados provided cheap forced labor for Portuguese administrators, traders, and farmers in Angola alone (Marcum, 1969:7). As late as 1961 a British team reported conscripts serving up to 18 months with women and children from eight years up being put to work on roads, mines, and coffee plantations (Marcum, 1969:7). We can but mention the Germans in Southwest Africa, and the plantation slavery of Fernando Po, first carried out by the Spanish and presently under the direction of an indigenous proprietor.

Finally, lest it be thought that the British escaped the laws of capitalist development in the periphery, it is evident that, like the other colonialists, the British also were able practitioners of the art of compelling labor to work without pay. A recent study has drawn our attention to the practice of forced labor in the Northern Territories of the Gold Coast (Thomas, 1973), but contemporaries have shown that the practice was widespread in British Africa (Buell, 1928:657; Orde Browne, 1933:37). In his contribution to this book Mason is concerned with how in Northern Nigeria the principle of a free labor supply (encouraged in the south) was abandoned in the face of labor scarcity for the building of that great colonial fetish, the railway:

Instead of creating the conditions for a free labor market, [Northern colonial officials] developed a system of forced labor which they disguised with the term "political labor." As the name implies, workers on the railway line were to be pressed into service by political means, that is, through the combined intervention of the European officials and the indigenous chiefs, the masters and the prefects joining together against what, in other colonial contexts, would have been regarded as the "boys."

PRECOLONIAL AFRICA

Let us turn now to the contrast between colonial and precolonial forms of exploitation. First appearances notwithstanding, our discussion of the incidence of compulsory labor is not designed primarily to provide a moral indictment of colonialism, because this has been done by many more ardent and practiced critics before us. What is more pertinent to the development of our subject matter—African labor history—is that we are successful in demonstrating that the spread of capitalism, even to a peripheral zone, detaches man from his product, from his habitual environment, and from his right to dispose of his labor power and his agricultural goods in his own right. It is in the scale and intensity of this dislocation and decomposition of domestic modes of production, distribution, and exchange that the colonial presence manifests itself. Only the most romantic of African nationalists would now seek to wrap the precolonial period in garments more suited to the Garden of Eden. Slaves were owned, raided, and traded before the establishment of formal colonial rule. According to Georges Balandier, modern studies have shown that in the Kingdom of the Kongo during the 16th to 18th centuries there was "a massive predominance of villagers of slave status in certain regions: this was the result of a gradual accumulation by an aristocracy which originally possessed only the advantage of freedom" (Balandier, 1968:11, Meillassoux, 1975). Favored categories of certain anthropologists such as kin groups, age groups, and lineage groups were often little more than masks serving to conceal from observed and dispossessed alike relations of dominance and disability, of, in short, the expropriation of surplus value through "class-like" social institutions (Meillassoux, 1977). The recent work of French economic anthropologists has done much to demystify these hitherto obscure social relationships. No doubt any complete labor history of Africa would need to include work on the precolonial period and perhaps to demonstrate the continuities and overlaps in the structuring of the relationships of superordination and subordination in the pre- and post-European conquest periods. As Dobb (1963:11) argues:

> Important elements of each new society, although not necessarily the complete embryo of it, are contained within the womb of the old; and relics of the old society survive for long into the new .... [but] there are crucial points in economic development at which the *tempo* is abnormally accelerated, and at which continuity is broken, in the sense of a sharp change of direction in the current of events.

That the establishment of colonial administrations on the ground propelled such a change in direction is our rationale for limiting our collection of materials to the colonial and postcolonial periods.

DOMINANT AND MIXED MODES OF PRODUCTION

We must now consider the final objection that was raised earlier—namely the survival of precapitalist modes of production, albeit in modified form, into the colonial-capitalist era. Dobb's view, usually so certain a guide in the case of metropolitan capitalism, that these can be considered as "relics" is far from satisfying. In the case of peripheral capitalism the dominance of the capitalist mode is usually established only at the point of distribution and at the point of industrial production. Agricultural production, though destined for the world capitalist market, often is conducted within the relations of production characteristic of an earlier period, while the "whole process of reproduction" (to use Marx's phrase) is normally left outside the capitalist mode of production. Adverbs such as "usually" and "normally" can themselves serve to mystify social precesses that often produce quite varied outcomes. With respect to African labor, three possibilities may be typified.

(1) The capitalist mode of production is dominant and, within the mode, a full time permanent urban proletariat is generated. Though in African countries this element is often only a small fraction of the population, it increases in widening circles as the administrative, commercial, and manufacturing sectors themselves expand.

(2) In the case of agriculture, capitalist control of the marketing and distribution of produce gives way to direct intervention in the quality of the product. Under colonial-capitalism this takes the form of introducing pest control stations, creating agricultural extension departments, subsidizing the sale of such items as fungicides, pesticides, and seeds. Direct intervention in the relations of production, notably the creation of a plantation system, is much less in evidence in Africa than in Latin America or the Caribbean; but insofar as direct intervention occurs, a rural proletariat is brought into being.

(3) Two modes of production, the capitalist and what for the moment can be called "the domestic," are coupled together in a mixed but asymmetrical form (Rey, 1976; Meillassoux, 1975a). In this case migrant labor represents the principal means of exchange between the two modes.

In this book each of the three possible outcomes is reflected by our contributors. The gradual creation of a stabilized urban proletariat is, for example, carefully charted by Hughes and Cohen in the case of pre-World War II Lagos. They deal with three aspects of class formation among workers—the nature of economic organization, the extent of industrial action, and the character of their political representation and association. By looking in some detail at Lagos in the early decades of this century, they have identified a working class not only in "quantifiable occupational terms," but they have also "sought to give flesh to the statistician's categories and to argue that the first hesitant steps along the long and tortuous path to class identity were taking place." Stichter is also preoccupied with how in Kenya "a peripheral capitalist economy based on parttime migrant labor began to evolve into one based on full time wage labor. Increasingly dependent on wages, drawn into the modern capitalist economy, but kept on the lower levels within it, the gradually forming African working class created a militant and nationalist labor movement." Militant interracial trade union organizations dominated the Kenyan political scene from the end of World War II to the Mau-Mau rebellion. The end of this "singular period" came with one faction of the labor movement being coopted by the increasingly sophisticated paternalism of the colonial government, and the other faction being actively involved in the Mau-Mau rebellion. The end of World War II was also a decisive period in the labor history of French West Africa, where a massive railway strike erupted. All four railway networks were involved, but the strike was centralized in Dakar where our author, Suret-Canale, was a close observer of the events he describes. His analysis clearly shows the organizational skills of the railway workers, their intense commitment to the objectives of the strike and their ability to sustain their struggle. Suret-Canale's contribution is the first serious attempt to look at this important event, which has certainly not received the attention warranted (other than by the novelist Ousmane, 1962).

The achievement of a degree of class and political consciousness by urban workers was inherent in their location in the principal African cities—the same milieu in which intellectuals and bourgeois elements created nationalist movements and looked to the urban mass as suitable supporters or voting fodder. It is perhaps more remarkable that in the one case of a wholly rural proletariat included in this volume, very high levels of political consciousness were also manifested. Using a case study of the Mazinde plantation in Tanganyika, Bolton shown how workers protested over many aspects of their working conditions. The interplay between workers in the sisal plantations on the one hand and employers, government, politicians, and union leaders on the other leads Bolton to the conclusion that ultimately the workers were on their own. When trade unionism on the plantations threatened not only the employers, but the nationalist leadership as well, the union leaders were isolated and frustrated. This cooperation in the 1950s between employers and politicians to isolate militant unionists and workers is interpreted by Bolton to presignify the limited and partial forms of socialism that postcolonial Tanzania has been able to effect.

The third possible outcome of the articulation of modes of production indicated earlier is the mixed mode, with the capitalist mode predominating. Here exchange between the modes, domestic and capitalist, is expressed primarily through part time, temporary, seasonal contract or migrant labor. Within the domestic mode the future labor power for the capitalist is biologically produced, nurtured, nourished, and educated—anticipatory socialization is so complete in the case of some Southern African peoples that manhood rituals, which previously comprised hunting an animal, now constitute working a contract in the dirty, degrading, and dangerous gold mines of the Witwatersrand reef. Some of the most powerful recent works on Southern African labor history have probed the full dimensions of superexploitation at the point of production combined with dependent, crippled, yet essential modes of production (Gordon, 1977; Johnstone, 1976; van Onselen, 1976; Perrings, 1977; *Review of African Political Economy,* 1976; Wilson, 1972; Wolpe, 1972).

The importance of the Southern African region in coupling together the most advanced forms of capitalist management and production is reflected in this collection in two contributions. Davies is concerned with the dramatic 1922 strike and armed uprising by *white* mine employees on the Witwatersrand. In a book on African labor history a concern with white employees may seem rather partial, though in fact the effects of the strike were to have dramatic repercussions on the whole character of white-black relations in the mining industry and in the wider social formation. The strike was broken with considerable force by the South African state, but in its final resolution the basis for an alliance between a racist, bureaucraticized, white labor movement and the state apparatus was laid, an alliance which has rebounded mercilessly on black labor. Our second Southern African contribution concerns a small mining town, Selebi Pikwe, in Botswana. Once again the most advanced fractions of capital are represented—this time in the form of a multinational nickel mining company (predominantly subscribed by American and South African capital) ranged with a state bureaucracy against Botswana mineworkers. As Cooper shows, an unsympathetic management combined with a predatory political class intent on building its own class interest through agriculture led to an explosive situation. Expatriate officials were beaten up, a white-dominated school was attacked, while 600 of the mines' 2,500 workers were instantly dismissed.

Though there have been strikes of greater economic significance conducted with greater violence in even more repressive states, the Botswana case study does illustrate what is increasingly evident as a general phenomenon in postcolonial Africa, namely the collapse of the political credibility of the postcolonial leadership in the face of mass demands. This is clearly illustrated in the careful and informed analysis of the class structure in Madagascar that Althabe, a direct witness, contributes. His account of the fusion and alliance between students, urban intellectuals, and fractions of the working class and sub-proletariat, provides a fascinating portent of the shape of postcolonial social conflict in Africa.

LABOR PROTEST AND POLITICAL AND CLASS CONSCIOUSNESS

Although all the papers are set in historically specific events, some of the larger issues will need further treatment. Specifically, these concern the reality of the existence of an African working class and its class identity and consciousness. While the editors have not included a specifically theoretical paper, each contributor had added to the debate by means of demonstrating how African workers have responded to their work situation, to deprivation and exploitation, and to the political authority of the colonial or neocolonial state. While the period covered by the contributors is indeed short in historical terms, Lagos in 1897 to events in Botswana in 1975, the evidence presented leaves little doubt that African workers, as workers, have a history of protest and strike action.

There are a number of ways of conceptualizing and analysing this history of protest. We could simply assert that colonialism and neocolonialism create an exploited proletariat, that such a class has its distinctive consciousness, and it protests the disadvantages of its economic and political subordination; or we can present the historical data, the explication of processes and their consequences, showing how, by stages and sometimes by leaps, distinct classes have come into being. It is this latter approach which most of the contributors have taken. From the data they set out, it is clear that strike action is deeply embedded in the uneven penetration of what has come to be known as peripheral capitalism and under-development; and that Africa's labor history must be seen in the context of regional and local forces which in turn are part of the uneven and selective incorporation of the continent into a world system of capitalism. It is because of this that labor protest has been difficult to conceptualize in terms of a single strand of its organization and expression. This accounts for the wide variety, scope, objectives, and meaning of strike action and protest by workers ranging from constitutional actions to achieve minimal reforms to revolutionary pressures, and from repeated efforts supported by a growing consciousness and coherence of class to prolonged periods of quiescence and less formal protest and resistance described by Cohen (1976) and van Onselen (1976). When forms of protest ranging from the adoption of religious beliefs to industrial sabotage and theft are taken into account, we can more easily explain the historically specific nature of political and class consciousness. Yet all the contributors are likely to support the view that where there are capitalists, expatriate or local, there are workers whose relations to the labor process acts as the driving force of their class position and their consciousness. It is thus the structural context which is all important and not exclusively the most obvious manifestations of labor protest and strikes.

The chapters in this volume do not suggest that an African working class has taken power over society, or even that we can invariably point to forces which will inexorably lead in that direction. What is clear, however, is that labor protest does point to the rise of a working class consciousness, both economic and political, "free from the mist of nationalism" (Braundi and Lettieri, 1964:598) and, one would hope, of narrow ethnic encapsulation. However, a trap is there which can create "heroic myths, or equally heroic oversimplifications, both of which the working class is quite capable of producing for itself without the aid of specialists" (Waterman, 1976:336). Clearly what is needed is a great deal more research on precolonial and colonial African economic and political history (one might test the proposition that the "true" history of colonial Africa is the history of labor), and the structure and objectives of the present neocolonial state. We need to analyse more precisely the relationship between the labor process and the selective incorporation and imposition of the African continent into the capitalist modes of production. Yet even at this early stage of documentation, the case studies presented show how wage workers have and do respond to their predicaments and that the processes of proletarianization have roots and are in full force at present. Thus Adrian Peace (1975:300) has observed (regarding Lagos workers) that:

> the wage earning class is continually involved in developing and refining those organizations which reflect a growing class consciousness determined by their consistently subordinate relationship to the industrial mode of production. [Class-based acts are] not to be seen as an isolated experience under exceptional circumstances ... more importantly [they are to be treated as] overt manifestations of ongoing socio-political processes.

We must also observe that the processes of class formation have followed different patterns and sequences in Africa than in Europe and North America. Hence we can expect different manifestations of consciousness. However, the problem is not whether a working class exists, but its size; not its internal divisions (be they ethnic, linguistic, religious, or cultural), but its homogeneity when called upon to express itself. Labor protest, the case studies reveal, is more than a consciousness of class and the ideology which informs it. As many of the authors make clear, labor protest is a reflection of conditions of life and work, and of the place of producers vis-à-vis managers and owners. It is easy to assert, and probably correct, that African workers are alienated from and by the economic and political environment in which they are trapped; yet it is remarkable how little we know about the daily life of Africa's wage workers, particularly those at the lower levels. Many Africanists, influenced strongly by past anthropological studies, subscribe to the conventional wisdom that exploitation is mediated by the embrace of kin and ethnic groups.

When labor protest occurs, as all the papers in this volume clearly indicate, it is revealed that workers not only perceive the extent of injustices, but they also have the courage and skill to organize themselves—and occasionally reject the authority of their leaders. Surely we must agree that there can be no effective labor action without a considerable sense of class consciousness. All the papers make this clear, although the contribution by Suret-Canale presents us with the most explicit example. This then indicates again that the issue is not whether an African working class exists, although editors and authors have little doubt, but rather what matters (particularly at this juncture of class formation and action in Africa) is what workers do (including ludditism) and, perhaps as much, what they do not(yet) do.

What most of the papers appear to indicate, even though we may legitimately speak of proletarianization as an ongoing process, is that the manifestation of political and class consciousness is often situational rather than an expression of the class struggle. Thus, the papers indicate that whatever the form of labor protest, reformism and populism seem at present to be more established than concerted and sustaining action to overthrow a particular regime. We should not speculate why this is so, but we can suggest that class consciousness and action are related to the specifics of the capitalist mode of production, how specific fractions are socially, politically, and economically related to this mode, the strength of unionization, the impact of foreign investment, and the legacy of particular colonial policies, be they relevant to housing or to the availability of credit. Once we know more about these matters, we shall better be able to understand what informs the ideas and actions of African workers.

The contributors may at times suggest that the African workers were drawn into wage labor relatively recently, at least in any significant numbers. Late 19th and early 20th century records are not easy to find. This should not lead us to conclude, however, that workers must inevitably pass through various stages. Rather than first learning to walk, they have had to run because they were left with no other choice. The labor process and labor protest will vary over time and place. Yet what appears certain is that class formation will increase and class and political consciousness will intensify not only over time, but also in the context of a particular labor protest. We must assume, despite past failures, that trade unions will more effectively promote the corporate interests of workers, while owners and managers will intensify their responses using the state apparatus to do so. Perhaps eventually labor parties and coordinated popular front attacks (hopefully of the left) might enter the political arena and increase political participation; such movements will almost certainly increase conflict and agitation. The actions of the African railway workers in 1947-1948 revealed an "incontestable significance," writes Suret-Canale in his paper. Is there any reason to believe that this will be less so in the future?

THE ANALYSIS OF THE WORKING CLASS AND CLASS STRUGGLE

Until recently social science research in Africa has revealed hesitant and contradictory attempts to deal with that very special object, the class struggle. In anthropology and sociology the working class becomes an "interesting case study" because of the growing interest in urban studies. In the case of British social anthropology, at least, this is the way the change took place. The study of the forced migration of Southern Africa revealed three major themes, which have been studied since the 1930s:[1] the social transformation of the rural universe, the migration itself, and the urban constraints.

Another impetus was given to the investigation of the class struggle by the study of the political and ideological movements for independence. This research dealt naturally with the function and nature of African trade unionism, one form of working class organization. However, there remains the problem: what do we mean by an African working class? To answer this question many ideological, theoretical, and practical ambiguities remain.

Most of the African nationalist or pseudo-socialist ideologies have never granted a specific place and role to the struggles of the working class, to those classes exploited by the capitalist system. Interpretations such as those of F. Fanon (the so-called theory of labor aristocracy) fall into this category because by and large the working class is seen as part of the dominant power group. Therefore, the ideology of the working class was never concretely considered as one of the means of achieving political and social class consciousness (Saul, 1975; Waterman, 1975). In terms of theory, anthropology can serve to demonstrate a more general weakness in the study of the working class. It has only lately begun to concern itself with the formal themes of sociology, hence the recent interest in the exploited labor force. The first Marxist essays dealing with African societies applied Marx and Lenin to the letter when studying the process of class formation and structure (from feudalism to capitalism, for example). That dogmatic brand of Marxism merely transferred European experience to Africa (Barbé, 1964; Woddis, 1959). Post-Stalinist Marxism evolved a more historical view of societies. However, most of the research fell into two categories: that of the macro-economy of peripheral capitalism, unequal exchange, and world capitalist relationships on the one hand, and that of precapitalist modes of production (African, Asiatic, lineage, etc.) on the other. The ordinary and concrete problems of contemporary African national societies have been ignored, because they are much more complex.

In practical and political terms it is not a simple matter to study urban exploited groups and classes in Africa. Political and police controls are often very tight concerning research at this level. One must also remember that the social scientists tended to show a marked preference for the country over cities and industrial regions, for the bush over shanty towns. Perhaps there was an exotic motivation for the African journeys of numerous anthropologists.

Even more recently history has come into focus: the history of anticolonial resistance, the history of the sociological formation of political and union organizations. The past appears more and more to be also a part of class struggle. This study of the past impels us to study the present in the same way, i.e., in a historical perspective. The phenomena of "periodization," process, transformation, and evolution are receiving more attention. That is why the study of peculiarly African social movements seems to have become more the province of history than of anthropology and sociology.

The crisis of the social sciences and the intensification of anti-imperialist struggles during the past ten years have sensitized social scientists who wish to understand why socialism has not yet succeeded in Africa. The investigation of authentic social movements, carried out independently of academic disciplines, of the dominant African ideologies and of the well-constructed theories (functionalism, structuralism, Marxism) has finally become a possibility. Major attention is paid to the visible protest movements (strikes, riots, etc.), to spontaneous expressions of popular grievances, and to concrete mass action. The analysis of institutions and organizations is, to some extent, being abandoned for the examination of the *real* content of declarations by "spokesmen." Groups are no longer identified with what "structures" them, with what "speaks" for them. Social scientists have at last become really curious and want to understand the point of view of those below (Gutkind, 1975).

Let us recapitulate. Although many have explained the social sciences as the "handmaiden" of colonialism and imperialism, the history and analysis of the movements and actions of the African working class have scarcely begun (Friedland, 1974). This is not to be explained by the subjectivity of the researchers or by the indolence of the directors of research in Western industrial sociology. It is to be explained rather by the fact that movements of class struggle have been hidden by the specific ideologies created by the transition to capitalism in the African context. The strategies of sub-imperialisms (South Africa, Zaire, Nigeria, Ivory Coast, Kenya), and the autonomous thrust of certain bourgeoisies (comprador, commercial or bureaucratic), determine a type of policy of law and order directed against the "dangerous classes." On the other hand, the success of the wars of liberation in Portuguese Africa or in Zimbabwe shows that revolutionary struggle and mass mobilization for overthrowing neocolonial and pseudo-socialist regimes are a very concrete and actual concern. While one can applaud the present interest in studies of resistance and protest, our problem is of a different nature—the analysis of the formation of a working class consciousness also contributes toward the creation of a tradition within this same class consciousness. The problem is not only to provide a written record of this tradition, but more fundamentally to clarify the role the working class plays in the creation of its own history. Past interpretations of the continent's labor history have not helped in this task. They have remained partial, incomplete, and locked within the two great cultural traditions, anglophone and francophone.

The Anglophone Tradition

Critics of colonialism from E.D. Morel to Basil Davison have focussed, quite correctly, on labor policies, laws, and conditions as magnifying the basic character of colonialism itself. Outside observers are paralleled by informed insiders. Among the more interesting of the colonial writers is Orde Browne, a progressive labor administrator whose reports on labor conditions spanned Malaya to the West Indies to West and East Africa (but see notably, Orde Browne, 1933). Among the hitherto little known inside critics of the system was Albert Nzula, the first black general secretary of the South African communist party. In a book first published under the title *Forced Labour in Black Africa* in Russian in 1933, and soon to be translated into English (Cohen, 1978), Nzula, with his Moscow colleagues, makes a devastating attack on the labor policies of each of the colonial powers in turn, while venting his special spleen on the racist practices of his white South African countrymen. There appears to be something of a hiatus in major studies of African labor until Noon's fairly indifferent study was published in 1944. Thereafter the selection of titles becomes somewhat haphazard though one can detect a movement from books conceived on a continental or regional scale (e.g., Roper, 1958; Davies, 1966) to those concerned with labor issues in one country (e.g., Friedland, 1969; Amsden, 1971; Bates, 1971; Cohen, 1974; Sandbrook, 1975).

Frequently, though not invariably, the studies of the 1960s and early 1970s were dominated by an institutional focus and in particular looked at the growth of the trade union movement, its leadership and organizational character, its success in wage bargaining, and the relationship it enjoyed with political parties or governments. In a later phase, there developed a tendency to disregard or minimize the importance of the organizations that purported to organize the working class, in an attempt to look at the texture of working class life from below and to plot more sensitively the forms of consciousness and action that develop below the control, and sometimes even the awareness, of the official trade union leadership. Several of the contributors in a recent collection deliberately lay stress on the popular "grass roots" character of their discussion (Lubeck, 1975; Peace, 1975; Jeffries, 1975), while others have focussed on periods before the development of organizations to service the demands and grievances of the working class (Stichter, 1975; Illife, 1975). This trend has gained the most considered and imaginative treatment in Charles van Onselen's work on mine laborers in Southern Rhodesia between 1900 and 1933 and in the more comtemporary study of a mine in Namibia (van Onselen, 1976; Gordon, 1977). The nature of van Onselen's investigation, in particular the repressive closed compounds, imposed to a large degree the view from below that van Onselen advocates. Nonetheless, his comments should be seen as laying the groundwork for a richer approach for the study of African labor protest (1976:227):

> In a labour-coercive economy . . . worker ideologies and organisation should be viewed essentially as the high water marks of protest: they should not be allowed to dominate our understanding of the way in which the economic system worked, or of the African miner's responses to it. At least as important, if not more so, were the less dramatic, silent and often unorganised responses, and it is this latter set of

responses, which occurred on a day-to-day basis that reveal most about the functioning of the system and formed the warp and woof of worker consciousness.

The Francophone Tradition

The differences between French-speaking and English-speaking African studies are quite significant and have a definite bearing on our knowledge of both French-speaking and English-speaking Africa.[2] With minor exceptions, [3] there is a notable lack of interest in labor history in Francophone African studies. Two convergent causes can explain this absence: the deficiency of urban anthropology or sociology and the backwardness of colonial historical research (see the works of P. Mercier, J.M. Gibbal, M. Vernière, and issue no. 51 of *Cahiers d'Etudes Africaines*, 1973). The second point is much more important for our knowledge of the beginnings of working class action and urban unrest. The study of the history of contemporary Africa is a very recent trend (Coquery-Vidrovitch and Moniot, 1974; *Cahiers d'Etudes Africaines*, 1976). It is mainly the history of the policies and decisions of the colonial administrations. Marxist influence led to the opening up of a new field of research, that of economic history, largely on the macro-structural level.[4]

Most of the research is oriented toward administrative and political history on the one hand, and economic history on the other. Social history as such (historical anthropology) is much more concerned with precolonial history or the very first beginnings of the colonial era. Thus the historiography of the working classes is still that of ideologies, parties, unions (Thiam Iba Der, 1972). At this point, however, we encounter some causes which are peculiar to the themes and theories of French history. The history of the French working class as such has been considered a serious topic for study only during the past 20 years or so. The history of working class organizations (parties, ideologies, unions, militants) is rather considerable. Yet the study of the working class as such (its actions, social consciousness, manner of living, etc.) is much more limited. The doctrinal content of Stalinist Marxism, influential in historical circles, explains this interest in an authoritative version of the class struggle (whatever the extent of that authority). As P. Anderson (1976) has suggested, the contrary seems to have been true in Great Britian. In France what is needed is a Hobsbawm (1964) or a Thompson (1968; Le Mouvement Social, 1977).

In the absence of a global historical perception of the working class or of a serious urban or industrial sociology (paradoxically ignored by the theoreticians of Marxism who are more preocccupied by precapitalism than by capitalism),[5] the theme of labor history and working class action is nonexistent.[6] The effect of this on African Africanists has been disastrous. The academic structure of universities in French-speaking Africa is closely modelled on that of French universities. The result is highly centralized administration and subordination of the universities and research institutes to local political powers, resulting in control and self-censorship of researchers. To this should be added the implicit influence of French intellectual trends and centers of interest. The official policy of France in the domain of *cooperation* and the control of African academic careers by the French Ministry of Education serves to suppress any sort of autonomous thinking. Then too there is the typical problem, quite important in Africa, of the bonds between the intellectuals and the working class. "Things are a-changin'," perhaps. Everything must have a beginning and social scientists should orientate themselves toward the creation of a theoretical, empirical, and political framework to study the class consciousness of the working class.

OUTLINE FOR A NEW PERSPECTIVE

The problems to be solved are situated at theoretical, practical, and political levels. At the present time the practical level is the most important. Documents are very rare. They have not been stored in administrative or police archives, as in Europe. The approaches are similar, whether we examine the past or the present.

J. Chesneaux says that "whole sections of world history are known only by what opressors have said or permitted to be said" (Petitjean, 1977). When we add to this aspect of the past the role of oral history, we understand why we possess so few documents of working class origin. Moreover, colonial administrations record mass movements less well than the administrations of developed capitalist countries. Consequently one of the most important sources of documentation concerning class consciousness and the real process of class action does not, so it seems, exist. Even within France we are reduced to reading the book by the French historian, Michelle Perrot (1974), who was able, by using a computer, to study in a very detailed and sociological way 2,923 strikes which occurred during the period preceding the one with which we are concerned (1870-1890). The quasi-absence until 30 or 40 years ago of working class organizations, or newspapers capable of describing the internal state of the working class, and of a trade unionist oral tradition have rendered things very difficult for both historians and sociologists. "An old man who dies is a library that vanishes." This well known statement by Amadou Hampaté Ba applies very well to the African worker.

When we tackle the investigation of present events (two remarkable examples are contained in this volume: Althabe, Cooper), we realize that major obstacles challenge foreign researchers. Working class militants do not transform themselves into memorialists for future historians. The rare written documents, the slight interest manifested in respect to working class problems (workers' education), the violence of repression—all these factors provide an African worker with little time and few means for meditating about his actions.

These pessimistic remarks do not intend to suggest that it is impossible to discover the traces of class consciousness. All the texts in this book prove that this can be done. But how can we go about setting up the oral archives of the African proletariat? This task is probably much more formidable than the collecting of classic oral literature.

THEORY AND PRACTICE

The theoretical level is just as important as the practical level. In fact, a careful scrutiny of the way this problem has been handled over the past ten years reveals clearly the importance of the choice of questions and the choice of their contents, for this choice has determined the discovery of new historical objects. These objects are also the result of a new intellectual orientation, the introduction of Marxism in the domain of African studies, but chiefly in Western academic circles. This Marxism is of a purely conceptual type, but unfortunately the revolutionary overthrow of neocolonial capitalism is not a theoretical concern. As J. Chesneaux (1976:140-141) has written:

> This effort is just as evident on the level of the themes studied: phenomena of the collective consciousness (fear, forgetfulness, memory, irrational pulsations); life of the people (work techniques, mentalities, popular culture, even if, over a long period, it loses political significance); forms of refusal and struggle (marginal members of society, bandits, rebels, convicts, prostitutes, and also peasant movements, workers' strikes, union activity). These new subjects are à la mode with young historians, but their real efforts to broaden their scope only ends up finally by renovating and consolidating the university institution.
> One must go still further. One must no longer be satisfied with "working" (another abusive misuse of language, since work is defined by its collective finality, its social usage)—working on peasant struggles, on utopian American communities. One must work with workers, peasants, the popular masses. That is much more difficult than to remain within an institution and succeed in arousing much curiosity with an "original," "suggestive," "stimulating" thesis. (The vocabulary of the university establishment is rich in such resources.)

There is also a theoretical task to be performed in relation to the problem of labor protest. Its emphasis should be on three points:

(1) the nature of peripheral capitalism and of the neocolonial state, i.e., the definition of the social formation and the mode of production;
(2) the character of the working class under the forms of capitalism prevailing in Africa; and
(3) the nature of class consciousness and class action.

It is not difficult to criticize mechanistic Marxism today, but neither the macro-economic view of the specialists of imperialism nor the anthropologism of the historians and anthropologists of precolonial societies can help us fill this gap. A sufficient number of studies have accumulated so that it is both necessary and possible to make a first synthesis.[7]

Other more typical problems have been raised by researchers, such as the relationship between social spontaneity, social organization and social expression. Raising the question of the theoretical implications of working class struggles leads in effect to the adoption of a political stand; in other words, advancing from the political questions of the researcher to the political problems of the object of research. The theme of this book is thus undoubtedly directly concerned with politics.

Let us cite once more J. Chesneaux (1976:178):

> But these techniques for research are justified only if there is a coherent political project. The technical division of labor and the utilization of the specialized skill of the historian can be very precious—*on condition that this division of labor be decided collectively by all those who are concerned, instead of being claimed as a right by the historian alone.* We must accept being at the service of a common reflection in order to imagine the present historically while imagining the past politically.
>
> The academic Marxist historians confuse the potential capacity of Marxism to analyse scientifically any zone of history, any society of the past with the concrete and preferential use of Marxism for studying those facts of the past susceptible in enlightening our struggles. They believe, as do other university historians, that all they need to do is to make themselves at home in a given speciality. In any case, according to them, these studies will contribute to the increase of the intellectual influence of Marxism within the university. Thus their social prestige will serve the cause of the working class and the revolution. Intellectual activity becomes a political objective in itself.

There is more and more agreement about these questions (Copans, 1974; Cohen, 1975; Echenberg, 1975; Leys, 1975; Waterman, 1977). Who should write this history and in what manner? This is a political question, but it concerns even the most radical authors. Questions as to methodology are political (what are the *good* documents?). Ethical questions are political too (how can we utilize our informants so as to protect the labor movement from repression?). The link between theoretical orientation and empirical research is a political one. The concentration of political power, and the hegemony of a dominant ideology, serve to constrain the raising of these subjects.

The real problem is the following: the evolution of African formations today assigns great responsibility to those movements, groups, and classes who wish to overthrow (in action and not only in words) the established neocolonial order. In such a perspective, an intimate knowledge of the system and a radical strategy for the mobilization of the masses are fundamental. Does this type of consciousness exist in the present historical period? The ambiguities of the anticolonial movement have not really helped the masses understand the condition in which they were making their own history. During the past 20 to 40 years, history has become the property of the specialists of the *modern world,* of the ruling class and its ideologists. This history has been massively inculcated into the people through official policies (schools, media) and has clearly played a planned role as an obstacle to the rise of class consciousness in a dominated working class. The mediation of bureaucracies and the limits of spontaneity (whatever its success or vigor) have contributed in either a negative or positive fashion to this phenomenon. To restore history to the exploited masses of Africa implies the creation of an authentic tradition of struggle and therefore full information about *their own struggles.* It should not come as a surprise that the very first elements of this history have been made in the academic world. Whatever their weaknesses may be, these first efforts are preferable to silence. Theoretical reformulation, the development of authentic African research, the establishment of a concrete link between this research and the needs of the present struggles and the forms of class consciousness—these are the basic elements of this program. We do not propose to substitute ourselves for those who "are making history," but we must attempt in a small way, with the best means and skills at our disposal (academic skills being what they are), to help bring about the creation of a tradition of analysis of working class struggle. It is not our role to define such a tradition, but we must raise the question publicly. Africanists have the privilege of freedom of speech and expression and should utilize this freedom to initiate debates and discussions around this very fundamental topic: what are the types of action, of class consciousness, of labor organizations through which the African working class can express its social needs and its political goals? We can at least describe the past and part of the present. The very action of investigating a theme gives it an "aura" of "scientific" interest, so it is unnecessary to justify one's research. In the present case, there is profound justification for our efforts—namely the political and social liberation of the African working class.[8]

In this volume the editors have sought to give an outlet to scholars who want to offer a fresher and more dialectical approach to the study of Africa's labor history. It is our hope that this book will shift scholarship within Africa away from nationalist myth-making and applauding the achievements of the elite into looking more closely at the history of the mass of their countrymen—workers in the fields, factories, and backyard sweatshops of African cities.

NOTES

1. B. Magubane has radically criticized the assumptions of this research and it is unnecessary to cover it again here (Magubane, 1971). It is even possible to escape dealing with political and ideological phenomena when studying workers. One example is Mitchell's failure to deal with class consciousness even though he deals with unions (Mitchell, 1956).

2. The equivalent of the *Review of African Political Economy,* a three-year-old independent Marxist journal edited from London, is unthinkable in France at the present time.

3. One excellent but little used source is *Presence Africaine* (1952). See also November (1965) and Meynaud and Salah-Bey (1963).

4. See the debate between C. Coquery-Vidrovitch and H. Brunschwig in *Cahiers d'Etudes Africaines,* 1976, Vol. 16, No. 61-62.

5. The relations (the articulation) between capitalism and precapitalism have been a central topic for some years (see Rey, 1976; Amselle, 1976; Meillassoux, 1975). On an empirical level one should notice the important work by P. Bourdieu and his team on the Algerian worker of 1960 (1966).

6. Three papers, including Gutkind's, have been published about this or a related subject in *Cahiers d'Etudes Africaines,* the leading French journal on Africa, over a span of 16 years. Only one was written by a French researcher!

7. See Copans's comments on Gutkind's paper (1975:44-55). See also Volume One of the Sage Series on African Modernization and Development.

8. The "style" of the research, the type of language can be very important. P. Waterman (1977) makes this point quite clearly in his paper.

REFERENCES

AMSDEN, A. (1971). International firms and labour in Kenya, 1945-1970. London: Frank Cass.

AMSELLE, J.-L. (1976). Les migrations africaines. Paris: Maspero.

ANDERSON, P. (1976). Considerations on western Marxism. London: New Left Book.

BALANDIER, G. (1968). Daily life in the kingdom of the Kongo. London: Allen and Unwin.

BARBE, R. (1964). Les classes sociales en Afrique noire. Paris: Editions Sociales.

BATES, R. (1971). Unions, parties and political development: A study of the mineworkers in Zambia. New Haven: Yale University Press.

BOURDIEU, P. (1966). Travail et travailleurs en Algérie. Paris: Mouton.

BRAUNDI, E., and LETTIERI, A. (1964). "The general strike in Nigeria." International Socialist Journal, 1 (5-6):598-609.

BUELL, L. (1928). The native problem in Africa (vol. 1). London: Macmillan.

CADBURY, W.A. (1910). Labour in Portuguese West Africa. London: Routledge.

CAHIERS D'ETUDES AFRICAINES. (1973). 13(3) (no. 51 Villes Africaines).

CHESNEAUX, J. (1976). Du passé faisons table rase? Paris: Maspero.

COHEN, R. (1974). Labor and politics in Nigeria. London: Heinemann.

_____ (1975). "Marxism and Africa: Old, new and projected." Working papers, no. 2. Montreal: Centre for Developing Area Studies, McGill University.

_____ (1976). "Hidden forms of labour protest in Africa." Discussion paper no. 30, Series C. Birmingham: Faculty of Commerce and Social Science, University of Birmingham.

_____, ed., (1978). Colonialism from below: Albert Nzula and the Moscow School of Africanists. London: Zed Press.

COOKEY, S.J. (1968). Britian and the Congo question. London: Longman.

COPANS, J. (1974). Critiques et politiques de l'anthropologie. Paris: Maspero.

_____ (1975). "Conscience politique ou conscience de la politique?" Cahiers d'Etudes Africaines, 15(1):44-55.

COQUERY-VIDROVITCH, C. (1972). Le Congo français au temps des grandes compagnies concessionnaires, 1898-1930. Paris: Mouton.

_____ and Moniot, H. (1974). L'Afrique noire de 1800 à nos jours. Paris: Presses Universitaires de France.

DAVIDSON, B. (1955). The African awakening. London: Jonathan Cape.

DAVIES, I. (1966). African trade unions. Harmondsworth: Penguin.

DOBB, M. (1963). Studies in the development of capitalism. New York: International Publishers.

ECHENBERG, M. (1975)."Consciousness and African historiography: Some suggestions for future research." Working papers, no. 6. Montreal: Centre for Developing Area Studies, McGill University.

FRIEDLAND, W. (1969). Vuta Kamba: The development of trade unions in Tanganyika. Stanford: Stanford University Press.

_____ (1974). "African trade union studies. Analysis of two decades." Cahiers d'Etudes Africaines, 14(3) (no. 55):575-89.

GORDON, R.J. (1977). Mines, masters and migrants: Life in a Nambian compound. Johannesburg: Raven Press.

GUTKIND, P.C.W. (1975). "The view from below: Political consciousness of the urban poor in Ibadan." Cahiers d'Etudes Africaines, 15(1):5-35.

HARRIS, J.H. (1913). Portuguese slavery: Britain's dilemma. London: Methuen.

"Histoire africaine: constatations, contestations." (1976). Cahiers d'Etudes Africaines, 16 (61-62).

HOBSBAWM, E.J. (1964). Labouring men. New York: Basic Books.

ILLIFE, J. (1975). "The creation of group consciousness: A history of the dockworkers of Dar es Salaam." In R. Sandbrook and R. Cohen (eds.), The development of an African working class. London: Longman.

JEFFRIES, R. (1975). "Populist tendencies in the Ghanaian trade union movement." In R. Sandbrook and R. Cohen (eds.), The development of an African working class. London: Longman.

JOHNSTONE, F.A. (1976). Class, race and gold: A study of class relations and racial discrimination in South Africa. London: Routledge and Kegan Paul.

LEYS, C. (1975). "Studying the political consciousness of workers and peasants in the third world: The problem of theory and practice." Working papers, no. 9. Montreal: Centre for Developing Area Studies, McGill University.

LOUIS, W.R., and STENGERS, J. (1968). E.D. Morel's history of the Congo movement. Oxford: Clarendon Press.

LUBECK, P. (1975). "Unions, workers and consciousness in Kano, Nigeria: A view from below." In R. Sandbrook and R. Cohen (eds.), The development of an African working class. London: Longman.

MAGUBANE, B. (1971). "A critical look at indices used in the study of social change in colonial Africa." Current Anthropology, 12(4-5):419-445.

MARCUM, J. (1969). The Angolan revolution (vol. 1): The anatomy of an explosion (1952-1960). Cambridge, Mass.: M.I.T. Press.

MEILLASSOUX, C. (1975). L'esclavage en Afrique précoloniale. Paris: Maspero.

_____ (1977). "La phénomène économique dans les sociétiés traditionelles d' autosubsistence." Pp. 21-62 in Terrains et theories. Paris: Anthropos.

_____ (1975a). Femmes, greniers et capitaux. Paris: Maspero.

MEYNAUD, J., and SALAH-BEY, A. (1963). Le syndicalisme africain. Paris: Payot.

MITCHELL, J. C. (1956). The Kalela dance. Rhodes-Livingstone Papers, no. 27. Lusaka: Rhodes-Livingston Institute.

LE MOUVEMENT SOCIAL (1977). No. 100. Paris: Editions Ouvrieres.

NEVINSON, H.W. (1906). A modern slavery. London: Harper.

NOON, J.A. (1944). Labor problems in Africa. Philadelphia: University of Pennsylvania Press.

NOVEMBER, A. (1965). L'evolution de mouvement syndicale en Afrique occidentale. Paris: Mouton.

ORDE BROWNE, G. St. J. (1933). The African labourer. London: Frank Cass.

OUSMANE, S. (1962). God's bits of wood. New York: Doubleday.

PEACE, A. (1975). "The Lagos proletariat: Labour aristocrats or populist militants." In R. Sandbrook and R. Cohen (eds.), The development of an African working class. London: Longman.

PERRINGS, C. (1977). " 'Good lawyers but poor workers': Recruited Angolan labour in the copper mines of Katanga, 1917-1921." Journal of African History, 18(2):237-259.

PERROT, M. (1974). Les ouvriers en grève, France 1871-1890 (2 vols.). Paris: Mouton.

PETITJEAN, G. (1977). "Les dynamiteurs de l'histoire et géo." Le Nouvel Observateur, Nov. 14:67.

Presence Africaine (1952). Le travail en Afrique noire. Paris: Presence Africaine.

Review of African Political Economy (1976). Special issue on South Africa. No. 7.

REY, P. Ph. (1976). Capitalisme negrier: Le marche des paysans vers le proletariat. Paris: Maspero.

ROPER, J. (1958). Labour problems in Africa. Harmondsworth: Penguin.

ROSS, E.A. (1925). Report on employment of native labor in Portuguese Africa. New York: Abbot Press.

SANDBROOK, R. (1975). Proletarians and African capitalism: The Kenya case. Cambridge, Mass.: Cambridge University Press.

_____ and COHEN, R. eds. (1975). The development of an African working class: Studies in class formation and action. London: Longman.

SAUL, J.S. (1975). "The 'labor aristocracy': Thesis reconsidered." In R. Sandbrook and R. Cohen (eds.), The development of an African working class. London: Longman.

STICHTER, S. (1975). "The formation of a working class in Kenya." In R. Sandbrook and R. Cohen (eds.), The development of an African working class. London: Longman.

THIAM IBA DER (1972). "La grève des cheminots d' Sénégal de septembre 1938." Unpublished M.A. dissertation, University of Dakar.

THOMAS, R.D. (1973). "Forced labour in British West Africa: The case of the Northern Territories of the Gold Coast, 1906-1927." Journal of African History, 14(1):79-103.

THOMPSON, E.P. (1968). The making of the English working class. Harmondsworth: Penguin.

VAN ONSELEN, C. (1976). Chibaro: African mine labour in Southern Rhodesia, 1900-1933. London: Pluto Press.

WATERMAN, P. (1975). "The 'labor aristocracy' in Africa: Introduction to a debate." Development and Change, 6(3):57-73.

_____ (1976). "Third world strikes: An invitation to discussion." Development and Change, 7:331-344.

_____ (1977). "Workers in the third world." Monthly Review, 29(4):50-64.

WILSON, F. (1972). Labour in the South African gold mines. Cambridge, Mass.: Cambridge University Press.

WODDIS, J. (1959). Africa: The lion awakes. London: Laurence and Wishart.

WOLPE, H. (1972). "Capitalism and cheap labour-power in South Africa: From segregation to apartheid." Economy and Society, 1(4):425-456.

1

AN EMERGING NIGERIAN WORKING CLASS:
The Lagos Experience 1897-1939

ARNOLD HUGHES
University of Birmingham

ROBIN COHEN
University of the West Indies

INTRODUCTION

This study is seen as an exploration of a still largely unmapped area of recent Nigerian social history—the emergence of a wage labor force in response to the economic changes brought about by the British annexation of Lagos (1861) and the gropings of this social aggregate toward some form of common identity born of its shared experiences and disabilities under colonial rule. Broadly, the time focus covers the first 40 years of the present century, taking up from Hopkins' earlier study of the Lagos labor force and ending shortly before World War II when more profound and widely recorded events were ushered in (see Hopkins, 1966; Cohen, 1974; Ananaba, 1969).

Before looking at the characteristics of wage earners themselves, we need to provide a broad picture of the social composition of the colony of Lagos. Periodic and not always reliable official statistics show a gradual change from a basically trading and commercial center to one in which government employment became a more and more common occupational category (see Table 1). Hopkins (1963:26), writing of 1881, noted that "about half the population was directly engaged in trade and that, indirectly, the greater part of the total population owed its livelihood to commerce." The situation in the inter-war period changed somewhat with a little over a quarter of the population claiming to be traders in 1921. The trading community, although a large one, consisted in the main of a few dozen prominent merchants and a large army of individuals working for either the most prosperous African merchants and European trading houses or themselves as petty-traders and street hawkers. Although swift to take advantage of opportunities afforded

AUTHORS' NOTE: This chapter is an amended and shortened version of an Occasional paper, published under a similar title by the Faculty of Commerce and Social Science, University of Birmingham (Series D, No. 7, November 1971).

Table 1. THE OCCUPATIONAL STRUCTURE OF LAGOS COLONY: 1881-1921

Occupations	1881	1891	1901	1911	1921
Traders	11,049	12,040	15,687	21,292	27,421
Farmers and fishermen	2,987	818	1,004	2,034	1,735
Traditional crafts (weavers and dyers)	——	1,212	1,016	700	537
Professional (higher professions)	333[a]	——	c.35	c.50	c.100
Civil servants	292	——	789	597[b]	2,009
Clerks	——	——	360	——	3,201
Skilled labor (mainly new trades)	5,713[c]	1,713	2,955	6,034	9,564
Semi-skilled and unskilled (general laborers cited for 1881 only)	3,822	909	2,447	4,019	5,837
Total population	37,452	32,508	41,847	73,766	99,690

NOTES:
a. A questionable figure which must include all the teaching professions. There is no separate entry for schoolteachers in any of the data.
b. Excludes the police and government printers and artisans.
c. Includes traders, manufacturers, mechanics, and artisans.
SOURCES:
Lagos Times, September 28, 1881.
Lagos Census Report (1911). Appendix C, p. 22.
P.A. Talbot (1926). Peoples of Southern Nigeria (Vol. IV). Lagos: Lagos Statistics.

by stabilized political conditions in the interior and the influx of people to the island, this large sector remained obdurately loyal to a way of life centered on family, clientage, and an autochthonous system of government based on the Oba (ruler) and the four grades of chieftaincy. Its economic activities and social bonds vitiated the emergence of social identity based on economic specialization and class solidarity.

Closely related to this main occupational and social category were those forms of employment which were indigenous to Lagos or which underwent partial transformation in response to new economic conditions. Farmers and fishermen, dyers and weavers were also closely bound to the pre-colonial way of life and many of those classified under skilled labor in Table 1 (such as gold and silversmiths, tailors, or shoemakers) would also associate themselves with, and be economically dependent on, the trading community.

The bulk of the colony's populace, while bound-up in the new colonial economy, maintained social relationships which were more in keeping with the slave-trading community of the past than with the bustling image of Lagos as the "Liverpool of West Africa," which the city's more "enlightened" inhabitants were at pains to portray. Nevertheless, the statistics do indicate the growth of another element in the population, a *servitor* sector, created by the colonial government and to a lesser extent the European commercial and humanitarian interests. In 1926, the government *Blue Book* (1926: Section 23,506,7) listed 5,800 established government employees, 5,533 skilled artisans working for the government, and 32,728 unskilled laborers in public employment. In 1938 (1938:W2-W5), 6,784 clerical workers and teachers were enumerated and some 9,000 artisans were listed, while daily paid and usually unskilled laborers working for the government numbered nearly 50,000 persons. In the same year about 3,000 clerks worked for private mercantile houses in Lagos. It must be remembered that, despite their low social overheads, colonial governments were probably more *etatist* than their metropolitan equivalent. Government's need for hired labor was varied and growing—it required substantial manpower to maintain the pax colonica, soldiers, policemen, and judicial functionaries. It needed legions of clerks to man the lower echelons of its large bureaucracy while specialists were sought or trained to maintain the technical adjuncts of the colonial state in the form of railways, harbors, and electricity plants. The acquisition of further territory inland stimulated the growth of Lagos into the main administrative center of Nigeria, while the building of the railway to Kano and the improvements to the Lagos harbor made it the country's commercial center as well.

Such was the demand for labor that the government was obliged to recruit widely along the West African coast and further afield in the West Indies. Kru labor from Liberia was often employed in the Marine and Public Works Departments (Burns, 1948:80), the Creole clerk from Freetown made an ubiquitous appearance in British West Africa, while West Indians were often recruited to work on the railways. Succeeding governors had a low opinion of locally recruited labor, which was felt to be expensive and of dubious quality. Fears were also expressed that any rise in the wage scale in Lagos would reduce the supply of agricultural labor and have a deleterious effect on the production of export crops, the taxation of which comprised a major source of revenue. The daily wage rate of one shilling was considered "absurd" by Governor McCallum in 1897 and Sir Frederick Lugard still thought it "preposterous" a few years later (Hopkins, 1966:135; Ananaba, 1969:8). Both pined for the passive and cheap labor of Asia, McCallum being particularly approving of what he called "the industrious and shifty Chinaman." Barring the introduction of some Indian clerks and printers as well as a company of Sikhs, however, the several official attempts to secure Asian labor were unsuccessful (Public Record

Office, Aug. 18, 1906: CO 520/36 Egerton to Elgin; Nigeria Times, Oct. 10, 1910).

As a result of the unprecedented need for both skilled and general labor, the ethnic homogeneity of Lagos gave way to succeeding waves of migrants drawn in the main from neighboring Yoruba country, but also from abroad and from other parts of Nigeria, particularly the southeast. The Ibo emerged as the second most numerous ethnic group in Lagos by 1931, but there were large representations from French Africa, Sierra Leone, and Liberia. By the 1930s, wage and salary earners in Lagos were a heterogeneous group drawn from three continents and some dozen territories. Themselves forming a minority of the total Lagos community, wage earners suffered from a number of internal divisions and cross-cutting ties with the indigenous trading society, which hampered the emergence of a common identity derived from common employment. The most prestigious and well paid employment was almost exclusively in European hands. There was no sense of identity between white colonial civil servants, who had their own association, and the African employees of government. The former saw the latter as a threat to their privileged position, because job equality was a frequently voiced demand of African civil servants who had seen their opportunities atrophy in the early 20th century. Further, white civil servants saw themselves as the government, not the governed.

Even within the African sector of the civil service divisions existed. The varied ethnic origins of public employees meant that the work force had a dual identity in that part of the time it was brought together in a common work situation, but at other times it identified itself with its separate ethnic components—Lagosian and a number of expatriate African communities. The Lagosian public employee usually retained strong ties with the indigenous trading community; ties of history, culture, and kin provided an alternative focus. The continued existence of family land tenure meant that this part of the work force was not entirely proletarianized. This was often the case with immigrant wage earners as well: rights in family land were not abandoned by distant employment.

Not only did these stranger elements form their own distinct pockets in Lagos, but in some cases they had a monopoly over certain occupations. Creoles from Sierra Leone were seen as occupying a great many of the remaining senior posts previously held by Africans, and it was a practice of the Fire Service to recruit exclusively from among Liberian Kru until 1933 when disaffection led the government to cease recruiting them. Kin and ethnic considerations in obtaining employment had a retarding effect on occupational consciousness.

There were also cleavages of an occupational kind within the African labor force, particularly in terms of status and remuneration. Government itself recognized divisions between relatively privileged salaried staff and wage earning, daily-paid, manual workers. While we argue later that distinctions among African employees were capable of being overcome and replaced by a common identity arising out of a shared awareness of being servitors of an alien government, job and status differences placed obstacles in the way. A major division was between clerical and manual workers. The former constituted the "salariat" of relatively better-off workers who aspired to some form of gentility based on imitating the lifestyles of European officials and the African middle class. While this stratum enjoyed more congenial conditions of work, its lower ranks, which were more extensive, actually received less pay than skilled artisans. The indebted clerk is a familiar figure in colonial society (and colonial courtrooms, as Joyce Cary's novel, *Mister Johnson,* exemplifies). Politically, the salariat often identified with middle class nationalist leadership, but, as will be shown, it was also quite capable of an independent defense of its working conditions.

Working class consciousness was, however, greatest at the level of skilled, semi-skilled, and unskilled workers, though subject to the mediating factors referred to above. While the unskilled wage earners lacked the job security and educational attainments of these other strata, they were not prevented from acting by themselves, or in concert with other manual workers, to protect their economic interests. Judging from the incidence of corporate action among wage earners, it was the skilled and semi-skilled workers who were most aware of their class interest. The most vigorous trade unions were to be found among them. Railway workers, as in other parts of colonial Africa, were particularly prominent in this respect, forming several unions and engaging in a number of labor disputes in the period under review. Whether such workers really formed an "aristocracy" of privilege as Fanon (1965:88) and Arrighi (1970:220-267) were later to suggest is questionable. (For a discussion of the labor aristocracy debate, see Sandbrook and Cohen, 1975.) Certainly in colonial Lagos, wage earners' supposed "privilege" did not prevent them from increasingly viewing themselves as badly served by government and repeatedly expressing their discontent in industrial organization and action.

Finally, every colonial society had its most depressed stratum, the lumpenproletariat, often emotionally defined as the dregs of society—the unemployable and the socially deviant. However, care needs to be taken in distinguishing the unemployed worker from those unable to find permanent wage employment. This becomes particularly relevant during times of economic depression and retrenchment—as was the case in Lagos in the early 1930s—when labor supply problems were over and unemployed workers mingled with rural migrants and the resident marginally employed. The lumpenproletariat is a complex stratum sharing the characteristics of both working class and petty bourgeoisie, often living off the bounty of the former and taking up transient occupations representative of the latter. Although uncontrolled migration to Lagos was discouraged by the government, after the depression years the flow of migrants into Lagos caused considerable fears in government circles about the volatility of the lumpenproletariat. Thus, the chief secretary warned the governor in 1938 (Gutkind, 1974:42):

> In Lagos and most other major towns law and order conditions have rapidly deteriorated. Government interest will have to be directed at the growing number of unemployed workers, at large numbers of vagrant children who throng the market places and at political agitators who prey on the ignorance and misery of the unemployed. Government will watch the political agitators who in recent years have shown greater daring and greater influence.

Having offered these general observations about the size and internal composition of Lagos society and of its wage labor sector in particular, we will now proceed to examine the various manifestations of a working class identity found there. Three aspects of this identity will be examined. First, the attempts at setting up economic organizations, namely trade unions, to defend and promote the corporate interests of wage earners. Second, the militancy and awareness of wage earners and trade unions as expressed in industrial agitation and, in particular, the use of strike action. Third, the efforts made to move beyond a purely economic and situational defense of wage earners through participation in the political sphere both as part of a general African reaction to colonialism and more specifically by recourse to the political organization of labor in its own right.

TOWARD A WORKING CLASS IDENTITY: ECONOMIC ORGANIZATION

The formation of trade unions in Nigeria was preeminently a feature of the public sector of the economy. Employment in the state sector often demanded the acquisition of new skills and attitudes, bringing together in the service of an alien administration an increasing number of Africans whose common employment over time led them to seek some form of corporate organization in defense of their new situation.

What forms of trade union organization had emerged before the Second World War? The standard literature tends to start from 1938 when legal protection and recognition for trade unions was granted under the Trade Union Ordinance of that year. This legislation was not the great releasing mechanism for trade union organization which later writers imply or state (Yesufu, 1962:37; Egboh, 1968; Ananaba, 1969:14). Rather it represented a kind of coming-of-age of Nigerian trade unionism, the birth and adolescence of which had taken place despite government hostility and nonrecognition. Legal protection undoubtedly helped the trade union movement by giving it the right to picket and to protect its funds from legal action by employers, but the ability to organize trade unions had been demonstrated some two decades previously. Recognition that is given to unionization in the pre-1938 period is confined to the "Big Three" unions of civil servants, railwaymen, and teachers. In fact, a number of trade unions did emerge over these years in addition to those most frequently commented on. We know for instance that as early as 1893 there existed in Lagos a Mechanics Mutual Aid Provident and Improvement Association and that a major strike took place in 1897. Early trade unions, as in Europe, combined the functions of a friendly society as well as the promoting of the job interests of their members.

The existence of a number of unions can be catalogued for these years commencing with the modest combination of mechanics through to the larger and more widespread organizations of the 1930s. For example, a strike on the railways in January 1920 was coordinated by the Nigerian Mechanics' Union, a body set up in September 1919 with about 800 claimed members and branches throughout the country. The union had as its patron Herbert Macaulay, the early nationalist leader who, so it appears from a reading of his private papers, clearly perceived the connection between worker protest and the nationalist struggle (Macaulay Papers, V,II). Taking the existence of the Nigerian Mechanics' Union alone, which during the course of the strike displayed a considerable degree of organizational coherence, the previously assumed hiatus in organizational activity is invalid.

In addition to the Mechanics' Union, there exists documentary evidence of at least three other unions organized on the railways *alone* prior to the formation of the Railway Workers Union. The Macaulay Papers contain the draft rules of the Nigerian Union of African Railwaymen, which were dated 1925 and signed by its general secretary, J. Adeyinka Olushola. The document sets out elaborate rules for the conduct of business in its branches and invites *other railway unions* to join it. In its section on political matters, the document anticipates many of the demands that were later to be made by the Trade Union Congress of Nigeria established in 1943 (see Yesufu, 1962:43-45). It demanded special representation for labor on the Legislative Council and local government bodies and proposed to use union funds to secure such representation. Olushola does not specify which "other railway unions" he is referring to, but he may have been thinking of the Station Staff Union, mentioned in the Macaulay Papers, or the Port Harcourt Mechanics' Union, from whom Macaulay received correspondence in

November 1923. Also, if the one case we found is anything to go by, trade union development was not confined to workers in the public sector, because in 1911 the Lagos Mercantile Clerks Association was formed to safeguard the interests of clerks working for the merchant houses (Lagos Standard, June 28, 1911).

In the area of trade unions operating internationally, the National African Sailors' and Firemans' Union established a branch in Lagos in July 1921. Though the headquarters of the Union was in Liverpool, the branches had spread all along the West Coast. Besides Lagos, the union operated in Freetown, Monrovia, Sekondi, Accra, and Bathurst (Macaulay Papers, V,II). Though viable enough structurally, the union made little impact, as far as we know, on working class attitudes in individual African countries. It was, like many other Sailors' Unions, primarily concerned with the welfare function.

The most frequently mentioned wage earner organization in Nigeria at this time was not strictly speaking a trade union. This was the Nigerian Civil Service Union. In keeping with metropolitan practice this was a staff association. It was only in 1946 that this and similar organizations of pensionable civil servants were allowed to organize on trade union lines.

Trade union organization was characterized in this period by a very heavy concentration in the public sector with the main center of activity among railway workers. Regrettably little is known about the distribution of unions though we know that, because of the colony-wide distribution of government departments, branches of unions existed throughout the country. Distinctions can be observed between white collar and manual unions, even within one area of activity such as the railways. The general impression is of a moribund and intermittent trade union movement without a central association, but this picture needs to be qualified in some respects. We know for instance that the Civil Service Union continued to exist during the 1920s and that branches corresponded with headquarters in Lagos. Further research may well reveal a more active existence than we can surmise at present. Railway workers were particularly active forming a number of unions determined by sectional occupation as well as by personality differences. Though admittedly in their infance and beset by a number of debilitating problems, trade unions did emerge to organize wage earning interests and to challenge employers in these forgotten years. Growing wage earner awareness was also to be reflected in other ways.

Toward a Working Class Identity: Industrial Action

The existence of trade unions may be inferred partly through remaining records of their organization and also through the job militancy of the wage earners. We know that a considerable number of work stoppages and strikes occurred between the strike of 1897 and World War II and that union organization lay behind a number of them. What we are not as clear about is how such industrial action was organized in the absence of formal trade union activity. The fact that industrial action could spread across occupational divides and often occurred beyond the confines of Lagos suggests a degree of coordination, if not a national organization. In particular, militancy in the Enugu coalmines occurred sporadically throughout the inter-war years. The incidence of industrial action is listed below:

List of Strikes and Other Labor Disturbances: 1897-1939

1897   Large-scale strike by artisans and laborers in the Public Works Department, Lagos (see Hopkins, 1966).

1899   Strike of government employed canoemen at Badagri (see Hopkins, 1966:Appendix).

1899   Warders in the Lagos Hospital came out on strike (see Hopkins, 1966:Appendix).

1902   A strike involving clerks working on the railways (see Hopkins, 1966:Appendix).

1904   A second and more widespread strike involving railway clerks, which spread to other employees (see Hopkins, 1966:Appendix); see also Public Record Office, C.O. 147/174; Lagos Weekly Record, Dec. 31, 1904).

1913   Eighty-three government printers came out on strike (Lagos Weekly Record, June 21, 1913).

1919   Strikes and other labor disturbances at the Lagos docks (Nigerian Pioneer, Jan. 31, 1919; West Africa, May 17, 1919).

1919   A strike by engineers employed by Elder Dempster (the shipping company) over inadequate war bonuses (Lagos Standard, May 14, 1919).

1919   Widespread strike action undertaken by railway employees at Iddo, Lagos (Nigerian Pioneer, Jan. 23, 1920; Lagos Weekly Record, Jan. 31, 1920).

1920   According to a newspaper account there was an "extensive" strike in Port Harcourt (Nigerian Pioneer, Feb. 27, 1920).

1920   A strike in the Marine Department, Lagos (Lagos Weekly Record, Nov. 6, 1920).

1920   A strike at the government-owned colliery at Enugu (Nigerian Archives, 1920).

1920   A strike in which "all the daily paid men in the employment of the railways and the Public Works Department are involved" (Nigerian Archives, 1920).

1919- 1927	Agitation over a lengthy period about pay and conditions of service (Macaulay Papers, file on the Nigerian Civil Service Union; Lagos Weekly Record, Jan. 24, 1920).
1921	Railway artisans were involved in strike action (African Messenger, Nov. 24, 1921).
1924	"Pit-boys" at the Enugu coal mines downed tools.
1926	"Tub-boys" came out on strike at the Enugu colliery.
1933	Disaffection among the Fire Brigade and Police (Public Record Office, 1933; Nigerian Pioneer, Apr. 28, 1933).
1934	A strike by bus drivers against Zarpas, a Lebanese-owned transport company (Lagos Daily News, July 24, 1934).
1935	Industrial unrest on the eastern section of the railway (Legislative Council Debates, Dec. 2, 1935).
1935	Strike initiated by lorry owners, but supported by drivers in protest against government measures to protect railways from competition by road transport (Legislative Council Debates, Sept. 21, 1936).
1937	Continuing strikes and unrest among coalminers at Enugu (Legislative Council Debates, Mar. 25, 1937).
1937	Produce laborers at Ijebu Ode refused to work in protest against "ill-treatment" (Legislative Council Debates, July 12, 1937).
1939	A strike in the Railway Foundry Shop, backed by the newly formed Railway Workers' Union (Emejulu, n.d.).

A breakdown of this list by departments, economic sector, and type of occupation involved is shown in Table 2. In terms of the geographical location of the strikes and unrest, 12 occurred in Lagos, four in the Western Provinces, six in the Eastern Provinces, while three occurred nationally. It should be added that the incidents tabulated are by no means definitive. They are merely those which gained enough prominence to be recorded in the local press and government files. It is likely that other strikes took place in these years and more than likely that numerous examples of labor unrest occurred.

A detailed description of the issues precipitating and the events surrounding each strike is impossible given the constraints of space and data. We will, however, give consideration to two strikes that occurred on the railways—one involving clerks and the other artisans—to illustrate the nature of the strikers' grievances and the character of the intervention of other agencies, like the government and members of the elite, in the settlement of the disputes.

The second strike of railway clerks in 1904 was connected with a protest against a new form of staff contract which, they felt, discriminated against Africans. The strike received a certain amount of support from the press and political leadership first, Hopkins (1966:155) surmises, because the strike involved white collar workers rather than (as in 1897) laborers, and second,

Table 2. BREAKDOWN OF STRIKE ACTION AND LABOR UNREST, 1897-1939

| STRIKE ACTION | | Proletariat | |
Public Sector	Salariat	Skilled	Semi/Skilled
Railways	x ----------x -------- x		
	x	xx -------- xx	
		x	x
Coal mines			xxxx
P.W.D.		x --------x	
Marine Department			x
Printing Department		x --------x	
Government hospital		x	x
Government canoemen			x
Private sector			
Bus drivers		x	
Docks and marine		x	xx
Produce laborers			x
LABOR UNREST			
Civil service	x		
Police		x	
Railway		x	

SUMMARY: Twenty strikes by employees, 15 in the public sector, 5 in the private sector. One strike involved nearly all wage earners. One strike among salariat only. Four strikes involved skilled workers only, while four involved skilled and semi/unskilled labor acting together. Ten strikes involved semi/unskilled labor only. In addition, there were three incidents of serious unrest in the public sector, one among the salariat, and three among skilled workers.

because one of the strike leaders was T.H. Jackson, whose father (J.P. Jackson) owned and edited the *Lagos Weekly Record.*

The strike seems to have begun entirely among the clerical staff on the railways, but spread to other classes of employee—a sequence which demonstrated that on occasions the white collar and unskilled laborers did not see their interests as being totally discrete. The clerical staff were being asked to sign a new form of agreement which the Chief Clerk in the Traffic Superintendent's Office, one Pearce, thought iniquitous. He telegraphed his colleagues at all the stations up-line advising them not to sign the new agreement until they had read a letter from him relating to the agreement. The railway administration considered that this behavior had placed him "in direct opposition to constitutional authority and (he) had misused his official position" (Public Record Office, C.O. 147/174). He was given the opportunity to apologize, sign the agreement, and retain his job. This he refused to do, and he was instantly dismissed. Within ten minutes of his dismissal the Accounts Office Staff headed by Jackson, the Chief Clerk, struck in sympathy, an action which was joined by the men in the printing press. The strikers handed in a document objecting to the terms of the staff agreement.

The same evening news of Pearce's dismissal was telegraphed to all stations (again using official lines of communication), which provoked a widespread strike affecting "even the menial staff who were in no way concerned." Petitions to the governor and a meeting with the general manager ensued; the railway administration apparently adopted a tough line—even to the point of introducing scab labor to replace some of the men who had struck. By December 27, 1904, the strike was broken. The strike had, however, highlighted some particular grievances of the railway clerks. They did not, for example, enjoy similar pension rights to other governmental workers and even the Colonial Office thought the clause in the disputed agreement that stopped pay when staff were off sick was too harsh. Perhaps the Colonial Office's show of moral sympathy was related to the adverse international publicity that the strike received, because included in the Colonial Office file is the comment that Reuters ought to be warned about the unreliability of their Lagos correspondent and that "they ought to change him." The man in question was none other than J.P. Jackson, editor of the *Lagos Weekly Record*. He had on one occasion specifically described the government's action as "incompetent" (Lagos Weekly Record, Dec. 31, 1904), but what enraged the Lagos officials was the connection they saw between the language of the strikers' petition and the criticism of Jackson's paper. In the Colonial Office file is the following elegantly penned note: "Special attention is invited to the objectionable phraseology of this document. Its rodomontade bears a strong family likeness to the lucubrations of the local press in its weekly record."

Unlike the 1904 strike, which appeared to have had little organizational coherence, the Iddo rail strike of January 1919, our second case study, was coordinated by the Nigerian Mechanics' Union, referred to earlier in this chapter. The strike originated, according to one press account, because of the stagnant wage rates which were insufficient to cover abnormally high living costs (Nigerian Pioneer, Jan. 20, 1920). It was compounded, however, by the arrogant and cavalier treatment that a white manager accorded to his African staff, a source of embitterment that was to continually poison management-employee relationships on the railways. On January 7, a white District Locomotive Superintendant told his men to go elsewhere if they were not satisfied by their wages. The railway authorities also apparently tried to get artisans to do laboring jobs. When they refused they were dismissed. By January 12, other artisans had stopped work because the authorities refused to pay extra for the extra work involved. As a result of these actions, railway traffic was dislocated. The Mechanics' Union asked for government intervention and the immediate increase of wages. The Lieutenant-Governor met them on January 15, promised an inquiry, and offered an increase of three pence in the pay of daily paid laborers. He warned, however, that a return to work had to precede the inquiry. A separate appeal to the General Manager of the railways met with a similar response: the General Manager wrote to the Union offering an inquiry and sympathetic hearing by the railway department itself, provided the strike was called off. The Union agreed to this, and work was resumed on January 19 (Lagos Weekly Record, Jan. 31, 1926).

In an attempt to get a settlement of the strike, several members of the Lagosian elite tried to make some political mileage out of the event. The Oba (traditional ruler) of Lagos was approached by the Union, almost certainly on Macaulay's advice (Macaulay was "Vice-Patron" of the Union) and asked to intervene. The matter was discussed at a meeting of the Central Native Council on January 13, and a meeting with Union leaders took place three days later. Macaulay was later to claim that Oba's action played an important part in persuading the workers to return, a claim that was hotly disputed in the columns of the *Nigerian Pioneer* (Jan. 23, 1920). The paper argued that industrial disputes could be settled without the intervention of such authorities and that the men had themselves rebuffed the Oba.

The incidence of industrial action that we have described demonstrates some capacity by wage and salary earners both to defend their situational interests and to organize effective demands despite distinctions of grade and status. A further index of growing class awareness may be sought in the wider political sphere, a topic to which we turn next.

TOWARD A WORKING CLASS IDENTITY: POLITICAL ORGANIZATION

The short-lived nature and limited success of industrial organization and action led some wage earners to seek a more specifically political solution to their occupational grievances. Three interrelated responses can be discerned: the first was an attempt to create an embryonic Nigerian "Labor Party"; the second was the more shadowy association with the international communist movement; and the third was that the representatives of the working class sought redress through a "Popular Front" approach in conjunction with the middle classes and their nationalist organizations.

A Nigerian "Labor Party"

Despite the fact that the Nigerian wage-labor force was less than 4% of the total population in the inter-war period (Coleman, 1963:68) and it was only partially and intermittently organized into trade unions, a number of militants sought to create a political movement to provide direct representation for proletarian interests. One of the leading advocates of such action was J.A. Olushola who, in 1922, established in Lagos the Nigerian Labor Corporation to "defend the Cause of Labour."[1] The following year he founded the *Nigerian Labour Bulletin* to popularize the Corporation's aims, but both enterprises soon collapsed, victims, according to Olushola (Nigerian Labor Bulletin, Mar. 17, 1930), of persecution at the hands of employers and of the misconceived demands of their followers who saw the NLC as a source of employment or financial assistance.

Apparently undeterred by his earlier failure, Olushola resuscitated both his creations in March 1930, renaming the NLC the Nigerian Labor Organization with himself as its labor organizer. He seems to have been moved not only by the usual sources of worker discontent, inadequate legislation to protect wage earners, and rising prices, but also (a portent of the times) by (Nigerian Labour Bulletin, Mar. 17, 1930):

[G]rowing unemployment [which] calls forth an action.... From Gambia right down to Nigeria, we hear of dissatisfaction among the laboring classes caused by the domineering attitude of the capitalists. Among the latter, we hear of, and see gigantic combines[2] and those who are affected are the African laboring classes. Something must be done to remedy the situation.

The solution lay with organizing the working class in its own defense.

African traders, artisans, Mechanicians, clerical workers and all down to the gutter sweepers should organize themselves into unions . . . NOW is the time . . . for us to organize . . . who will lead?

Although preaching industrial combination, Olushola asserted that "it is not the policy of this journal to teach or encourage strikes . . . rather to teach the dignity of labour and to bring about understanding between employees and employers." Few appear to have taken up his message and once more, and this time for good, the NLC and its mouth-piece sank into oblivion.

Others quickly stepped into the breach because on June 2, 1931, the inaugural meeting of the African Workers Union was held at the Lagos premises of the Nigerian Press Ltd. The driving force behind it appears to have been the radical Sierra Leone journalist, I.T.A. Wallace-Johnson,[3] then editor of the *Nigerian Daily Telegraph,* which was owned by the Nigerian Press Ltd. The chair was taken by Dr. Hamed Tinubu (the first Lagos Muslim to qualify as a medical doctor) and speakers included Wallace-Johnson, two struggling journalists, Deniga and Babamuboni, and a Julius Ojo Cole. The main themes of the speeches were the need for racial and economic solidarity in bringing about an end to foreign exploitation. As if anticipating difficulties with the authorities, the meetind ended on a loyal note. Attendance was apparently disappointing although 200 people were enrolled, each promising to pay the very substantial monthly subscription of 1/3d.

The aims of the AWU are outlined in an advertisement in the *Telegraph* and they seem to include not only the comprehensive protection of the rights of wage earners, but also the encouragement of native industries and the promotion of mass education, particularly in the technical field (Nigerian Daily Telegraph, May 28, 1931). Once more, by attempting to appeal on as wide a basis as possible, unrealistic goals were sought and, despite the support of a few members of the Lagos elite, the AWU ran into trouble with the authorities who were suspicious of the intentions of its General Secretary. Wallace-Johnson's house was raided by the police in October 1933 (indicating that the AWU might still have been in existence) who were searching for books and publications "containing seditious documents" (Macaulay Paper, V,II; Public Record Office, C.O. 583/195). A copy of the prescribed communist paper *Negro Worker* was found, but no action was taken against Wallace-Johnson, who left Nigeria the following month. It seems that his departure at a time when unemployment was at its height and worker demoralization widespread left an organizational vacuum which was not to be filled until the Second World War.

Relations with the International Communist Movement

A little researched area in recent African political history is the extent of the contact between the international communist movement and colonial Africa (but see Meli, 1970; Langley, 1969; Wilson, 1976). From its foundation the Soviet Union displayed considerable interest in the colonial and semicolonial world which was viewed as the exploited and vulnerable periphery of the capitalist-imperialist world. The main instrument for building up a following among proletarian and trade union movements in these dependent territories was the Profintern (Krasnyi International Profsoyuzov or Red International of Labor Unions), which was set up in 1921 in opposition to the "reformist" Amsterdam International and active until the end of 1937 (see Bol'shaya Sovetskaya Entsiklopediya, 1953:23,275). The Profintern directed and coordinated the activities of a range of subordinate occupational and geographical bodies from South America to Australia and from the U.S.S.R. to South Africa. Colonial Africa, if not a main center of Profintern activity, was recognized as "one of the most down-trodden branches of the world labour army" (Trud, May 27, 1930).

As early as 1926 the Profintern established a subsection called the International Committee of Negro Workers to which two African trade unions were affiliated, but its main attempt to gain a foothold in Africa occurred two years later when George Padmore, the Trinidadian Marxist, established the Negro Workers' Bureau at Hamburg to recruit African and West Indian cadres and to disseminate Marxist literature in black colonies (see Hooker, 1967: chapter 2). Through such bodies as the International of Seamen and Harbor Workers and the British section of the League Against Imperialism, Padmore was able to make contact with Africans, though in 1930 he managed to travel incognito the length of the west coast of Africa recruiting six delegates for the International Negro Workers Conference held in Hamburg that year (Gambia Record Office File, 4/38). In the same year the Acting Governor of Nigeria, Sir Frank Baddeley, went so far as to accuse the *Negro Worker,* Padmore's principal organ edited from Hamburg, of having contributed to the Aba riots in that year. According to Baddeley, the journal had been discovered "among the workers of Lagos" and the government "was adopting precautionary measures to combat the spread of Bolshevism among the natives." This speech was later reported in the *Negro Worker* with barely concealed satisfaction (Wilson, 1976:219–220).

Padmore's companion during his underground West African journey was Frank Macaulay, eldest son of the veteran Nigerian nationalist, Herbert Macaulay. Although there is little in Frank Macaulay's public pronouncements (he worked on his father's *Lagos Daily News* and had his own column, "The Joker") or lifestyle to associate him with international communism, he nevertheless attended the Hamburg Conference and from there proceeded to Moscow to attend, as one of four African regional delegates, the Fifth Congress of the Profintern. He stayed on in Moscow for several months to study the printing trade and then returned to Lagos. In 1931, shortly after his return from the Soviet Union, Frank Macaulay died as a result of a domestic mishap so that a new intermediary became necessary (Macaulay Papers, III,28, which included Frank Macaulay's obituary in the London *Daily Worker*).

The obvious successor was I.T.A. Wallace-Johnson, who as we have noted, already had a reputation in West Africa for radical journalism and trade union organization. The peripatetic Wallace-Johnson was not to remain in Nigeria for long; he spent much of 1932 travelling in Europe and attending the International Labor Defense Congress in Moscow. Already under police surveillance he returned to Lagos the following February, but nine months later came the police raid on his house and his rapid departure for the Gold Coast, possibly hurried on by official pressure. With his departure, independent action by wage earners along either reformist or radical lines seems to have come to an end. Pressure from employers and government, the incomplete consciousness of the wage earner, and the debilitating effects of the Great Depression all played their part in tying the working class to the political apron strings of the middle classes. Despite the raising of bogies by the government, communist infiltration of Nigerian society was minor and had nothing to offer the politically influential, but constitutionally minded middle class.[4] Perhaps what is significant was the degree of contact Nigerian labor organizers were able to maintain with the distant and disapproved Soviet Union and that some of them at least saw their predicament in a global class context.

Relations with the National Bourgeoisie

While we have sought to show a certain capacity for independent political and industrial action among the wage labor force, the limited success of such action and the failure of outside working class organizations to provide support inevitably meant that periodically the Nigerian wage earners had to turn to their "class enemies," the national bourgeoisie, for help. Hopkins, examining the events of 1897 in Lagos, stressed the class antagonisms which led the African merchant community to support the government in its dispute with its employees. Apparently antagonisms between the various elements of the proletariat were overcome on this occasion, but the middle classes sent an address of loyalty to the governor and were bitterly resentful of his failure to notify them (as opposed to the European merchants) of the possibility of rioting. Constitutionalist attitudes were also shared by leaders of the popular elements in Lagos (Hopkins, 1966:151-152):

> Even Macaulay, the acknowledged leader of the "agitators," disapproved of strike action and took care not to become too closely involved with the urban workers, lest he should encourge the growth of a power which could not be confined within the limits of his own political programme and organization.

In addition to their tepic support for working class demands, some rich Lagosians were directly engaged in the exploitation of African labor on their cocoa and kola farms in Agege (near Lagos), with the colonial government acting in the capacity of "protector of the poor." Wages on these farms were not only low (15/- per month for laborers), there were also complaints that they were not paid at all, and because the provisions of the Labor Ordinance did not apply to contracts entered into under Native Law and Custom, there was little the colonial government could do to prevent the abuse of cheap farm labor (Nigerian Archives, 1930: CONCOL I, 1097). For the most part, however, we would agree with Hodgkin's (1956:115) assertion that:

> The fact that the economic claims and interests of different sections of African society . . . may be divergent is of subordinate importance, so long as for all sections the colonial regime is regarded as the main obstacle in the way of economic progress.

It is in this context of "we are all Africans" that class relations must be examined. There was a measure of interdependence between bourgeoisie and proletariat in colonial society born of a common subordination to alien rule and perceived injustice. There was also a complementarity of resources: the wage earners provided a suitable mass to flatter the bourgeoise leaders and substantiate their claim to be representative of wider sections of society: Skilled workers and the more senior of the salariat qualified for the franchise (which required an annual income of £100) and could therefore vote for the bourgeoise parties, such as Herbert Macaulay's Nigerian National Democratic Party, while all could be asked to contribute to campaign funds. Macaulay in his turn could put his intellectual and organizational skills at the service of wage earners, often on an entrepreneurial basis, by writing petitions, providing newspaper coverage in his *Lagos Daily News* for workers' grievances, and raising questions in the Legislative Council through the elected members of the NNDP. In this way a class-cutting patron-client relationship could prove beneficial to both interests in the short term. Thus, we find a railwayman and trade unionist involved in setting up the Railway Workers Union of 1931 praising Macaulay for his help (Emejulu, n.d.:10):

> One of the moving spirits of this giant in an embryo [the RWU] was the late M.H. Macaulay . . . he charged very modestly for the petitions he put up . . . and His Newspaper was constantly championing the cause of Railwaymen.

Let the trade unionists contemplate strike action, however, and Macaulay's personal and editorial wrath would descend on them. Awolowo ruefully recalls Macaulay's reaction to the Transport Owners strike in January 1937,[5] and the numerus editorials in the *Daily News,* although sympathetic to the worsening plight of wage earners, came out strongly against direct industrial action. "We want at the present time, *no strike action in Nigeria"* (Lagos Daily News, May 30, 1934). Instead Macaulay advised the workmen to make further constitutional representations against the sackings and short time, which were prevalent for most of the 1930s.

In spite of his undoubted talents, Macaulay was able to do very little for the working class in the long years of the depression (1930-1935). Endless questions were raised about unemployment in the Legislative Council and editorials and petitions sought to persuade government to wield its retrenchment axe less savagely. The NNDP even arranged a meeting with Governor Thompson in 1930 to discuss the growing problem of unemployment but, when asked to submit proposals of its own, the NNDP failed to satisfy the Governor as to their relevance[6] (Legislative Council Debates, Feb. 8, 1932). With the very economy of the state facing bankruptcy, Governor Cameron was compelled to reduce government expenditure by mass sacking, pay cuts of up to 26%, and short time working. Europeans as well as Africans were dispensed with in these years, the nadir being reached in 1934. There was a gradual recovery in 1935, but as late as 1938 wages were still being docked. Some indication of the effect of the vicissitudes of these years on the living conditions of the working man may be gleaned from the official reports of the time.

At the insistence of the NNDP members in the Legislative Council, the government agreed to set up an Unemployment Inquiry Commission in April 1935. It was charged with assessing the extent and causes of unemployment (particularly among the semi-educated), and to propose remedies for it (Lagos Daily News, Apr. 5, 1935). The committee was unable to assess the scale of unemployment, let alone suggest means of reducing it, and so the government was obliged to invite the unemployed to register during mid-April. Eventually it obtained some statistics on unemployment and made several suggestions in the light of them.

It was estimated that about 56% of the total of about 4,000 self-registered persons were born in Lagos and that 3.3% of the population of Lagos was unemployed (Nigerian Legislative Council, 1935). This in itself was not a startling figure compared with other parts of the world at this time, but of particular concern was the high number of skilled and clerical workers registered as unemployed and the failure of school-leavers to find work. Compassion for their plight was strengthened by the substantial increase in criminal offenses at this time (Annual Report of the Police Department, 1934). It was recommended that government should repatriate those unemployed living off their relatives in Lagos and that the state should set up agricultural settlements in the Ilaro Forest to provide work (and a suitable geographical distance perhaps) for unemployed youth. Other than this, the committee suggested approaching the Lagos Youth Movement to establish a Labor Bureau.

It seems significant that it was the Lagos Youth Movement, not the NNDP, which was invited to establish a Labor Bureau because it reflects a swing in Lagos politics away from Macaulay's Democratic Party, increasingly identified as a party living off its not particularly glorious past, to a new organization representative of a younger section of public opinion. The old political leadership, it was claimed by its youthful opponents, had failed to tackle the problems of life in the Depression, and should give way to "youth." The Lagos Youth Movement was founded in 1934 (it became the Nigerian Youth Movement in 1936) by a group of "new men," some of whom were scions of the existing social elite, but others were representative of the increasing number of Yoruba and other provincials now to be found in Lagos.[7] The Youth Movement, through its lively journal, *Service,* and in its celebrated *Youth Charter,* outlined comprehensive reforms for Nigeria, not simply in the political sphere, but also in economic matters (Macaulay Papers, IV,19). Its "Economic Charter," which was part of the Youth Charter, consisted of 22 subsections dealing with all the current ills and offering to cater to the interests of all elements in Nigerian society. It strongly upheld the existing land tenure and the rights of the farming community; African cooperatives, credit houses, and craft industries were prescribed to create a "contented peasantry." It opposed foreign monopoly capital and came to the defense of the African businessman and trader; it sought to build up indigenous capitalism through thrift clubs and a grandiose "Five Year Plan" to promote basic industries. Finally, it did not neglect salary earners. Higher salaries and increased Africanization of senior administrative posts were urged and better terms of employment for those working in the commercial houses were also mentioned as an objective. Wage earners were never specifically mentioned in the charter, though unemployment was to be tackled, commencing with the setting up of the NYM Unemployment Bureau, which it was hoped would be converted into a labor exchange. Scientifically managed state farms were seen as a means of combatting unemployment among school-leavers, but silence on artisans and clerks was a recognition of the inability of the NYM to tackle this intractable problem.

Politically, the Youth Movement took an active part in supporting cocoa farmers and transport owners, and members such as Akinsanya and Awolowo were employed as labor organizers. It sought to replace the NNDP as the protector of labor and ties were established with the Railway Workers Union, one of the more militant and influential trade unions in Lagos in the 1930s (Emejulu, n.d.:15). Union members were persuaded to buy shares in the Service Press Ltd. and the *Daily Service* and NYM leadership were expected to support the railwaymen. During the unsuccessful Foundry Shop strike of 1939, two NYM leaders, H.S.A. Thomas and Sam Akinsanya, interceded unsuccessfully with the management. In the crucial Legislative Council elections of 1938, the NYM swept the NNDP out of three seats and in the municipal elections of the same year won three out of four seats. All the candidates fielded were professionals except for a chief and Akinsanya, who claimed to be a labor organizer. He was the only one to lose although he gave the veteran

NNDP leader, Dr. Adeniyi-Jones, a close run for his money.

How significant working class support was for the NYM is impossible to say, but with votes being expressed in hundreds rather than thousands, the backing of a small number of the enfranchised workforce could make a substantial difference. The NYM failed to live up to its promise and fell victim to internal splits in the war years, but by then trade unionists were once more looking elsewhere for a political ally, which they were to find in the National Council of Nigeria and the Cameroons.

CONCLUSIONS

Our purpose in writing this paper has been to focus attention on a neglected social formation which emerged from the colonial situation in Nigeria, namely wage workers. While much has been written about the response of precolonial society to European contact and hegemony or on the rise of an educated elite, far less has been published about the origins and growth of a wage labor force. In addition, there has been a tendency to minimize the importance of this category and to see it as a product of the social and economic changes ushered in by the Second World War. By looking in some detail at the British Colony of Lagos in the early decades of this century, we have tried to show not only the existence of such a formation in quantifiable occupational terms, but we have also sought to give flesh to the statistician's categories and to argue that the first hesitant steps along the long and tortuous path to class identity were taking place.

Class identity requires more than the existence of new economic relations; it demands the recognition of shared economic interests within the new social formation and the willingness to act in the pursuit (or defense) of these comprehended interests. Perception and action we believe existed in this period as we have tried to show by reference to the public utterances and activities of workers or their representatives. Economic organization in the form of trade unions, the recourse to strike action in defense of a newly acquired corporate interest, and the quest for a political identity as manifested in the innovations and alliances described above are indicative, we believe, of a nascent class consciousness among the labor force of colonial Nigeria.

In using notions of class and class conflict in the face of much conventional literature that questions whether such concepts have any relevance to Africa, we have been guided above all by the view that class "is not a thing, it is a happening" (Thompson, 1965:357), moreover a happening expressed in terms of shared values, feelings, interests, life experiences, and set in concrete historical events and processes. Our Nigerian data does not allow us to describe the "feelings" of wage earners with any degree of confidence; we have to infer the extent of their class consciousness from a reconstruction of the actions that they engaged in and the growth of institutions designed to serve their needs. We are nonetheless aware that a number of mitigating and mediating factors exist in a colonial situation to prevent the uncomplicated formation of a class. Colonial society is a syncretic one: the old way of life refuses to give way and adapt itself to change. In Lagos the indigenous community is a case in point. Exposed to the fiercest blast of westernization, a large part of the population did little more than modify its way of life and even that section of the population which directly concerns us was also subject to older loyalties. An element of duality prevails among both indigene and immigrant employed in the wage labor force, a source of comfort as well as mystification for the wage earner. The colonial-racial nexus further erodes class awareness by stressing the common identity of all Africans in their subordination to and exploitation by an alien hierarchy. In such situations political initiative is often snatched by the middle classes who appeal for the support of wage earners on the basis of racial solidarity. A nefarious clientage system is created which fragments any unity among wage earners and stultifies the growth of leadership within this group.

The "invasion" of working class society by elements of the middle classes is encouraged by the constraints on independent economic and political action by wage earners. Until 1938, the imperfect industrial legislation allowed considerable scope for victimization of labor militants while the high-income franchise prevented wage earners from having direct representation in the colonial legislature. The middle classes alone (with the exception of one chief) were elected to the Legislative and Municipal Councils and the major political organizations of the period were also firmly under their control. Employed labor was also divided among itself into white collar, artisan, and laboring strata. On several occasions concerted action between these strata took place, but there was a real cleavage between the office-bound salariat and the proletariat. Vitiating imported social distinctions robbed the wage earners of the full support of the better educated salary earners; and always there loomed the "reserve army" of the unemployed to threaten the jobs of the literate as well as the illiterate workers.

Yet despite these obstacles and diversions progress was made toward a class consciousness. Trade unions did emerge to promote the interests of wage earners and numerous examples of industrial action occurred. It is true that these tended to be short lived and on the whole localized—there was no general strike or trade union congress in this period—but we do find successful strike action and persisting union activities. Even the failures helped sharpen antagonisms and provided a martyrology for later acolytes, though it would perhaps be oversimplifying to argue that the unfolding of consciousness *always* progresses in a unilinear fashion toward greater and greater class crystallization. Spontaneity often characterized the wage earners' behavior in their occupational struggle, whereas their efforts at creating a separate political identity had limited success. Symbiotic and often dependent relationships existed with the middle classes. Several features of the prewar situation persist today among Nigerian wage earners, while the possibilities of independent class action still remain contingent on the extent to which workers can free themselves from the politics of bourgeois clientelism.

NOTES

1. Fragmentary information regarding Olushola can be found in the columns of the *Nigerian Labour Bulletin,* March-June 1930. Olushola is the same individual mentioned earlier in connection with trade union organization among railwaymen in 1925 and who sought direct working class representation on the Legislative Council. Garbled information about his activities seems to have spread to Eastern Nigeria because there is a letter in the *Macaulay Papers* (V,II) from the Port Harcourt Mechanics Union dated November 1923, pledging its support for Macaulay's "Nigerian Bulletin Corporation" (clearly a confusion both of leadership and of the two enterprises run by Olushola).

2. This is an allusion to the 1929 amalgamation between the African and Eastern Trading Company and Lever Bros. This, together with the earlier amalgamation which led to the creation of the A & ETC, had resulted in job rationalization and the dismissal of many African staff.

3. Wallace-Johnson, at this time actively connected with the Comintern, was the scourge of colonial officials not only in Nigeria, but also in the Gold Coast (where he was tried for seditious publication together with Nnamdi Azikiwe in July 1936) and in his native Sierra Leone where he spent part of the war years in detention. (For an official account of his activities in these years, see Gambia Record Office 4/73, "Activities of Wallace Johnson and the International African Service Bureau.") Wallace-Johnson was also the West African correspondent for *The Negro Worker,* a Profintern journal which, according to Wilson, carried "action programs . . . particularly for workers in the principal ports of Nigeria, Senegal and other colonies of West Africa . . . sometimes on the basis of surprisingly detailed information from the field" (Wilson, 1976:217).

4. In 1930 the Nigerian government banned Padmore's main journal, *The Negro Worker,* for publishing an anti-British article on the Aba Riots. At the same time Wallace-Johnson's *Nigerian Daily Telegraph* was reprimanded for relaying material criticizing British policy in India, supplied by the German Communist news agency ANKO (see Public Record Office File, C.O. 583/174). Sir Frank Baddeley's widely publicized speech in London warning of communist subversion in Nigeria was answered in the *Lagos Daily Record* (July 28, 1930) when it stated: "We can assure all the scare-crows that so-called Moscow propaganda cannot flourish in or vegetate under West African soil. What is really needed is sympathetic liberalism in the treatment of the natives, especially the progressive ones."

5. "We were thoroughly let down by Herbert Macaulay . . . when he learnt that we had also enlisted the assistance of Sir Adeyemo Alakija, he was enraged, drove us from his house, and threatened to break the strike. He then wrote an article in his paper calling upon the government to enact a law making strikes illegal" (Awolowo, 1960:127). This incident also shows how the interests of the wage earners (and in this case transport owners) could become secondary to rivalries within the bourgeoisie.

6. In fact, several broad suggestions were made by the NNDP in 1929 which sought to ameliorate the economic situation through cutting down expenditures on European salaries and fringe benefits and using this money to revive old industries, expand public works, and set up an institute akin to that at Tuskegee in the United States (Nigerian Archives, 1929-1931: COMCOL, 894, vol. 1).

7. Its originator was a doctor, J.C. Vaughan, and a member of a leading Lagos family, but other prominent figures in the LYM/NYM were neither Lagos Yoruba nor drawn from wealthy backgrounds, such as Ernest Ikoli (an Ijo teacher turned journalist), Samuel Akinsanya (an Ijebu clerk turned labor organizer), and Nnamdi Azikiwe (an Ibo journalist-businessman).

REFERENCES

African Messenger (November 24, 1921).
ANANABA, W. (1969). The trade union movement in Nigeria. London: Hurst.
Annual Report of the Police Department (1934). Lagos.
ARRIGHI, G. (1970). "International corporations, labor aristocracies, and economic development in tropical Africa." Pp.220-267 in R.I. Rhodes (ed.), Imperialism and underdevelopment: A reader. New York: Monthly Review Press.
AWOLOWO, O. (1960). Awo. Cambridge: Cambridge University Press.
Blue Book: Nigeria (1926). London: Colonial Office.
_____ (1938). London: Colonial Office.
Bol'shaya Sovetskaya Entsiklopediya (1953). Moscow: vtoroe izdanie.
BURNS, A.C. (1948). A history of Nigeria. London: Allen and Unwin.
CARY, J. (1969). Mister Johnson. New York: Harper and Row.
COHEN, R. (1974). Labor and politics in Nigeria, 1941-1971. London: Heinemann Educational Books.
COLEMAN, J. (1963). Nigeria, background to nationalism. Berkeley and Los Angeles: University of California Press.
EGBOH, E.O. (1968). "The early years of trade unionism in Nigeria." African Quarterly, 8 (April/June): 59-69.
EMEJULU, L. (n.d.). Brief history of the railway workers's union. Lagos: Author.
FANON, F. (1965). The wretched of the earth. London: MacGibbon and Kee.
Gambia Record Office (4/38).
_____ (4/73). "Activities of Wallace Johnson and the International African Service Bureau."
GUTKIND, P.C.W. (1974). "The Emergent African Urban Proletariat." Occasional Paper Series, No. 8, Montreal: Center for Developing-Area Studies, McGill University.
HODGKIN, T. (1956). Nationalism in colonial Africa. London: Frederick Muller.
HOOKER, J. (1967). Black revolutionary. London: Pall Mall.
HOPKINS, A.G. (1963). "An economic history of Lagos, 1880-1914." Unpublished Ph.D. dissertation, London University.
_____ (1966). "The Lagos strike of 1897: an exploration in Nigerian Labor History." Past and Present, December: 133-155.
Lagos Census Report (1911). Appendix C:22.
Lagos Daily News (1934, 1935).
Lagos Daily Record (1930).
Lagos Standard (1911, 1919).
Lagos Times (1881).
Lagos Weekly Record (1904, 1913, 1920).

LANGLEY, J.A. (1969). "Pan-Africanism in Paris, 1924-1935." Journal of Modern African Studies, 7(1):69-94.

Legislative Council Debates, Nigeria (1932, 1935, 1936, 1937, 1938).

Macaulay Papers. III,28; IV,a; IV,19; V,11. File on Nigerian Civil Service Union. Ibadan: Ibadan University Library.

MELI, F. (1970). "The comintern in Africa." African Communist, 43:81-99.

Negro Worker (1929-1931).

Nigerian Archives (1920). CSO/1/32. Clifford to Secretary of State for Colonies.

———— (1929-1931). COMCOL 894, vol.1.

———— (1930). COMCOL I, 1097.

Nigerian Taily Telegraph (1931).

Nigerian Labour Bulletin (1930). Ibadan: Nigerian Archives.

Nigerian Legislative Council (1935). Report of the Committed appointed by His Excellency the Governor to inquire into the question of unemployment. Lagos: Sessional Paper No. 46.

Nigerian Pioneer (Lagos) (1919, 1920, 1933).

Nigerian Times (Lagos) (1910).

Public Record Office, London (1906). C.O. 520/36, August 18, Egerton to Elgin.

———— (1904). C.O. 147/174.

———— (1933). C.O. 583, 191/1142, August 18, Cameron to Cunliffe-Lister (and enclosure).

———— (1930). C.O. 583/174.

———— (1933-1934). C.O. 583/195.

SANDBROOK, R., and COHEN, R. (eds.) (1975). The development of an African working class: Studies in class formation and action. London: Longman.

TALBOT, P.A. (1926). "Peoples of Southern Nigeria." Vol. IV. Lagos: Lagos Statistics.

THOMPSON, E.P. (1965). "The peculiarities of the English." Pp.357 in R. Miliband and J. Saville (eds.), The socialist register. London: Merlin Press.

Trud (May 27, 1930).

West Africa (May 17, 1919).

WILSON, E.T. (1976). Russia and Black Africa before world war II. London and New York: Holmes and Meier.

YESUFU, T.M. (1962). An introduction to industrial relations in Nigeria. London: Oxford University Press.

2

WORKING ON THE RAILWAY:
Forced Labor in Northern Nigeria, 1907-1912

MICHAEL MASON
Concordia University

> *The treatment of the workers by the*
> *privileged classes may be taken as a*
> *criterion of the ethical standard attained*
> *by a community. [Forward by Lord Lugard*
> *in G. St. J. Orde-Browne,* The African Labourer, *1933:v]*

By the beginning of the present century in Nigeria forced labor had become one of the twin forms of labor exploitation wrenched from the dying body of slavery. Alongside its sibling, wage labour, it provided the muscle which was demanded by the colonial regime to install the infrastructure required for domination and appropriation. While the Hercules of wage labor was emerging from its infancy in the second and third decades of the present century, forced labor still held on grimly to life. Clearly the two were not contradictory in an economy which was primarily centered on staple production. The contradiction, as we shall see, was between the aims of increased agrarian production and the labor requirements implicit in the building of a system of transport to evacuate the fruits of that production.

Each form of oppressed labor sets in motion its own opposition. Students of slavery, especially in the New World, have diagrammed the means, both violent and passive, by which slaves resisted the demands of their masters. Even more massively studied is the universal struggle between wage laborers and their bosses. However, the forms of oppressed labor which rose in places where the development of wage labor was stunted by different forms of colonial rule—such as indentured labor in Mauritius and the Caribbean and contract labor in Southern Africa—have until quite recently been neglected. It is the aim of this chapter to consider the question of the origins of forced labor and the opposition which it generated within a single colonial realm, Northern Nigeria. Here, consistent with the policy of effecting colonial rule through an indigenous hegemonic class, the epigones of Sir Fredrick Lugard devised a form of forced labor which they sought to camouflage under the designation "political labor." This mode of expropriation achieved a meteoric dominance in the building of the "pioneer lines" in the region over the period 1907-1912, but was perceived as being so contradictory to the main aim of the colonial state—the production of agricultural staples—that it was denounced almost as soon as it had achieved its first major task. In spite of this, it was still widely used in the 1920s and almost certainly even later.

As long as Northern Nigeria remained marginal to the "world" economy the exploitation of labor power took on essentially precapitalist forms. The creation of a wage labor force became contingent upon the establishment of a British colonial government, which was effected by 1903. Shortly thereafter two main types of colonial labor emerged. By 1902 the British had secured control over the Jos tinfields and had begun to employ indigenous workers in the minefields there. By 1907 they had begun to drive local peasants and slaves to build a river port at Baro on the Niger and a railway line to link that town to the ecomonic heart of the Protectorate, Kano. In this chapter we are primarily concerned with the second of these labor forces.

The two main lines constructed in Northern Nigeria were the Baro-Kano Railway, which roughly bisected the region and gave it access to the sea via the Niger river, and the Lagos Extension, which was built to connect the Baro-Kano line with the Lagos Railway that ran inland from the coast. The political history of the Baro-Kano line has already been studied and need not detain us here (Tamuno, 1965; Oyemakinde, 1970). It may be noted in passing that it was seen by its advocates at the time as both assuring cut-price hegemony in the area and as providing a pipeline for the pumping out of the region's surplus wealth and the pumping in of imported goods, particularly those from Britain.[1] The invocation of Baro as a river port did not follow the same economic pattern of capitalist logic. Instead, it seems to have been due largely to the myopic illusion of Sir Fredrick Lugard who aimed to establish a kind of colonial absolutism in the north as independent as possible from the kinds of transformations taking place in the south (see Nicholson, 1969: chapter 6)

By the time the Baro-Kano Railway was begun the line from Lagos had been slithering northward for over a decade. It had been built by local labor, both skilled and unskilled, most of which had been employed by local petty capitalists who had been contracted to build earthworks. Of these skillful men and their methods, Dr. Oyemakinde (1970: 28) has

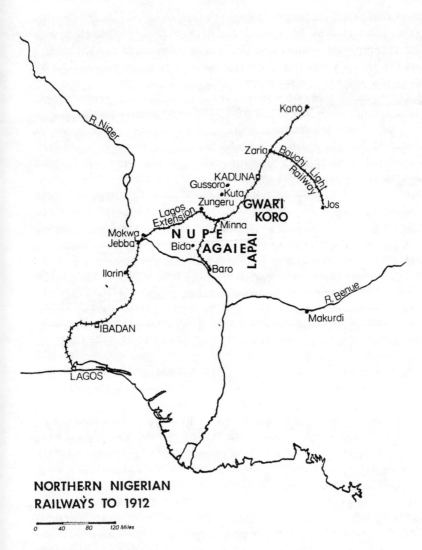

R. Niger

Kano

Zaria   Bauchi Light
Railway

KADUNA
Gussoro   Jos
Kuta
Zungeru   GWARI
Lagos   KORO
Extension   Minna
Mokwa   N U P E
Jebba   Bida   AGAIE   LAPAI
Baro

Ilorin

R. Benue

IBADAN   Makurdi

LAGOS

NORTHERN NIGERIAN
RAILWAYS TO 1912

0   40   80   120 Miles

written that they "made considerable fortune especially as they multi-
plied their net gains by the clever device of drafting their wives along with
other cheaply paid women and children to participate in earthwork."
More skilled work, like track laying, was supervised and paid directly by
European foremen.

Until the end of 1903 labor supplies on the southern line were adequate
in spite of the fact that between June 1900 and January 1902 approximately 6,500 laborers left Lagos to work on the railways and in the mines
of the Gold Coast (Hopkins, 1966). After this labor shortages began to be
felt. Skilled working men found better pay and conditions in the
departments of the colonial government and with the expatriate firms.
Unskilled labor found the newly commercialised agriculture more
attractive. In 1904 the first strike of railway workers took place
(Oyemakinde, 1970: 43-48), a sign of the growing consciousness that
working on the railway was not as it might be.

The historical trajectory of the lands north of the Niger-Benue valley
was quite different from that in the southern provinces of Nigeria. The
colonial administration which was established there, and which was
highly militaristic, found a political structure that it imagined as being an
African variant of European feudalism. The economy was essentially
precapitalist and locally oriented, except for the areas near the rivers on
which the Royal Niger Company had operated, and its social and
political formations were virtually unaffected by those western elements
which had pierced the towns on the coast and in the Lower Niger.

The British who ruled the Protectorate of Northern Nigeria generally
regarded those Africans who had become involved in mercantile capitalism as petty traders or who had mission education as being irre-
mediably corrupted. As one of the distinguishing orthodoxies of colonial
rule in the north, this view originated with Sir Fredrick Lugard. Lugard's
specific phobia regarded the colony of Lagos and its inhabitants, of whom
he wrote disparagingly that the British had spent nearly a million sterling
"to create a spurious civilization" among a "debased population"
(Anjorin, 1965:281). His successor, Girouard, a willing convert to the
dream world of colonial absolutism, carried the fantasy of an Islamic
Camelot a step further by arguing for the exclusion, especially in the
Hausa emirates, of not only southern Nigerians, but of European
missionaries as well. In his view, "the best missionary for the present will
be the high minded, clean living British Resident" (Girouard, 1908-
1909).

We have diverged to discuss some of the more salient features of the
colonial policies in the north because it is only against this background
that we can see the colonial government's attitude toward labor. It is

evident that the divergency between labor policy in the north and in the south is but one facet of more general policies determined by quite contrary historical circumstances. For instance with regard to petty commodity trade in the hands of Africans, which Lugard and his successors attempted to discourage, the more liberal governor of Southern Nigeria, Sir Walter Egerton, wrote (Anjorin, 1965:344): "The greater the trade, the greater the revenue, and the greater the revenue if it is well spent, the better the lot of the people we govern."

Consistent with their aim of maintaining an embalmed facade of indigenous autocracy, the colonial rulers in the north were able to demand that the system of labor contractors employed in the south should be disallowed on the Baro-Kano line and permitted only in a modified form on the Lagos Extension, which was started soon after. Instead of creating the conditions for a free labor market, they developed a system of forced labor which they disguised with the term "political labor." As the name implies, workers on the railway line were to be pressed into service by political means, that is, through the combined intervention of the European officials and the indigenous chiefs, the masters and the prefects joining together against what, in other colonial contexts, would have been regarded as the "boys." The workers recruited by means of political coercion were not expected to remain on the line of rail for more than a few weeks at most. Supervised and paid directly by British foremen, they would in this way, it was asserted, be saved from exploitation by either southern contractors or by local despots. Like other forms of paternalism, this system was devised to assure low wages and the absence of any form of labor consciousness.

It was openly accepted that forced labor was necessary in all African colonies, particularly in the earliest stages of colonial rule.[2] Porterage and road maintenance were the most universal forms of compulsory labor. (Orde-Browne, 1933:39-41). When it proved appropriate to the requirements of regional colonial interests, forced labor was employed for other purposes as well, such as in the mines of Southern Rhodesia between 1903 and 1912 (Van Onselen, 1976: chapter 3). In Northern Nigeria, however, mines never assumed the dominance in the colonial economy that they did in Central Africa. There was never a problem for this reason of a massive supply of cheap labor beyond the building of the colonial infrastructure.

Compulsory native labor in Northern Nigeria was at first only permitted for purposes specified in the Roads Proclamation of 1903.[3] When in early 1907 the Colonial Office sent a circular dispatch to governments of all British colonies and territories inquiring about the subject, the High Commissioner of Northern Nigeria was able to reply in tones of hurt innocence that in his territory compulsory labor was employed solely in road making and in accordance with the Roads Proclamation, that is, never for more than six days a quarter. As for recruitment and labor movement, he said the former was done through local chiefs and so in the case of the latter there was no movement of labor outside the villages from which it was drawn. When the Attorney General of the Protectorate was asked in a minute about punishment for misconduct and desertion, he replied that up to that time no convictions had been upheld for either of these. Thus by mid-1907 Northern Nigeria appeared to have been one of the islands of serenity in a continent in which the most brutal abuses of labor of all sorts were regularly practised. This was to change so suddenly in the next half decade that by 1912 even the colonial administrators in Northern Nigeria themselves were to complain about the deleterious effects of the forced labor system.

The government of Northern Nigeria was informed by the Colonial Office on August 8, 1907, that approval had been given to build a "pioneer line" from Baro to Kano. Prior to this, survey work had already been carried out.[4] The decision to start construction had come after a debate on the subject, which had begun as early as 1903, the year the Protectorate had been brought, more or less, under British control. As a preliminary to the recruitment of a massive labor force, the governor toured Nupe Province through which the first stage of the railway from Baro was to pass. Purred the Resident of that province:[5]

> Your Excellency's tour through Nupe . . . and interviews with the chiefs of the Province has had a striking effect in impressing on them the magnitude of the work that had been commenced. The Agaie and Lapai Emirs were especially glad at being accorded the honour of a personal interview.

The Emir of Lapai, at least, had much to be glad for. By the end of the 19th century many of the villages over which he had previously exercised a slack but oppressive hegemony had been in a state of revolt. Even as late as 1904 a patrol of the colonial West African Frontier Force had to be sent out to enforce the payment of tribute by some of his resentful subjects. To the Emir, as to other rulers in Northern Nigeria, this lesson in the value of dependency was learned quickly. The honor of the personal interview established quite unambiguously the relationship between the governor and the emir. It was one between sovereign and prince in an absolutist system; and among other obligations of princes was the supply of labor along the line of rail. However, the British were not so perfidious as to ignore their own obligations. In mid-1908, when the people of one of the districts administered by the emir attempted to resist his despotic sway, the Resident of Nupe Province assured the High Commissioner that support of the emir was warranted: "He had been of real assistance to the administration, and his services have been invaluable to the Railway."[6]

After the governor's visit to the emirs, the districts which comprised the province were toured by one of the political officers who appointed district headmen "from the ruling Fulani classes." In Lapai Emirate there were four districts on the line of rail and, besides the Fulani headmen, the sub-district heads, each with 15 to 20 villages under his charge, were called up and urged as to the necessity of promptly supplying the labor required. In Agaie the same procedure was carried out. As with the emirs, the British were aware that, by appointing district heads from among the ruling stratum,[7] they would find the "keenness and interest in their work" which they desired. The enthusiasm of these petty officials was understandable: in their new, colonially sanctioned offices they had a chance of regaining the authority and status which they had lost on the arrival of the British, or often never really had.[8]

Figures for labor on the Baro-Kano railway are not available for the last part of 1907.[9] From early 1908 we can see them rise rapidly, remaining at a constantly high level from February through June, that is, well into the agricultural season.

Table 1. LABOR FIGURES ON THE BARO-KANO RAILWAY, 1908.

Jan.	Feb.	Mar.	Apr.	May	June	July	Aug.	Sep.	Oct.	Nov.	Dec.
2426	4364	4822	3820	4264	4362	—	—	—	4798	5146	2734

Up to May most of the recruits had been Nupe, most probably from the emirates of Lapai and Agaie. From the end of May the Gwaris became increasingly important as the earthworks moved northward. We have seen that the recruitment of Nupe labor was through existing political structures, stiffened and made more assertive by British support. Among the Gwaris no such analogous structures existed so the railway builders had more difficulty recruiting. For this reason it was more necessary for the direct intervention in the recruiting process of the European political agents.[10] Perhaps as a reflection of the new difficulties, in late 1908 we see labor being sent from the emirate of Abuja to the east where the political means existed to force men out to work. Whatever the case, by the end of the year the Baro-Kano line was seen to employ laborers who were of fairly mixed ethnic origins—Nupe, Gwari, Koro, Yoruba, and Hausa. Generally the most unskilled work, the building of earthworks, was done by the first three groups, while Yorubas were engaged in the more skilled tracklaying, and "wandering" Hausas were used as carriers of tools and materials.[11] Each gang of 25 men worked for four complete weeks before being replaced by another gang from the same district.[12]

By October 1907 a second railway line had been sanctioned for Nupe Province. This was known as the Lagos Extension and it was intended to link the Baro-Kano line with the Lagos Extension which had reached Ilorin. It was to be built north of Ilorin to Jebba and then diagonally across Nupe to join the Baro-Kano near Minna. North of the Niger in the section from Jebba to Zungeru, the northern capital, the policy of labor recruitment seems to have been a modification of the "political" system used on the Baro-Kano line. South of the Niger sub-contractors were employed exploiting labor from north of the river. This led to a certain amount of friction between the political officers from the north and the European railway builders from the south.[13] The Resident of Nupe Province excitedly denounced the exploitation of "his" Nupe laborers by the Yoruba contractors. He provided evidence that these men worked their gangs from dawn to dusk with only two half-hour stops for food, and that some laborers worked for as long as four weeks and were paid as little as 8/6d while others received only 1/- for a week's work. It was also indicated that some of the workers had been beaten by the contractors.[14]

By the beginning of 1908 the Lagos Extension was employing 2,750[15] laborers although by the third quarter of the year it appears that this number had fallen to around 1,000.[16] Judging from the tenor of official reports, and especially the tone of implicit self-congratulation in the northern officers' condemnations of the labor contractors south of the river, it might be assumed that all was rosy in the northern domains, but outside observers put a different coloring on the subject.

The Protestant missionaries in Northern Nigeria had been encouraged by Sir Fredrick Lugard, himself, although his successor, Girouard, developed an ill-concealed antipathy toward both their methods and their ambitions. His complaints against them were grounded in the fear that their activities might provoke a "fanatical outbreak," a Mahdist Mutiny, among the Muslims of the Hausa emirates. But in Nupe, which of course counted as a Muslim area, missionaries had been established for several decades prior to colonial rule, so there was no question of impeding their activities. Like missionaries elsewhere in Africa, those in Nigeria were mainly sympathetic to colonial rule; and in the north any criticisms they might have had of the forms of colonial policy were less likely to emerge for fear of increasing the hostility of the unsympathetic High Commissioner. Nonetheless, given the evangelical basis of the missionaries in Nupe, including the Church Missionary Society (C.M.S.), and their exaltation of personal moral consciousness, there was no way of assuring that protest, however undiplomatic, could be effectively stifled. Nowhere is this more evident than the reaction of the C.M.S. evangelists to the abuses of labor.

The Rev. J.D. Aitken was the Superintendent of the Mokwa District of the Church Missionary Society's Northern Nigerian Mission. It was through this district that the Lagos Extension was built. Moved by the palpable horrors of railway building, he wrote the Resident at Bida a number of letters condemning both the European supervisors and the African labor recruiters for extortion and exploitation of various sorts. Among the explicit charges made were those that the Europeans made "requests for virgins to be supplied to them" and claimed that "fowls had been requisitioned and not paid for" and, more generally, that "harsh and unjust treatment was being meted out to the chiefs in connection with the provision of labour for the railway."[17] He also suggested extortion by the African headmen.[18]

Before the tempest which followed blew itself out, the High Commissioner had been consulted and the secretary of the local Executive Committee of the C.M.S. had been called to Bida. If any understandings were reached between the mission and the government, they are nowhere preserved. At a meeting subsequently called by the Executive Committee at Lokoja, the Reverend recanted in the most enigmatic terms and was immediately transferred out of Northern Nigeria.[19] To assume that pressure was put on him by his fellow missionaries whose dominant concern was to accommodate the colonial regime may not be wholly unjustified.

That at least some of the charges were just cannot be doubted. The political officer in charge of the area in question admitted that the African agents were exploiting the laborers, although he remained mute concerning the involvement of the Europeans with regard to laborers, chickens, or virgins. It becomes apparent that the system of labor recruitment had ultimately depended on the local district heads employing subordinates to do the job of forcing men out of the villages and onto the railway earthworks. These clients of the local autocrats rewarded themselves by extorting money both from the villages and from the laborers, although how much they kept and how much they passed on is unknown. Mallam Isagi, an agent of the Nakorji who had charge of the village of Wagbe, took six pounds from one gang of laborers as they returned home. Another follower of the same titleholder "owned to having taken various presents and gowns from several Yeti villages." One of the Benu's recruiting staff, Mallam Ibrahim, confessed to extorting 12 shillings from a Bete village.[20] It becomes apparent that the forms of extortion were almost unlimited. Most commonly men were made to pay 3d a week in "dues." In some cases further sums were demanded at the end of the compulsory period of labor before the workers were let off, and then again once they reached home. In the latter case this might amount to three shillings per head, that is, the equivalent of a week's wages *before* dues.

Although the claims of Rev. Aitken were withdrawn and their author humiliated, they were in fact investigated by a spy paid on the Secret Service account. At least one malefactor was arrested and sentenced to prison, probably no less a figure than the brother of the Emir of Bida.[21] At the same time the Resident's scorn toward missionary intervention was unabated just as his interest in the protection of the railway navvies was unexceptional. "I am of the opinion," he wrote, that "our responsibility ends in seeing that the individual is paid, if he likes to pay his village or District Chief 3d per week—probably for some service rendered—it is certainly no concern of Mr. Aitken's and I even doubt the wisdom of the Political Officer stopping this voluntary gift."[22] Plainly in the paternalistic scheme of the Resident, subjects had a clear obligation to resign their labor to the new colonial state and their wages to their traditional masters.

While the complaints of Rev. Aitken were thus abruptly and peevishly dismissed, other complaints regarding the mistreatment of workers made by the Right Reverend Bishop Tugwell were afforded the extreme unction appropriate to a cleric of his status. In September of 1909 Tugwell addressed himself quite informally to the Acting High Commissioner, Sir William Wallace, on the question of the workers at Baro, Northern Nigeria's aborted little port.[23] The burden of his letter was that the working conditions there were "difficult to distinguish . . . from slavery." He made four points explicitly: first, "the men do not volunteer their services but are forced to render service"; second, "although they are nominally paid six pence a day, they do not actually receive this amount. A large part of their earnings do go to the men who drive them to their work"; third, the men worked for nine or ten hours a day under revolting conditions, sometimes carrying heavy rails through deep mud without a break; fourth, "whilst carrying these heavy loads, if a man slacks or slips he is most cruelly beaten by those who are his overseers. Whilst if a man escapes from Baro and runs to his village, he is sent back by his overlord, possibly after further beating."

Reacting to this severe criticism of what the Bishop regarded as an unjust *system,* namely that of forced labor, Wallace ordered an inquiry to be held at Baro to answer the *specific abuses* cited by Tugwell. The cast of witnesses was not notably unbiased: Mr. Eaglesome, the Director of Railways, Northern Nigeria; Mr. Higgins, Surveyor of Works; Mr. Graham, the Paymaster; Lt. Cripps, the Marine Superintendent; Mr. Taylor, the Assistant Accountant; Dr. Chartres, the Senior Medical Officer; and Capt. Osborne, the District Superintendent of Police were the principal ones. In a supporting role were a number of Africans including the son of the Emir of Lapai, the cousin of the Emir of Agaie, and the son of the Yerima of Bida, all of whom were connected with labor recruiting. The chairman of the inquiry was the Resident of Niger Province, Herbert Goldsmith. It was Goldsmith, remember, who had earlier expressed the view that the Rev. Aitken had no business complaining about abuses on the Lagos Extension. In support of the official inquiry, independent testimony was provided by Father Schirer of the Roman Catholic Mission at Lokoja. The conclusion of the inquiry contained few surprises. It noted that:

(a) "It is true that labour (natives) supplied through the Political Staff are not volunteers in the sense of their being recruited in the open labour market," but they were not physically forced. The lack of physical coercion was attributed to the chief's lack of power.

(b) The laborers received 9d a day *while engaged in discharging railway material,* not 6d as Bishop Tugwell alleged.

(c) Men were not driven or exploited although it was true that in parts of the province men were paid 3d per week, which was generally used to pay for food supplied by the chiefs or for taxes.

(d) Working conditions were not as Tugwell had described and, contrary to his affirmations, no serious accidents had been brought to the notice of the senior medical officer.

(e) Finally, although "a certain amount of ill-treatment of labour is bound to occur at times," men do not "escape from Baro," but are relieved every three or four weeks. Father Schirer testified that, in several visits to Baro, he had "never seen the least sign of ill-treatment inflicted upon any native."

The matter thus officially closed.

Although no further questions were raised publicly, Bishop Tugwell privately dissented from the choral unanimity expressed at the inquiry. In a private letter to Wallace after it was all over he reasserted his original view that it was cruel to employ unskilled labor to unload iron rails and iron sleepers and that eight hours in tropical conditions was too long to employ men who were ill-fed, ill-clad, and unused to strenuous and continuous exertion. While admitting misinformation on some points, he argued that if the pay and working conditions were as the report affirmed, it was difficult to see why so few men, in the testimony of the report, were willing to return after working the mandatory three-week period. Further, he was able to cast plausible doubts on the quality of the testimony of both the African agents and the Resident himself. He contradicted the agents' denial that the laborers had paid no part of their earnings to them. He cited the testimony of Goldsmith himself, who admitted that he had recently learned (probably from Rev. Aitken) that such payment had been made. To the Resident's conclusion that men never fled from Baro he cited the testimony of the Nakorji of the town of Etsu Gaie who admitted that "I have only known one or two cases of men who actually ran away from the work. They were always sent back."

Although Bishop Tigwell could not have appreciated it, the government itself produced evidence of the exploitation of workers by agents. In the Niger Province report for the final quarter of 1909 was the statement:[24]

> The supply of labour for the railway has given opportunities to native staff subordinates to practise a system of extortion on unwilling recruits. Native agents would go to villages and give an order in the name of the District Chief for so much labour to be supplied, but it would appear, from certain cases tried in the Provincial Court, that these agents were quite prepared to accept a cash equivalent as a substitute for an unwilling recruit.

It is likely that Bishop Tugwell had at least momentarily embarrassed the colonial regime in Northern Nigeria; but he had done little more than that. With Resident Goldsmith serving the complex but complementary roles as witness, advocate, and judge, it would have been surprising if the hearing convened at Baro did not fall short of even the most modest standards of impartiality. Even so, there is little indication that the Colonial Office, to whom both Goldsmith and Wallace were ultimately answerable, was especially concerned with the form of forced labor which had emerged in Northern Nigeria.

Within the Nupe section of the railway line there is no evidence to suggest that resistance to the demands of the labor recruiters took forms other than flight. In large part this may be explained by the highly organized system of political oppression which existed in the Nupe emirates. From the Resident down through the emirs to the village heads ran a chain of authority which as securely linked those who had an interest in labor recruitment as it shackled those upon whom the burden of labor fell. In all of the Nupe emirates force and extortion had been fairly well developed in precolonial times. After the emirates had virtually collapsed in the 1890s, the British reconstituted them in the early part of the 20th century. The coercion which they were able to employ was thus stiffened by both the newly formed emirate police, who were controlled by the local political coalition of emir and political officer, and the West African Frontier Force, which backed up the police.

Leaving Nupe, the railway line moved into the lands inhabited by the Gwari people. Here political structures were almost completely different because well-organized government based on political hierarchy and sustained by military superiority was virtually nonexistent. This created at least temporary problems both for administration and for the exploitation of labor, as we can see in the Resident's complaint:[25]

The provision of labour in the Gwari country, split up as it is into a number of different communities, is a totally different problem to the labour question in Nupe where the Emir of Bida is paramount Chief and where in consequence organisation can be effected through him as a central authority. More political officers are obviously wanted where there are many independent Chiefs than in a state where there is only one.

It would seem that by 1909 labor demands all along the line had reached a high level. The conscripts from Lapai and Agaie working at Baro had been told that they would be allowed home in time for the planting season of 1909, but when the time came they were made to stay.[26] Further north where some 1,752 Gwaris and Koros (the latter being a less numerous people who lived interspersed among the Gwaris) had been brought to build earthworks,[27] the first signs of large-scale resistance became evident. The Koros of the Paiko and Fuka districts of Kuta Division deserted en masse to their homes at the beginning of the rains and refused either to turn out for work or to pay the tribute due for the previous year.[28] The British administration could do nothing about this because it was too short staffed. Whatever explanations the political officers conceived for the Koros' nonconformity, the disinclination to work on the railway was probably more connected with poor wages than a passion for village life. In the Niger Province Report for the June Quarter of 1909 the Resident noted that food along the line of rail was scarce and prices high because of the large demand. He estimated that food could cost 4d to 5d per day and was quick to conclude that a 6d daily wage was insufficient.[29] The real daily wage would have been even less if the workers, like their brothers in Nupe, were forced to remit a part of their pay to their exploiters.

By June 1909, the semi-annual report for Niger Province finally admitted "a lamentable spirit of discontent amongst the Gwaris." Recognition of this required little acuity of perception, because in the previous month the men of the village of Gussoro in the Kuta Division had shot and killed the Political Officer, Mr. Vanrenen, as well as 11 African policemen accompanying him. Although this revolt has received almost no attention in the histories of this period, it was one of the most vigorous attempts at resistance to colonial rule to succeed the Satiru and Hadejia rebellions of 1906.[30]

The Gussoro revolt was served up to the Colonial Office in an ample sauce of mystification.[31] In a letter forwarded by the Resident to the Acting High Commissioner, Sir William Wallace, it was explained that the revolt had its origins in a dispute over the office of village chief. The logic of village politics was presented as being as inscrutable as the colonial subjects themselves: "They maintained that it has always been their custom to grow tired of their Chief and to drive him out and kill him."[32] Although it was claimed that the chief had taken more money from the people than had been required for tax purposes, the Resident emphasized that this charge was unjustified. It was thus, it appeared, in an attempt to comb out the tangled skein of village politics that Mr. Vanrenen, the local political officer, had taken a party of 35 policemen. The villagers, 100 strong, but armed only with bows and arrows, were determined to prevent the return of the unpopular chief who was with Mr. Vanrenen's party. A skirmish ensured at the end of which an estimated 40 Gussoro men were killed and the same number wounded. On the colonial side Mr. Vanrenen and 11 African policemen lost their lives.[33] In the retaliatory exercise that followed, in which the colonial force was more massive and heavily armed, according to different estimates between 75 and 200 villagers were either killed or wounded.[34]

The retaliatory expedition was not the end of the process of colonial justice. In the aftermath of the second attack on Gussoro, seven Gwari men were captured and brought to trial for their part in the rebellion. All were found guilty and sentenced to hang by the Resident, Mr. Orr. At the same time the remaining people of Gussoro were evacuated and the village apparently destroyed.[35] This was the same fate which had befallen the rebel village of Satiru near Sokoto.[36]

For the Gussoro seven there was reprieve, however. Their sentences were commuted to life imprisonment by the Acting Chief Justice. Still, Mr. Orr, who expressed regret that at least four of the malefactors were not to be hanged, consoled himself with the reflection that the site of Gussoro town had become inhabited solely by monkeys.[37]

Two weeks after the first letter to the Governor at Zungeru, which was forwarded to London, the Resident wrote again. A copy of this letter did not reach the Colonial Office. In it the Resident accepted the unpopularity of the chief of Gussoro as being not entirely due to Gwari arbitrariness. He explained:

> For many years he (the chief of Gussoro) has always tried to carry out the Resident's orders, and there has always been a large faction in the town which passively resisted him. But towards the end of last year this resistance increased, owing apparently to orders being issued for the Gussoro people to build some canoes for placing at the various rivers where the railway would cross, and the hostile faction increased in the early part of this year when Gussoro was called on to supply labor for earthworks.

The Resident did not think the demands from Gussoro to be excessive. From inquiries he learned that no more than 200 of the 1,000-odd men of Gussoro were ever forced to work on the railroad and that in April, the month for planting, only 150 men were at work. All of these walked off the job in early May.[38]

Why had the Gussoro men, alone among all others, undertaken armed resistance? Obviously we must look beyond the simple answer that they sought to avoid the oppression of forced labor because the same oppression affected people who did not revolt. The resistance by the Gussoro men, we must assume, was borne of a combination of factors which were quite specific to time and place. Of these the political factors were determinant. We have seen that the structure of coercion in Gussoro was not as well grounded as it was in the villages of Nupe, all of which had in precolonial times been forced to submit to the authority of centralized political systems, the emirates. Nupe village chiefs could rely on the support of other chiefs, the district heads, the emir, the political officer, and the colonial police. Behind them was not merely moral pressure, but physical force. Gwari villages were, on the other hand, all independent of one another, or at most were organized in small groups. They had no hierarchies analogous to the ruling elements which had arisen in the Nupe emirates in the 19th century.[39] Thus the Gwari chiefs were a long way from the Nupe emirs. Opposition to them in Gussoro, as we have seen, and presumably elsewhere, was effective and difficult to crush.

That the events of May were not spontaneous is seen in the fact that in March the Gussoro laborers had also abandoned railway work under the leadership of one of the chief's rivals, a man who seems to have been one of the village leaders.[40] We find no analogy to these strikes in Nupe, because leadership of the railway gangs was imposed from above and was loyal to the government. In fact, so close was the supervision of Nupe labor that one of the emirs, Lapai, moved from his traditional capital to a camp near the railway line.[41] So in Gwari not only was traditional authority much less well entrenched, but even the British political officers were too few to see to the collection of taxes and the raising of labor levies.

While the political structure of Gussoro determined that there could be resistance, it was economic circumstances which dictated the timing of the revolt. The laborers who abandoned the line in March returned due to the persuasion of Mr. Vanrenen. Those who left in May could not have returned if they were to plant their crops; thus they were more determined to stay in Gussoro. These factors and others which remain invisible determined passive resistance. Active resistance was defensive and it was only brought about when the village was approached by the European in charge of "political" labor accompanied by a body of armed African policemen.

Labor problems on the Baro-Kano line persisted beyond the crushing of the "Gussoro Revolt." Resistance spread and became more determined. Mr. Gill, one of the political officers on the railway in southern Zaria Province, reported 300 "desertions" from the line while another officer complained of 800.[42] The British attributed these desertions to "underground mischief" and connected them with the resistance at Gussoro. Fears that widespread resistance would lead to questions being raised in England were aired in official correspondence. A suggestion was made that detachments of the colonial army should be sent to "steady" the Gwaris and that these should be large lest the Gwaris "try conclusions" with the government. However, such notions were unrealistic and accepted as such by the Acting High Commissioner. The lesson of Gussoro was not that more force should be used to recruit labor, but that "it is madness to take large levies during the farming season from pure agriculturalists like the Gwaris, far better go slow till dry weather." The Acting High Commissioner was not alarmed at the reports of massive desertion, although he admitted that "what happened at Gussoro makes one careful of expressing opinions."[43]

By March 1909 the railway line had entered Zaria Province. The labor force recruited from that province swelled from 300 men in March to 3,191 by the end of the year. In Zaria town itself, work was begun at the end of July with 470 men. By the end of the year this force had risen to 4,100 men.[44] A third province, Kano, became involved in April 1910, the roll of laborers here being swollen from 500 at the start of the year to 8,000 at the beginning of July.[45] So by April-May thousands of men were toiling on earthworks which stretched from the Niger, through Nupe, Gwari, and Zaria to Kano, the commercial capital of the Central Sudan. The total workforce at this time may have been as many as 15,000 men.[46] Even this was not the climax of Northern Nigeria's frenzied railway boom, however, because in March 1911 the Bauchi Light Railway line was started. This was aimed at connecting the Jos tinfields with the main line by means of a narrow gauge feeder which branched eastward at Zaria. Unlike the main line, which was built for the general purpose of exploiting Nigeria, the Bauchi line was built expressly to accommodate the mining interests on the plateau. These were doubly favored by the colonial rule—first they got control of the mines and the cheap labor to exploit them, and second they got forced labor to build a railway to export the tin from those mines. In addition to the more than 8,000 men working on the main lines in the spring of 1911, 5,000 were at work on the Bauchi line.[47]

By 1912 the boom in railway building appeared to be finally at an end. In Niger Province (originally called Nupe Province) where it had started in late 1907, 251,443 laborers had been recruited over a five-year period.[48] At least partly as a result of the demands for railway labor, political unrest still seethed in the Gwari districts and military patrols were maintained there as a regular feature of colonial administration.[49]

As late as March 1911, for instance, the Gwari village of Taberma had been burnt to the ground and five of its leaders executed for killing a government agent.[50]

Although the railway was officially opened by early 1912, there still lingered in the minds of some administrators the apprehension that continued demands for compulsory labor would be made. This moved the Acting Resident of Niger Province to indicate the past evils of the labor system in order to urge the government to let the railways secure their own labor, in future, on the open market. His evidence against a continuation of compulsory labor was that it undermined agricultural production, led to depopulation through flight from labor exactions, and permitted extortion by headmen. He cited uncleared and unmanned farms in Kuta, a town near Gussoro, where crops were being sown by very little boys; emigrations from the Trans-Kaduna area, where the Lagos Extension was being built to Pategi on the other side of the Niger; and the trial of two court messengers for extortion to prove his point. Concluding his case against compulsory labor, he sounded a note of unconsciously ironic morality:[51]

> The wealth of the people in this Province is increasing; liberal ideas, the offspring of our rule, on the right every man has to the free use of his own intelligence and labour are spreading very rapidly; and it becomes increasingly difficult to reconcile compulsion with our precepts.

From the response of the government at Zungeru we can only conclude that his complaints fell on ears already sensitive to the problem. The administrator of the northern government cabled his opposite number in Lagos to inquire whether the question warranted the initiation of an inquiry to see if there might be alternative means of raising labor to work on the railway line.[52] He drafted another letter to the Acting Chief Director of Railways in Kaduna that was less tentative and more threatening:[53]

> The natives who entered enthusiastically into the scheme cannot fail to be disgusted if their services are continually being requested at prices which are not those prevailing in the labour markets. This disgust will inevitably burn to unrest.

As correspondence on the subject accumulated, it became apparent that "unrest" was not a threat for the future, but an existing condition. The second quarterly report from Zaria Province had already noted the resistance to labor demands and wholesale emigration from that province. A partial list compiled by the Emir of Zaria indicated that 639 families had abandoned Zaria for Kano, Katsina, and Bauchi. Working conditions on the line in Zaria bear more than a superficial resemblance to those uncovered by Bishop Tugwell in 1909. Laborers who resisted conscription were punished by the Emir. Those who did not were exploited by their own headmen or other usurers so that when they were paid at the end of the month they had to hand over two thirds of their inadequate wage.[54] Wages had not increased since 1907 when they were set at 6d per day, although mine labor was earning 1/- a day.[55] Not unnaturally did men avoid working on the railway.

Perhaps the whole debate about "political" labor was aired when it was because there was a general realization that the peak demand had passed. Thus for the administration there was an inclination to get on to other things—especially "development." For the railway officials, however, although the demand for labor had dropped from a peak of 16,000 to somewhere around 4,500, supplies were still short.[56] The mines had drawn off most of the free labor with their better wages and possibly less oppressive conditions. This conceivably might have suggested raised pay for the railway workers, although to Mr. Bland, Acting Director of Railways in the north, such a suggestion should be adopted only in the last resort. His view of the question was one which may be seen as representing the classical colonial labor theory and is worth citing. It was premised on the colonial commonplace that (NAK SNP 7/13 3436/1912, Memorandum):

> The peasant in Northern Nigeria as long as he can grow enough food to supply his own and his family's needs has not the slightest inclination to leave his farm. His wants are few; he can grow his own cotton, weave it and clothe himself, he breeds a few sheep and goats, occasionally visits the nearest market, does a small amount of trading and is quite satisfied with life in general.

Not surprisingly he was not motivated by money. More likely to move him from his stagnant Eden were taxes. Alternatively, Mr. Bland suggested, the government could encourage agricultural productivity. This would lower farm prices and drive the marginal farmers into the waiting arms of the labor recruiters. Otherwise a labor bureau might be set up with incentives given to recruiters or even forced movements of population undertaken in order that every section of the line might be assured of an ample working population to draw on. Only if all else failed should wages be raised. "If the country is to develop along economical lines," he asserted, "it is most necessary that the cost of labor . . . be kept down during the early days." And lest it appear that he did not have the Africans' best interests at heart, he added, "Any increase now would I maintain find its way into the pockets of the big trading firms and thence to England or the continent without benefiting the country in the slightest."[57]

Mr. Bland's schemes were ignored, however. Replying to his proposals the governor explained:

We have no alternative whatever before us but to do away with every kind of forced labour or whatever term is used to apply to it. There is no doubt at all that the "political labour" is not voluntary.

He thought the best solution was to pay the men more.[58]

Thus, the end of political labor was signalled. By the last quarter of 1912 the payment of 8d per day had been promised in the hopes of attracting more volunteers.[59] Still the railway remained unpopular, as the Resident of Zaria concluded:[60]

There is more labour for the mines and other requirements than can be employed, and yet practically none have come forward to work on the Railway which shows some.

The completion of lines linking Kano to the south did not put an end to the inexorable demand for northern labor. With the opening of the Bauchi line the demands of the minefields increased voraciously. In 1910 the mines employed around 1,500 men; by 1912 this had risen to 10,000;[61] Still new projects were undertaken. By 1914 Zaria labor was expected to be fully employed on the new line from Eastern Nigeria, Kano was being asked to provide the manpower to build the new capital at Kaduna, and Niger was being asked to provide the men to build the new railway headquarters there;[62] but forced or political labor was losing its popularity. One of its critics was Mr. Gowers, the influential Resident of Kano. Concerning future supplies of labor he wrote:[63]

I presume that the labour needed is to be engaged in the open market and that 'political' labour is not required. . . . I do not think it is necessary for me to enter on the subject of the abuses to which the recruiting of unwilling labour gives in the Province, . . . the use of 'political' labour from Kano for departmental works is, in the present stage of development and in view of the degree of economic education that the population of this province has now attained, neither advisable nor justifiable.

However, as long as wages were kept low and working conditions were scarcely tolerable, forced labor would continue to be necessary. As late as 1925 there were still over 3,000 men forcibly recruited to work on the railways in Northern Nigeria. At the increased rate of 9d a day, men were paid just enough to feed themselves, although food shortages were still experienced. The mortality rate, perhaps a reflection of the combination of wages and working conditions, stood at 24 deaths per thousand workers, per annum not as damning as the 70 per thousand rate for Mozambique workers in the Rand or the appalling 80 per thousand in Kenya and the Cameroons, but much higher than the 8 per thousand in the Belgian Congo (Buell, 1928:658-659; Vail, 1976:399). Given that the railway laborers in Northern Nigeria remained on the earthworks for only a month at a time and were not subject to the same long-term effects of strenuous labor, deficient diet, and dehumanizing environment as were the mine laborers in southern Africa, these government figures themselves remind us that even in West Africa, the exploitation of labor under conditions imposed by the colonial state was systematically ruthless.

The day of the brave but primitive revolt of men like the Gwaris of Gussoro had dawned at the same time as a new light was breaking. Of the thousands of peasants conscripted to work on the railway lines from 1907 most returned to the oblivion of rural life with little more than a sharpened awareness of the conspiracy of exploitation which had developed between their chiefs and the Europeans. Nontheless, the railway which they themselves had built was to become the nursery of a new class which was not to dissolve so conveniently into rural incoherence. The most notable members of this class were the railwaymen. North of the Niger their numbers were probably conspicuous at such depots as Minna, Zaria, and Kano. By 1911 the Emir of Zaria was heard to complain that his influence over his subjects was waning because of the railway. The British Resident at the time was also aware of a novel response to traditional oppression. He cautioned that a *"talaka* [peasant] who did not wish to do what he was told merely cut himself adrift from his village knowing that he could be quite independent and earn good money as a railway labourer."[64]

A higher level of political awareness is evident as well among the permanent gangs on the Baro-Kano line and on the Lagos Extension who refused to pay taxes to local native authorities. We should be mindful of the fact that this took place in a part of Niger Province where traditional authority was most well established. That railway workers refused to pay taxes (which were legal) in precisely the same areas as those in which peasants had been unable to resist extortion (which was, at least formally, illegal) seems to suggest a consciousness among the former of which the latter was devoid. Such a consciousness was the necessary basis of class coherence. A class happens, in E.P. Thompson's (1968:9) words, "when some men, as a result of a common experience, (inherited or shared) feel and articulate the identity of their interests as between themselves and as against other men whose interests are different from (and usually opposed to) theirs." If it is the case that class experience is determined by the productive relations into which men enter, then we can acknowledge in the case of the railway workers the beginnings of a class, although hardly, as yet, one for itself. The struggles in which a specific class consciousness was forged were yet to come.

NOTES

1. Sir William Wallace who served at different times the Royal Niger Company and the Protectorate of Northern Nigeria and so, presumably, saw the question from both the commercial and the political viewpoints, wrote "The construction of the railway is justified first and fully upon military and administrative grounds" (C.O. 446/83 Wallace to C.O. July 11, 1909). This is not to suggest that behind the railway's apparent military value there was not a more significant economic concern, but merely to note that *at the time* the military ends were seen as being dominant.

2. Buell (1928:657) noted that "under certain circumstances, the administrators in every colony in Africa oblige the natives to work for public purposes." A few years later this was repeated by another author, a colonial labor official (Orde-Browne, 1933:37).

3. National Archives, Kaduna, Nigeria (hereafter NAK) SNP 7 2089/1907, Girouard to C.O., June 21, 1907; this was incorporated into Proclamation No. 12 of 1904.

4. NAK SNP 7/9 4341/1908, Baro Kano Railway, Progress Report for the Half Year ending June 30, 1908.

5. NAK SNP 7 4014/1907, Nupe Province, Report for September Quarter, 1907.

6. NAK SNP 4108/1908, Niger Province, Report for June Quarter, 1908.

7. The Hausa word "sarakuna" is used in the correspondence.

8. The local rulers were also directly remunerated for their services. In the first half of 1908 the Lapai District chiefs had been paid a total of £52.6.0 and the Emir of Lapai £12.12.10 by the railway. NAK SNP 7 41083/1090, Niger Province Report No. 1 for Quarter Ending June, 30, 1909.

9. Labor figures are printed in NAK SNP 7/9 4241/1908, Baro Kano railway, Progress Report for the Half Year ending June 30, 1908, and telegram from Girardin to Secretary, Zungeru, May 18, 1909. I have found no figures for the third quarter of 1908 in either the reports in the Kaduna Archives or the published Annual Reports for Northern Nigeria.

10. I derive this assumption from the comments of the Resident, Niger Province, in his Annual Report for 1908. Here he mentions the "splendid service" of three political officers, including Mr. Vanrenen, "for the very difficult task of organizing the Gwari labour, and in gaining the confidence of native tribes which have barely been a year under control" (NAK SNP 7/10 1896/1910).

11. NAK SNP 7/9 4241/1908, Baro Kano Railway, Progress Report for the Quarter ending December 31, 1908.

12. See the article by John Eaglesome (1912). Until research work is done in the field, it will not be possible to know the precise relations between laborers and chiefs. Were the former mainly clients, pawns, or slaves?

13. NAK SNP 7/9 5893, Niger Provincial Report, September Quarter, 1908.

14. For the catalogue of complaints presented by the Resident to the High Commissioner, see NAK SNP 7 1694/1908, Railway (Lagos Government) Northern Extension.

15. NAK SNP 7/9 2838/1908, Railway (Lagos Government) Northern Extension.

16. NAK SNP 7/9 5893, Niger Provincial Report, September Quarter, 1908.

17. CMS G3 A9/0, Alvarez to Baylis, April 12, 1909.

18. NAK MINPROF 252/1908, Complaints made by Mr. Aitken regarding Extortion by Headmen on the Railway. Rev. Aitken's own letter is missing.

19. CMS G3 A9/0, Northern Nigeria Executive Committee, Feb. 1909, Rev. J.D. Aitken, Questions Affecting. The reverend's picaresque retraction ran: "Dear Sir, I am a cad and have behaved like a cad. I am very sorry and wish to withdraw all I have written." However, neither he nor anyone else actually suggested that his accusations were without basis.

20. NAK MINPROF 252/1908, Complaints Made by Rev. Aitken.

21. CMS G3 A9/0, Tugwell to Baylis, Mar. 8, 1910.

22. NAK MINPROF 252/1908.

23. The Tugwell-Wallace correspondence, excepting Tugwell's reply to the inquiry,

may be read in C.O. 446/85. Tugwell to Wallace, September 1909 enclosed in Wallace to C.O., Nov. 4, 1909. The full correspondence, including Tugwell's parting shot, is in NAK SNO 6/5 127/1909, Labour Conditions at Baro: Bishop Tugwell Complains.
24. NAK SNP 7/10 1106/1910, Niger Province, Report for December quarter.
25. NAK SNP 7/10 2888/1909, Gwari Labour for Railway.
26. NAK SNP 7/10 3713/1909, Niger Province, Report for June Quarter.
27. Out of a total labor force of 4,067. NAK SNP 7/10 3713/1909.
28. NAK SNP 7/10 3713/1909.
29. NAK SNP 7/10 3713/1909.
30. The revolt is neither mentioned in comtemporary historical studies, such as Charles Orr's *The Making of Northern Nigeria,* 1911, or in William Geary's *Nigeria Under British Rule,* 1927, nor in more modern studies such as Michael Crowder's *West Africa Under Colonial Rule,* 1928. It is, however, noted in the *Gazetteer of Nupe Province* (1920, E.G.M. Dupigny, ed.) where in the account of the colonial period in Kuta Division we are told: "The only serious opposition to the British administration in the Division came from the independent Gwari town of Gussoro . . . in May 1909. The trouble was entirely local and due to domestic intrigues for the chieftainship."
31. C.O. 446/83, Wallace to C.O., June 4, 1909.
32. C.O. 446/83, Orr to Wallace, May 22, 1900, enclosed in Wallace to C.O. June 4, 1909.
33. C.O. 446/83, Orr to Wallace, May 22, 1900, enclosed in Wallace to C.O. June 4, 1909.
34. C.O. 446/83, Williams to Wallace, May 18, 1909, enclosed in Wallace to C.O. June 4, 1909. Williams, who commanded the Gussoro Expedition, estimated 73 killed and an unknown number wounded while "native spies" estimated total casualties at round 200. In a telegram to the C.O. Wallace indicated that 200 had been killed. C.O. 446/84, Wallace to C.O. August 25, 1909.
35. C.O. 446/83, Chief Justice to Wallace, July 27, 1909, in Wallace to C.O. June 4, 1909.
36. NAK SNP 7/10 5979/1909, Niger Province Report, Quarter ending Sept. 30, 1909. The suggestion that the village was destroyed comes in Dupigny, 1920:44.
37. NAK SNP 7/10 2888/1909.
38. NAK SNP 7/10 2888/1909, Resident, Niger to Governor, May 29, 1909.
39. Because no serious study of any part of Gwari has ever been attempted, it is impossible to comment here on the political structure of that community. A superficial account, based on colonial assessment reports, may be found in Gunn and Conant, 1960:95.
40. This was the Madaki. See SNP 7 1888/1909, Orr to Governor, May 23, 1909.
41. NAK SNP 1106/1910, Niger Province, Report for December Quarter 1909.
42. NAK SNP 7/10 2888/1910.
43. NAK SNP 7/10 2888/1910.
44. NAK SNP 7/10 986/1910, Zaria Province Annual Report, 1909.
45. NAK SNP 7/10, Kano Province (Half Yearly), June 30, 1910.
46. This rough estimate is based on the 4,100 men working in Zaria Province at the end of 1909, the 5,228 in Niger in March 1910, and the 8,000 in Kano in July 1910.
47. NAK SNP 7/12 2136/1911, Zaria Province Report, March Quarter 1911.
48. NAK SNP 7/12 1855/1911, Niger Province, Summary of Principal Events to 1912.
49. NAK SNP 7/12 2047/1911, Niger Province Annual Report, 1911.
50. NAK SNP 7/12 2047/1911, Niger Province Annual Report, 1911.
51. NAK SNP 7/13 3436/1912, Railway labor, Withers Gill to Administrator, June 19, 1912.
52. NAK SNP 7/12 2047/1911, Niger Province Annual Report, 1911. Acting Chief Secretary, Zungeru to Colonial Secretary, Lagos, July 10, 1912.
53. NAK SNP 7/12 2047/1911, Niger Province Annual Report, 1911. Chief Secretary, Zungeru to Acting Director Railways, July 13, 1912.

54. NAK SNP 7/12 2047/1911, Niger Province Annual Report, 1911. Extracts from Resident E.H.B. Laing's report on Zaria Province for Quarter ending June 30, 1912.

55. NAK SNP 7/12 2047/1911, Niger Province Annual Report, 1911. Memo on the Question of Railway Labor enclosed in Acting director of Railways to Chief Secretary; Aug. 15, 1912. The exception to this seems to have been the Lagos Extension where 8d was paid. Ibid. General Manager, Nigerian Railways to Director of Railways, Oct. 25, 1912.

56. Around 2,500 were needed to maintain the railway and another 2,000 for new works. NAK SNP 7/13 3436/1912, Memorandum.

57. NAK SNP 7/13 3436/1912, Memorandum.

58. NAK SNP 7/13 3436/1912, Memorandum. Chief Secretary to Director of Railways, Kaduna, Aug. 29, 1912. Specifically, he wrote, "We should try to obtain voluntary labour for a little over 6d."

59. At the same time government unskilled labor was being paid 9d a day everywhere else in West Africa (Sandbrook and Cohen, 1975:15). Richard Jeffries stated in the same work that in the Gold Coast railway wages for unskilled workers stood at 9d to 1/3 per day (1975:44).

60. NAK SNP 7/13 6607/1912, Zaria Province Report, September Quarter 1912.

61. NAK SNP 7/13 3436/1912, Extracts from Mr. F.D. Bourke's Report on the Naraguta Mine.

62. NAK SNP 8/1 50/1914, Railway Circular re "Enlisted" and "Casual" Labour in Secretary, Zungeru to Resident, Kano, Feb. 5, 1914.

63. NAK SNP 8/1 50/1914, Resident, Kano to Secretary, Mar. 17, 1914.

64. NAK MINPROF 344/1912, Taxation of Railway Labour.

REFERENCES

ANJORIN, A.O. (1965). "The British occupation and the development of Northern Nigeria, 1897-1914." Unpublished Ph.D. dissertation; University of London.

BUELL, L. (1928). The native problem in Africa, Vol. 1. London: Frank Cass.

CROWDER, M. (1928). West Africa under colonial rule. London: Hutchinson.

DUPIGNY, E.G.M. (1920). Gazetteer of Nupe Province. London: Waterlow and Sons.

EAGLESOME, J. (1912). "The system of recruiting native labour for the construction works on the Baro-Kano Railway, Northern Nigeria." The African Mail, 453: Aug. 16.

GEARY, W. (1927). Nigeria under British rule. London: Frank Cass.

GIROUARD, P. (1908-1909). "Correspondence." Rhodes House, Oxford, MSS British Empire, S.63.

GUNN, H.D., and CONANT, F.P. (1960). "People of the Middle Niger region of Northern Nigeria." Ethnographic Survey of Africa, Part XII. London: International African Institute.

HOPKINS, A.G. (1966). "The Lagos strike of 1897." Past and Present, 35:47.

NICHOLSON, I.F. (1969). The administration of Nigeria. Oxford: Clarendon Press.

ORDE-BROWNE, G. ST. J. (1933). The African labourer. London: Frank Cass.

ORR, C. (1911). The making of Northern Nigeria. London: Frank Cass.

OYEMAKINDE, J.O. (1970). "A history of indigenous labour on the Nigerian railway, 1895-1945." Unpublished Ph.D. dissertation, University of Ibadan.

SANDBROOK, R., and COHEN, R. (eds.) (1975). The development of an African working class: Studies in class formation and action. London: Longman.

TAMUNO, T.N. (1965). "The genesis of the Nigerian railway, II." Nigeria Magazine, 84:31 (Mar.).

THOMPSON, E.P. (1968). The making of the English working class. Harmondsworth: Penguin.

VAIL, L. (1976). "Mozambique's chartered companies." Journal of African History, XVII(3):399.

VAN ONSELEN, C. (1976). Chibaro: African mine labour in Southern Rhodesia, 1900-1933. London: Pluto Press.

3

THE 1922 STRIKE ON THE RAND: White Labor and the Political Economy of South Africa

ROBERT DAVIES

INTRODUCTION

On March 10, 1922, the South African Prime Minister, Smuts, dispatched a force of 7,000 troops supported by bomber planes and armored vehicles to put down an armed uprising by white wage earners employed in the goldmining industry. It was the dramatic climax of a struggle which had begun two months earlier when some 25,000 white mine employees had come out on strike demanding the restoration of a job color bar agreement unilaterally abrogated by the Chamber of Mines. After four days of armed struggle, during which 153 people were killed and over 500 wounded, the strikers' forces were eventually subdued. Five thousand of their number were immediately arrested, several hundred of these were subjected to penalties ranging from fines and imprisonment to (in four cases) death, and on March 16 the mines were finally reopened on terms dictated by mining capital.

Although the strike itself was defeated, it was nonetheless one of the crucial watersheds in the evolution of social class relations in the South African social formation. It had decisive long-term effects both on the structuring of the relations between capital and white wage earners, and on the rate and trajectory of capitalist development in the social formation. This chapter will attempt to analyze and explore some of these consequences of the 1922 strike, concentrating particularly on its effects on the structuring of relations between capital and white wage earners. It will begin with a general analysis of certain of the structures and contradictions of South African capitalism in the period 1896–1924. It will then proceed to examine the immediate causes of the strike of 1922 and its immediate effects in producing a realignment of class forces and a change in hegemony in the power bloc. And it will finally examine the effects which this realignment of class forces and change in hegemony had, firstly, on the rate and trajetory of capitalist development and, secondly, in bringing about a particular form of incorporation of the "white labor movement" into the state structures.

CONTRADICTIONS BETWEEN MINING CAPITAL AND WHITE WAGE EARNERS, 1896–1924

To understand the causes and consequences of the strike of 1922, we have to understand something of the changing relations of production in the mining industry in the period between 1896 and 1922, something of the position of mining capital in relation to other capitals during this period, and something of the rhythm of two particular contradictions arising therefrom. To begin our analysis of the changing relations of production in the goldmining industry and the contradictions arising therefrom, we need first to refer to the specific constraints within which capitalist production in the South African goldmining industry took place. Essentially as Johnstone (1976: 13-20) has shown, there were two major technical and price constraints: first the goldbearing ore of the Witwatersrand, though plentiful, was and indeed still is of a low average grade, mostly located in narrow broken seams far beneath the surface; second, the price of gold, as the international money commodity, was internationally determined and set at a fixed level over long time periods. Capital accumulation in the South African goldmining industry was therefore from the outset critically dependent on two factors: on the ability of the mining capitalists to obtain the relatively large amounts of advanced capital necessary to bring the mines into production, and on their ability to bring about the extreme minimization of the costs of production necessary to make the production of gold from low grade seams and within fixed price constraints possible. The net effect of both these factors was to bring about an early transition from competitive to monopoly capitalism beginning within ten years of the opening up of the Withwatersrand goldfields in 1885.

If we follow the analysis of Poulantzas (1975:116-138), the phase of transition from competitive to monopoly capitalism is a phase of capitalist development during which there occurs a two-fold change in the relations of production. Firstly, it is a phase in which the capitalist centers exercising *the powers of economic ownership* (i.e., the powers to assign the means of production, resources, and profits to this and that use) are rapidly concentrated into a smaller number of units. But, secondly, it is also a phase in which capital effects a greater concentration of *the powers of possession* (i.e., the powers related to the direction and internal organization of actual labor processes) in order to gain the advantages of large scale socialized production. In other words, the phase of transition to monopoly capitalism involves, in addition to a change in economic ownership, a reorganization of actual labor processes: in particular it involves an enlargement of the size of the actual productive units, and a socialization of labor processes hitherto performed under the real control of skilled craft workers. However, for a number of reasons which cannot be discussed here, this concentration of the powers of possession generally proceeds at a slower pace than the concentration of the powers of economic ownership.

In the case of the South African goldmining industry the concentration of the powers of economic ownership characteristic of the phase of transition to monopoly capitalism began in about 1896 and was virtually completed by about 1910. One observer described the juridical form which the process assumed as follows (Frankel, 1938:84):

> Out of the 576 goldmining companies floated on the Rand during the period 1887-1932 . . . only 57 remained in existence in 1932. . . . The 57 goldmining companies in existence in 1932 were, with some minor exceptions, controlled by six finance houses or groups. The process of amalgamation and financial concentration had taken form by 1897 and the group system can be regarded as having been firmly established by the time of Union [i.e., 1910—R.D.].

However, the concentration of the powers of economic ownership in the industry had, characteristically, advanced at a faster pace than the concentration of the powers of possesion, which was in fact only completed after 1922. To understand the particular form of the contradictions arising in the South African goldmining industry at this particular phase, however, we have to understand how agents of production of particular racial groups had been combined in the industry's division of labor at the beginning of the period.

Essentially the production of gold required the coordination of a number of labor processes. In the mine itself the rockface had to be drilled and blasted, the ore had to be shovelled into trucks, trammed to the winches, and then hoisted to the surface; the mine also had to be ventilated, pumped, and provided with timber supports. Development work required, inter alia, shafts to be sunk, pipes to be fitted, tracks to be laid, and winding engines to be installed. Above ground the ore had to be sorted and crushed and the metal extracted. But while a number of these processes had been organized on the basis of socialized production under capital's real control at least since the beginning of "deep level" mining in 1896, at the start of the phase of transition mining capital had been compelled to rely upon skilled craft workers both to organize the method of work (conceptualize), and to actually perform (execute) a number of other key functions. These included a number of important functions in the amalgamation and reduction process, in other surface tasks and, underground, the operation of much of the technical equipment including (at first) machine drills.

Capitalist production in the South African goldmining industry had, therefore, at the start of the phase of transition to monopoly capitalism, required the incorporation of agents of production into three distinct types of places in the division of labor. Firstly and most importantly, it had required the incorporation of agents into various places in socialized groups of direct producers (known locally as gangs). Secondly, it had required the incorporation of skilled craftsmen to perform the various productive tasks enumerated above. Finally, it had required the incorporation of agents to perform the dual function of supervision under capitalist social relations, i.e., to coordinate the labor processes (a productive function necessary to the production of use values), and to exercise surveillance and control over direct producers (a function arising out of the antagonistic nature of capitalist social relations necessary for the extraction of surplus value).[1]

For the first category of agents of production (direct producers in socialized work groups) mining capital turned to Africans, and indeed steadfastly refused to employ in these places the increasing number of "poor white" proletarians drifting into the towns through the spread of capitalist relations in agriculture (see Johnstone, 1976; Davies, 1976). The reasons why these particular places in the industry's division of labor emerged as "all black" are essentially to be located in the differing conditions under which white and African proletarians had become proletarianized. As several writers have shown at length (see Bundy, 1972; Legassick, 1974, 1975; Johnstone, 1976), the proletarianization of Africans in South Africa came about through the deliberate, purposeful intervention of the dominant classes (foremost among them mining capital). As such, it had been a process accompanied by an intense and protracted struggle on the part of the dominant classes to ensure that it took forms most beneficial to the needs of capital accumulation. At the most visible level this had involved the establishment by the dominant classes of a number of coercive/repressive apparatuses which functioned both to ensure a supply of African workers and to ward off various forms of resistance by them. Among these were the use of taxation to force the sale of labor power by Africans in the "reserves," the promulgation of pass and vagrancy laws which had a similar effect on those living in the towns, and the promulgation of laws and regulations subjecting various forms of resistance (e.g., striking, desertion, or "insubordination") to criminal as well as civil penalties. At another level it involved the creation of particular structures which enabled capital to minimize the costs of reproduction (value of labor power) of African workers. These have been most extensively analyzed in the work of Wolpe (1972, 1974, 1975) who has argued that the notorious migrant labor system involved a particular pattern of articulation between capitalist and precapitalist (African) modes of production. In the most developed version of his basic thesis (1975), Wolpe has argued that the conservation and restructuring by the dominant classes of the productive capacity of the precapitalist (African) modes of production enabled capital to avoid the costs of generational reproduction of the African working class, while still ensuring that the workers' families fulfilled their essential role of producing and reproducing the recruits to replace the "worn out" members of the working class. In other words, through the migrant labor system, capital was able to reduce the value of African labor power (and hence the wage level) to the costs of reproducing the worker from day to day. Moreover, as Legassick (1975) had indicated, through the operation of the compound system mining capital was able to minimize those day-to-day costs of reproducing African migrant workers for which it remained "responsible." In the first place the compound system enabled capital to assume direct control over the pattern of consumption and to regulate with some precision the quantities and qualities of the various items of consumption to the minimum levels required to rejuvenate the worker as a "muscular machine." Secondly, it meant that the mining capitalists became large institutional buyers and were thus able to secure discounts, savings, and other "economies of scale." The net effect of these factors was that the costs to capital of reproducing African labor power under these conditions was far below the minimum subsistence costs of reproducing the fully proletarianized, urbanized "poor white" families—1/2 to 1/6 according to various contemporary estimates. To have employed whites in these places would therefore have run counter to the prime imperative of capital accumulation in the industry—to bring about an extreme minimization of the costs of production.

In respect of the other two categories of agents of production (skilled craftsmen and new petty bourgeois supervisors), however, mining capital had turned to whites. In the case of skilled craftsmen the reasons for this were relatively straightforward: there were at the time when the mining industry was being developed few skilled, experienced miners available in the social formation and mining capital was therefore obliged to import skilled labor power from European social formations. In the case of supervisors there were essentially two reasons, deriving from the dual character of the supervisor's task, why mining capital had turned to whites. Firstly, because the productive function of coordination, originally a far more important part of the supervisor's task than it became later on, required the exercise of considerable mining skill and experience; and secondly, because under the prevailing political and ideological conditions, whites had an assumed authority over blacks which was considered by mining capital to be indispensable in the exercise of surveillance and control over black workers. As one influential American consultant put it in 1905 (Browne, 1905:1595):

> He [the black man] has to be controlled and efficiency of control demands . . . the supremacy of the white race [and] a distinct line of separation between skilled white and unskilled coloured labour.

At the beginning of its phase of transition to monopoly capitalism, therefore, the mining industry was characterized by a racial division of labor in which blacks were assigned to places in socialized groups of direct producers and in which whites (paid wage rates averaging between eight and sixteen times the average African wage per shift) were assigned to artisanal and supervisory places. The concentration of the powers of possession, characteristic of the phase of transition to monopoly capitalism, took the form essentially of a struggle by mining capital to bring about a reorganization and socialization of labor processes involving the transfer of productive functions from white artisans to socialized groups of African direct producers. It did not, however, ever become a struggle for the elimination of white wage earners from the industry altogether (as contemporary trade union rhetoric suggested). Neither did it become (as the "conventional wisdom" of liberal historiography has tended to assume[2]) a struggle to establish a nonracial structure of relations of production. The employment of whites in the tasks of supervision continued, for the reasons mentioned above, to be necessary for the extraction of surplus value in the industry. Therefore what the struggle for the powers of posession in the mining industry entailed was a struggle in which capital took the offensive seeking to bring about a greater separation between the tasks of conception and control on the one hand and productive manual labor on the other in order to restrict white employment to new petty bourgeois supervisory places.

As Legassick (1975) has indicated, this pattern of struggle is most vividly illustrated in the case of the rock drilling process. Originally large rock drilling machines had been operated by white artisans assisted by one or two African "helpers." It had soon become apparent to mining capital, however, that the African "helpers" were in fact quite capable of operating the drill on their own. Thus, even before 1900 the process had, after a brief struggle, been reorganized so that the Africans became the actual operators and the white a supervisor of two drills operated by five Africans. At this stage, however, the white supervisor combined his supervisory duties with the performance of one or two productive manual tasks. He was, for instance, required to rig up the drill preparatory to its operation and to assist in its operation from time to time, as well as to handle the blasting of the ore.

By 1907 it had become apparent that many of these residual manual tasks could also be handled by Africans. Accordingly, after a fairly intense struggle, the process was again reorganized so that most of these tasks (except for blasting) were transferred to Africans or eliminated altogether by the introduction of smaller drills, and the white "rock-driller," relieved of these duties, became a supervisor of three drills instead of the previous two. However, at this stage the performance of the productive task of coordination was still an important part of the white "rockdriller" supervisor's duties. Thus, according to one contemporary description he was required to "watch" the African drillers, occasionally "if the rockdrill went out of order," helping "to put it right." But he was also required to exercise judgment, to know how "to put in his holes to best advantage and to utilize his explosives in the best possible manner"; in the view of one consulting engineer this was "highly skilled work" (Ross Skinner to 1913 Select Committee: 2 and 14).

In later periods the degree to which he performed even this remaining productive task—coordination of the labor process—was reduced. By 1914, for example, white "rockdrillers" were to be found supervising up to ten drills, as Africans increasingly took over the tasks of coordination as well. By 1922 they had lost even their specialist identification with a particular productive task. As the Mineworkers Union put it in a submission made in 1926 (Statement to *Mining Industry Arbitration Board* 1926/1927:408):

> Prior to the 1922 strike the rock breaker did rockbreaking, the timberman timbering . . . [etc.]. Today the general rule is that the rockbreaker in addition to rockdrilling has to do [read supervise—R.D.] one or more of the jobs enumerated above, and it is no exaggeration to say that the rockbreaker of today is doing the work which it formerly took two or three men to do.

What happened in the case of rockdrilling was repeated in the case of a host of other departments and processes ranging from the operation of engines and underground hoisting equipment and the performance of tasks in the amalgamation and reduction process to tasks like drill sharpening, truck repairing, and even compound maintenance.

For the white employees in the mining industry this process of deskilling/restricting white employment constituted a threat to their position. In the first place the transformation of white employees into supervisors was not a process in which each individual white employee was reassigned to a supervisory place. On the contrary, by increasingly transferring the productive tasks to Africans, mining capital was able to increase the ratio of productive workers to supervisors. It was therefore, inevitably, a process in which white labor was shed as Table 1, showing the trend toward a reduction both in the absolute number and in the proportion of whites employed in the industry, clearly indicates.

Table 1. SOUTH AFRICAN GOLDMINING INDUSTRY SELECTED EMPLOYMENT STATISTICS

Year	Whites	Blacks	Ratio White:Black	
1910	25,634	198,713	1 :	7.75
1915	22,901	206,354	1 :	9.01
1920	22,837	184,971	1 :	8.10
1922	14,681	171,658	1 :	11.69

SOURCE: Union Statistics for Fifty Years (Jubilee Issue, Pretoria, 1960).

Even where redundancies were not an immediate prospect, this pattern of labor reorgnization still remained a potential threat to the position of white wage earners. From the outset white employees in the mining industry had relied upon capital's dependence on their skills to secure and defend their relatively high wages. They were therefore faced, through the deskilling inherent in this process, with the loss of one of their most important bargaining advantages as well: a factor which mining capital was not slow to recognize.

This last point is perhaps most vividly illustrated by the events of the 1907 strike. Before 1907 mining capital had recruited the overwhelming majority of its white employees from among the skilled miners of the European social formations and had, as we have already seen, relied upon them to perform a number of productive tasks. When these employees struck against the reorganization of the rock drilling process, mining capital soon recognized that with the white "rockdriller's" task deskilled, the strikers were vulnerable to the effects of the (white) reserve army of labor. Unemployed whites were invited to scab on the strikers, which they did in sufficient numbers for the strike to be defeated. They were not taken on at the same rates of pay as the previous incumbents, however, with the result that mining capital was able through this maneuver to reduce the median white wage from 18 shillings and 6 pence to 17 shillings and 7 pence a shift.

For these reasons mining capital was resisted by its white employees at each stage of its attempt to reorganize labor processes along these lines. The form which this resistance took was that in opposition to mining capital's attempt to transfer as many of the productive tasks as possible to African workers, they (the white wage earners) put forward the counter-demand that a range of specified tasks and functions be reserved exclusively for whites. The demand by the white miners for job color bars was thus not simply an expression of some irrational racial prejudice which for some reason or other the mining capitalists did not share. Rather, it was as Johnstone put it (1976:74): "a response to a specific class problem, produced by the system of production and class structure from which that problem itself derived." It was a demand which reflected both the nature of the white wage earners' incorporation into a racist hierarchical division of labor, and the degree to which, despite the frequent claims to be socialists, their perspectives failed to transcend the prevailing structures of capitalist social relations.

THE CONTRADICTIONS BETWEEN MINING CAPITAL AND OTHER CAPITALS, 1896–1924

Having indicated something of the nature of one of the contradictions which concerns us here—that arising between mining capital and its white wage earning employees during the mining industry's phase of transition to monopoly capitalism—we now have to briefly examine the other—that arising between mining capital (identifiable as a fraction of imperialist or "foreign" capital) on the one hand, and capitalist agriculture and industrial capital (identifiable as fractions of national capital) on the other.[3] This contradiction essentially arose from the uneven development of the different capitalist fractions during this period and the particular imperatives of mining capital. Capitalist agriculture and industrial capital were during the first quarter of the 20th century, by and large, internationally "cost inefficient" and their particular fractional class interests therefore lay in excluding from the local market the products of "more efficient" foreign competitors. Mining capital's interests, on the other hand, lay in minimizing its costs; both its direct costs (in the form of the items of constant capital) and its indirect costs (in the form of wage goods). It was therefore generally opposed to the exclusion of cheaper imports. Thus, as Kaplan (1974, 1976, 1976a) has shown, the major contradiction arising within the dominant classes at this stage—arising of course in the context of a wide range of common interests related to the preservation of their domination over other classes—took the form of a struggle over alternative economic policies: the policies of protection and subsidization favored by national capital or the policy of "free trade" favored by mining capital.

Before concluding our analysis of the period prior to 1922, we need to indicate how the particular contradictions which we have examined were condensed into determinate social relationships *at the level of the state.*

This has to be understood by reference to the principal and overdetermining role of the state in a capitalist social formation generally, which is (following Poulantzas, 1973) to act as the factor of cohesion in a social formation characterized by class domination and class contradiction through politically organizing the dominant classes and politically disorganizing the dominated classes. Like other capitalist states, therefore, the South African state was involved during the period prior to 1922 in the dual task of politically organizing the dominant classes and politically disorganizing the dominated classes.

In respect of the first task—the political organization of the dominant classes—the South African state acted in a number of ways to overcome the isolation effects arising from capitalist property relations and to realize the common political interests of all the different dominant capitalist classes and fractions (both "foreign" and "national"). In so doing, however, it did not dissolve all the contradictions existing between them. As in all capitalist social formations, the dominant classes in South Africa came together in a contradictory unity (what Poulantzas calls a power bloc) under the hegemony of one particular fraction which had been able in the class struggle to assert the primacy of its own particular interests. In the period prior to 1924 hegemony lay with mining capital, and it was thus its particular interests which prevailed over those of the other fractions. More particularly with respect to the differences between the dominant fractions over the state's economic policies ("free trade" or "protection"), it was the "free trade" policies of mining capital which prevailed. Protective duties did exist, but by way of compromise concessions to members of the power bloc, which fell far short of meeting the basic demands of the fraction of national capital.

In respect of its second task—the political disorganization of the dominated classes—the state's principal role was of course related to the defense of the political interests of the dominant classes against the struggles of African classes, the principal dominated. However, it also had to defend the dominant classes against the political threats posed by the struggles of the white wage earning classes: particularly those arising from the struggles over the powers of possession in the mining industry.

We have already seen that white wage earners in the mining industry were a minority of the total labor force whose role in the actual production process was diminishing over time. One important consequence of this was that they were, to an increasing extent, placed in a position in which strike action by individual groups was unable to seriously disrupt production. As the Secretary for Mines put it in 1913 (Department of Mines and Industries Report for 1913:10):

The bulk of the manual work is being done by the coloured or aboriginal workman. . . . His presence makes it possible for a mine . . . to continue work for a time at all events, although half its white employees may go on strike.

For these white wage earners to be in any way successful in a strike, two things were required: first, that they mobilize the support of a comparatively large proportion of their number; and, second, that they prevent capital from utilizing the scab labor to which they were as nonproducers particularly vulnerable. There was thus a structural tendency for the strikes of the white wage earning employees in the mining industry to assume the form of large-scale general strikes in which the strikers adopted a particularly militant anti-scab stance. Having achieved a degree of trade union organization at a very early stage, this structural tendency had, prior to 1922, become an actuality for white workers on two occasions following struggles over the powers of possession—the first being in 1907 and the second in 1913. On both occasions strikes arising from some specific issue related to the reorganization of labor processes rapidly escalated into a general strike of all white mine employees during which there were major confrontations over the use of scab labor, riots, and even, because the white miners had access to explosives, bombings.

The state's initial response to these strikes had been basically to intervene directly to defend the immediate interests of the dominant class fraction involved (in this case the hegemonic mining capitalist fraction) through expediting the defeat of the strikers and attempting to undermine trade union combination. It had on both occasions deployed its armed forces to defend strike breakers against pickets, and used various laws to break up gatherings of pickets and strike meetings. It had become increasingly apparent in the course of these struggles, however, that the state could not defend the interests of the power bloc through such means alone. Indeed, it had become apparent that direct intervention in support of the *economic* struggles of the hegemonic fraction were having the effect of undermining certain of the power bloc's *political* class interests. The power bloc needed, given the absence from the social formation of such "traditional" supportive classes as a small holding peasantry, some degree of support from all white classes, and direct state interventions of this sort were having the effect of undermining efforts to organize the white wage earning classes as a supportive class for the form of state. Furthermore, large scale strikes, whose outbreak was not actually being prevented by such repressive measures, were seen as having potentially serious effects on the struggles by the African, principal dominated, classes. Firstly, they were seen as having a possible catalytic demonstration effect which might prompt similar strikes by Africans. Secondly, the massive redeployment of the state's repressive forces required to defeat major strikes by white wage earners was seen as leaving the power bloc particularly vulnerable to an uprising by the African masses. As one government commission stated (Report of the Native Grievances Inquiry, 1914:67):

> If as is most probable a native outbreak takes place as a result of disturbances among the Europeans . . . forces are almost certain to have been diverted to deal with the latter. In the case of serious riots among whites, it may easily be impossible to keep in reserve for a further contingency any part of the force available.

Following both major strikes in the mining industry, therefore, the state had become involved in seeking an alternative means of defending the power bloc's political interests against the effects of militant struggles by white wage earners, viz. the incorporation of the "white labor movement" into various racially discriminatory "industrial relations" apparatuses (racially discriminatory at the insistance of capital [see Davies, 1976a]) whose role would be to delimit the form of struggle by white wage earners, in part by making available certain economic concessions through institutionalized forms of struggle which did not constitute a threat to bourgeois political interests. An act suspending the right to strike and providing for the establishment of "conciliation boards" in the event of a "dispute" had been passed in the Transvaal in 1909, and a bill providing for the registration of trade unions and their recognition within a "standing conciliation board" system had passed through the House of Assembly in 1914. Neither of these specific legal mechanisms was particularly successful, however, in bringing about the desired institutionalization of the struggles of white wage earners. The system provided for under the Transvaal Act was rejected after it patently failed to yield significant concessions, and a number of strikes proceeded, despite several prosecutions, without any reference to "conciliatory boards" whatsover. The 1914 bill failed to become law, technically because it failed to pass through the Senate before the end of the parliamentary session, but more fundamentally because it too, like the 1909 act, failed to gain the necessary degree of acceptance among a still militant white labor movement, which such ideological apparatuses need to gain to be effective.

More significant during this period were the various attempts to incorporate white wage earners into various "industrial relations" apparatuses established by individual capitalists and fractions of capital acting at the industrial level. For example, when the 1914 bill failed to become law the Chamber of Mines announced its willingness to recognize white trade unions and through agreements with various unions set up a comprehensive "conciliation board" and "boards of reference" system, providing for negotiation over wages, conditions, and job color bars as well as for arbitration over "grievances" raised by individual white employees. Similar moves were also made in other industries and sectors, for instance in the printing industry where an "industrial council" was set up in 1918.

However, once again although such apparatuses were by 1920 fairly widespread, and although they were by that year being seen as having a significant effect on reducing the number of strikes (see Department of Mines and Industries Labor Division Report for 1920:105), nevertheless the institutionalization of the "white labor movement" remained incomplete. The contradictions arising between mining capital and white wage earners during the mining industry's phase of transition to monopoly capitalism placed limitations on the degree of "acceptance" of bourgeois ideological apparatuses by white wage earners, and this meant in particular that the effects which the incorporation of trade unions into such apparatuses had in disorganizing rank and file white wage earners as a militant social force was fairly limited. Under conditions where there was still resistance to institutionalized bargaining procedures, and where involvement in such procedures depended very much on enticement, even though the structures were themselves hierarchical and bureaucratic, neither capital nor trade union "moderates" were able to structure relationships within them in such a way that they decisively subordinated the rank and file within trades unions. On the contrary, rank and file organization remained fairly solid and militant as evidenced, for example, by the militant shop and shaft stewards' movement on the mines (see Mining Industry Board 1922:220-221).

Thus, to summarize: during the period under review, the South African social formation was characterized by two main secondary contradictions (in addition to the principal contradiction between capital and the African dominated classes). One was the contradiction between the different capitalist fractions in the power bloc arising from their different interests with respect to "free trade" or "protectionist" economic policies. The other was the contradiction arising between the dominant capitalist classes (foremost among them the hegemonic mining capitalist fraction) and white wage earners. With respect to the second, there had been a number of attempts by the dominant classes to institutionalize their conflicts with the white wage earning classes in such a way that (a) politically damaging forms of struggle were avoided, and (b) that the white wage earners emerged as a supportive class for the form of state. Although by 1920 a number of apparatuses had come into existence which were functioning with some degree of effectiveness in this regard, the institutionalization of the struggles of white wage earners nonetheless remained incomplete, principally on account of the antagonisms arising during the mining industry's phase of transition to monopoly capitalism.

THE CRISIS OF 1920-1924 AND THE HEIGHTENING OF THE SECONDARY CONTRADICTIONS

Having indicated something of the nature of the major secondary contradictions arising in the South African social formation during the first quarter of the 20th century, we are now in a position to approach an analysis of the crisis of 1920-1924, the high point of which was the general strike and armed uprising of 1922. Ultimately the effect of this crisis was to heighten both of the above described secondary contradictions to the point of rupturing social relations as they had existed previously.

Like a number of other crises affecting the South African social formation, the particular crisis of 1920-1924 had its origins in a more generalized crisis affecting the whole of the imperialist chain. After a period of steeply rising prices—caused by the massive expansion of credit in the imperialist metropolises during the First World War and immediate postwar years—the early 1920s was a period of worldwide recession during which world prices slumped dramatically.

Capital in the subordinate South African social formation had been far from immune to the effects either of the wartime inflation or of the subsequent recession. It was dependent on the imperialist metropolises for a wide range of imported materials, and it had as such been obliged during the inflationary period to pay higher prices for its imported materials. In fact, the index of imported prices nearly trebled from 1,106 in 1914 to 3,185 in 1920. Furthermore, higher import prices had reflected themselves in higher prices for wage goods, and under the conditions of class struggle prevailing in the social formation at the time, capitalists had been obliged to concede a number of money wage increases to their white (and also to a limited extent to their black) wage earning employees. Between 1914 and 1920, for example, wage rates rose in money terms by 54% for white miners, by 78% for white employees in manufacturing, and by 14% for black workers (the latter representing a fall in living standards in real terms).

During the war and immediate postwar inflationary period, these increases in costs had not posed any particularly serious problems for any fraction of capital in South Africa. In the case of industrial capital and capitalist agriculture they were more than offset by the "artificial protection" which they had enjoyed in these years through the disruption of trade routes and higher export prices, and the period had accordingly been one of overall expansion for both fractions. Even mining capital, normally extremely vulnerable to the effects of rising costs, had been cushioned by Britain's temporary abandonment of the gold standard which had the effect of raising the price of gold to a "premium price" of between 116 and 114% of its normal price of £4.28 per ounce.

However, with the recession beginning in 1920, the picture began to change abruptly, and in particular as all major fractions of capital began to experience particular (though rather different) restraints of the prices of their products, the effects of previous cost increases began to pose serious problems for capital accumulation. Capitalist agriculture experienced the effects of the recession most directly through a disastrous fall in prices on the world market (the price of wool, for example, fell from 33 pence per pound in the early part of 1920 to 11 pence in 1921). Mining capital experienced the recession through a fall in the "premium price" for gold, which fell from a high of £5.59 per ounce in 1920 to £4.61 in 1922. Industrial capital experienced it through the effects of intense price competition from abroad as trade routes were reopened and world prices slumped.

Although the recession hit each of the major capitalist fractions in a similar manner, it could not be resolved by any common economic policy which did not differentiate between them. For capitalist agriculture and industrial capital, the fractions of national capital, an important part of any solution to their class problems was the introduction of more effective tariff protection to insulate them from the effects of falling prices; but this was directly contrary to the interests of mining capital, which stood to gain nothing from protection except a further increase in its costs which would exacerbate its problems still further. The state's economic policies during the crisis therefore depended on the outcome of a struggle within the power bloc and, during this phase of mining capital's hegemony, it was mining capital's interests that remained dominant. The demand by national capital for increased protection was effectively denied and, indeed, for some elements of national capital (notably beef and wheat farmers), the recession period was a period in which they lost some of the protection which they had hitherto received.

One of the consequences of the recession was that it divided the fractions in the power bloc still further and intensified the struggle between them. This took the form of intense debates over economic policies and it also led at the party political level to most fractions of industrial and agricultural capital deserting the governing South Africa Party for the Nationalist Party, which became in consequence the authentic party of national capital.

However, while the denial of protection to national capital was of some benefit to mining capital in its struggle to maintain its rate of profit during the crisis period, it could not provide a solution on its own. Under conditions where mining capital was experiencing a sharp fall in the "premium price" for gold, the imperatives of capital accumulation demanded that there be some reduction in its major cost item (which was also the cost item that had risen fastest during the inflationary period): its white wage bill.

As Johnstone (1976:119-125) has shown, there were in principle three possible ways in which white wage costs could be reduced: first, by reducing the rate of wages; second, by reorganizing and socializing labor processes still performed by white artisans or "semiskilled" white workers (transferring the functions to gangs of lower paid African workers); and, third, by amending the mining regulations to transfer productive functions, still performed by white, new, petty bourgeois supervisors along with their supervisory duties, to Africans.

In pressing its demands against its white wage earning employees, however, mining capital's initial approach involved the studious observance of the procedures of the various "industrial relations" bodies established after previous struggles. The mining capitalists and their political representatives were well aware that their demands could provoke potentially damaging defensive action, and they were therefore concerned to preserve as far as possible the efficacy of the various apparatuses and institutions concerned. The struggle began accordingly with a process of negotiation with the white trade unions. Agreement was reached over one of the least painful options as far as white wage earners were concerned—the transfer of a few minor functions from white supervisors to Africans—as well as over a small wage reduction. From August until December 1921 mining capital and the white trade unions engaged in a protracted process of negotiation over more substantial wage cuts and modifications to labor processes; but the contradictions were too great for mining capital to secure the kind of economic changes it needed to make at the expense of its white wage earning employees and at the same time preserve intact the efficacy of the particular ideological apparatuses in question. As the gold price continued to plummet, mining capital became less and less able to tolerate the inevitably lengthier process of negotiation and eventually it announced on December 8, 1921, that the negotiations had not produced a sufficient reduction in its costs and demanded further wage cuts, the removal of a large number of whites from various forms of "semiskilled" work (whose places had previously been guaranteed by a 1918 agreement), and a blank check to reorganize underground work.

When the unions refused, mining capital announced its intention to implement its demands unilaterally and eventually in January 1922 this move was met by a general strike. During the early stages of the strike there were still some further attempts at negotiation, but when these came to nothing the Chamber finally announced in a particularly forthright statement that it would no longer negotiate with the South African Industrial Federation. Thenceforth the struggle passed into a new phase. The leadership of the strike passed from the more "moderate, augmented executive" of the SAIF to the more militant "Action Committee" and the strike commandoes—bodies of armed strikers—began to get involved in "pulling out scabs" and attacking Africans who tried to go to work. Eventually, as we indicated earlier, the state's armed forces intervened and after a four-day battle the strikers' forces were defeated and two days later the mines were reopened on terms dictated by mining capital.

Mining capital's victory over its white employees in 1922 was far from being a Pyrrhic victory as it is sometimes described. It secured a number of far-reaching economic gains which were either not reversed or else only partly reversed during the later Pact period. Among these were a reduction in the white wage rates of between 25% and 50% and the withdrawal of two paid holidays. However, the most important gains made by mining capital in 1922 were those made in terms of its control over the labor process itself (the powers of possession). Through its defeat of its white employees, mining capital was able to remove a number of barriers to its assumption of certain powers of possession and was thereby able to bring about a number of changes in the relations of production such that it passed into its phase of monopoly capitalism proper. Indeed, the gains made in this respect through the victory in 1922 were so far reaching that capital accumulation in the goldmining industry has been able to proceed to this day without any further major restructuring of the relations of production.

With the defeat of the strike, the agreement of 1918, which had obliged mining capital to employ whites in certain semiskilled manual places, was annulled and in 1923 the color bar regulations in the Mines and Works Act were declared by the courts to be ultra vires and therefore invalid. In addition shaft and shop stewards, regarded as having "encroached upon . . . managerial authority" through their activities on local grievance committees, had their recognition withdrawn—with, according to one commission "most beneficial effects of efficiency" (Mining Industry Board, 1922:20-21). Whites previously employed as semiskilled manual workers performing such functions as drillsharpener, wastepacker, enginedriver, pumpman, and handyman were correspondingly replaced by Africans, and the production processes in most of the departments were reorganized so that whites were restricted to the performance of (an extended range of) supervisory duties. Moreover, the mining regulations were amended to permit Africans to begin work without a white supervisor being present (thereby lengthening the African working day). Through these changes mining capital was also able to introduce new, more productive technologies in the form of the jackhammer drill and the corduroy blanket reduction process.

Significantly, however, mining capital never made any attempt to put Africans into supervisory, new petty bourgeois places, despite being technically free to do so with the legal invalidation of the job color bar regulations in 1923. As indicated earlier, the maintenance of the racist hierarchy in the industry's division of labor was in mining capital's class interests. What had been sought and achieved in 1922 was a modification to, not an elimination of, the racist hierarchical division of labor: a modification in which almost all the white mining employees emerged as a supervisory new petty bourgeoisie.

However, these economic gains by mining capital had been brought about at the cost of the near total destruction of the various "industrial relations" apparatuses. The negotiating system in the mining industry was totally destroyed as was that in the railways (where a similar series of struggles had taken place). Moreover, the strike of 1922 had been the most serious ever in terms of its adverse effects on the power bloc's political interests. Not only had it been a particularly vivid indication that a significant proportion of the white wage earning classes had withdrawn their support for the form of state, but it had also come very close to provoking a militant uprising by Africans. On the one hand attacks by strike commandoes had brought them (Africans) very close to the point of retaliation, and on the other hand there was the concern expressed by the Martial Law Judicial Commission (1922:26) that some of the strike leaders had contemplated some sort of approach to Africans calling on them to join in common political struggle.

Because continual repression was seen to be impossible, it thus became incumbent on the state, as the factor of cohesion in the social formation, to intervene and attempt to effect some restructuring of the particular ideological apparatuses concerned. The years 1922 to 1924 were accordingly years of major new forms of state activity in this connection. The Mining Industry Board—the commission appointed to investigate the economic issues at stake in the 1922 struggle and which unanimously endorsed practically every one of mining capital's economic gains—was also given the task of working out a new "industrial relations" system for the mining industry. The Industrial Conciliation Bill, based initially on the recommendations put forward by this commission, was introduced in

1923, and became, after some modification, the Industrial Conciliation Act of 1924. However, the restructuring of these ideological apparatuses did not simply involve their reestablishment in the form in which they had existed prior to 1922. Capital, particularly mining capital, had a number of specific demands related to the new conditions of class struggle, and the new apparatuses reflected these demands and thus the improved position of capital in the class struggle.

The system established in the mining industry (which functioned from 1922 until the late 1930s) specifically withheld recognition from shaft and shop stewards, and before conceding recognition to any union, required that that union include clauses in its constitution providing for a secret ballot before strike action could be taken and to suspend any strike action until negotiating procedures had been exhausted. The Industrial Conciliation Act also excluded any direct shop floor involvement by prohibiting any small group from obtaining access to negotiating bodies. Like earlier legislation of this sort, it also suspended the right to strike until negotiations within standing "industrial councils" or ad hoc "conciliation boards" had been exhausted. It also provided, furthermore, for the registration of trade unions, which although not compulsory was a precondition for recognition under the system. Registration was to be denied to any union which did not meet certain requirements in terms of membership and constitution (in particular which did not exclude "pass bearing natives" from membership).

Despite this restructuring of the various "industrial relations" apparatuses and despite their acceptance by a number of white trade union leaders, the state under the hegemony of mining capital remained unable in the aftermath of the 1922 strike to regain a sufficient degree of support among the white wage earning classes to bring about a really effective incorporation of the organizations of these clases into the particular apparatuses in question. Widespread antagonism continued to exist among white wage earners to mining capital and the regime and through them to the institutions and apparatuses of the bourgeois state. Furthermore, the disruption caused by the state had the effect of deepening the recession, thus further heightening the contradictions between mining and national capital. With the position of mining capital severely weakened by its inability to restore white wage earners to their position as a supportive class and with continuing deep divisions within the power bloc, the conditions existed in the period following the strike of 1922 for a reorganization of the power bloc. In the aftermath of the strike national capital entered into alliance with the reformist (social democratic) factions within the white labor movement (manifested at the party political level in the formation of the electoral pact between the

Nationalist and Labor Parties in 1923). For national capital this alliance offered additional support for its struggles in the power bloc and also enabled it to put itself forward within the power bloc as uniquely placed to "restore order" after the crisis of 1922. For the social democratic factions of white labor, it offered the prospect of reasserting themselves within the white labor movement after having been somewhat eclipsed during the course of the strike. They could now offer an "alternative" within capitalist society (an alliance with national capital in its struggle for a more "progressive" capitalist society) to the programs of the radicals and communists (calling for militant struggle either in alliance with the African working class or "independently" against capitalism itself).

Eventually this alliance succeeded in its immediate objectives. A "shock defeat" of a cabinet minister at a byelection in 1924 provided a particularly dramatic index of the degree to which the party of mining capital had failed to restore the support of white wage earners at least for a state under the hegemony of mining capital. In response to this result Prime Minister Smuts decided to call a snap election to "test" his support in "the country at large." When the results came in on June 18, 1924, they indicated that his party had lost and the pact parties had won. It was an event which had more than mere party political significance. It was an index that hegemony in the power bloc had passed from mining to national capital.

THE HEGEMONY OF NATIONAL CAPITAL AND THE RESTRUCTURING OF SOCIAL RELATIONS

The achievement of hegemony by national capital in 1924 resulted, as indicated earlier, in a twofold change in social relationships in the social formation. Firstly, it enabled the national capitalist fractions to assert the primacy of their own particular fractional interests over those of "foreign" capital, and thus to modify the rate and trajectory of capitalist development. The period of the Nationalist-Labour "Pact" government (1924-1933) thus saw the introduction of a number of new policies clearly favoring national capitalist interests. More particularly it saw the introduction (against the opposition of mining capital and its allies) of a number of protectionist measures which created the conditions necessary for the beginnings of the process of national capitalist industrial and agricultural development, which has marked out the South African from other social formations in Africa. Among the more important of the new measures were: the Custom Tariff Act of 1925 which radically overhauled the customs tariff, imposing protective tariffs on items previously imported free of duty or at a low revenue duty; the removal of rebates previously granted to British products under imperial preference; the granting of a wide range of subsidies to agricultural capital; and the granting of special forms of protection to particular elements within agricultural capital, such as beef farmers who were protected by an act prohibiting the importation of cheap Rhodesian beef. Another important form of state intervention to benefit national capital was the establishment (again against the opposition of mining capital) of the state-run Iron and Steel Corporation (ISCOR), set up as part of the necessary infrastructure for local industrialization in 1927. Partly as a consequence of these measures, industrial output increased from £26 millions in 1923/1924 to £38 millions in the predepression year of 1928/1929, and agricultural output increased from £42 millions to £46 millions over the same period.

Secondly, the change in hegemony and the change in regime in 1924 also enabled the state to assert the necessary degree of relative autonomy to bring about the incorporation of the "white labor movement" into the state structures. The change in hegemony and change in regime enabled the state to set itself up as the representative of the (white) nation/people as a whole and even, with Labour Party representation in the cabinet, to *appear* as a state in which white labor's interests were placed above those of mining capital. It should be emphasized that the apparent dominance of white wage earners' interests was only an appearance. In reality the state remained a capitalist state dominated by a power bloc of capitalist classes under the hegemony of a capitalist fraction, and its role thus remained to protect and guarantee the essential interests of the members of the power bloc against the demands of all other classes, including those of the white wage earning allies of the hegemonic fraction. In seeking to incorporate the "white labor movement," therefore, the state was fundamentally acting, as in the period of mining capital's hegemony, to defend the political interests of the power bloc against the threats posed by the militant struggles of white wage earners. In fact, in its struggle to bring about the incorporation of the "white labor movement," the Pact regime took over and administered practically unchanged the Industrial Conciliation Act, passed, as we saw, toward the end of the period of mining capital's hegemony.

One thing that had changed, however, by the time the Pact regime came to administer the Act was that, in the wake of the strike of 1922, there was a much greater level of political commitment on the part of the dominant classes to making an "industrial relations" system work effectively. This was true of all fractions and was already evident at the drafting stage of the Industrial Conciliation Bill when within limits certain concessions had been made to make the system acceptable to reformist trade unionists; but it was particularly true of the national capitalist fractions, which had put forward and achieved hegemony at least partly on the basis of their "unique" ability to restore order and stability to the social formation.

The Pact period thus saw a much greater level of state activity in connection with "making the conciliation system work." On the one hand this involved the state arranging for a number of further economic concessions to be made available to white wage earners within institutionalized bargaining procedures. White miners, for example, received a wage increase after pressure from the state on mining capital, and they also received statutory protection for their occupation of their existing places in the division of labor in the form of a color bar act (the Mines and Works Amendment Act) passed in 1926. Once again, however, it must be emphasized that these concessions remained strictly limited to those compatible with the maintenance of the essential requirements of capital accumulation. The white miners' wage award, for example, was less than 1/20 of the sum demanded by the Mine Workers Union and fell very far short of restoring wage rates to their pre-1922 levels in either real or money terms, and the job color bar act covered only certain supervisory places which mining capital had no intention of transferring to Africans and it therefore did not amount to any real loss by mining capital of the powers of possession it had gained after the 1922 strike.

Furthermore, "making the conciliation system work" also involved placing obstacles in the way of other forms of struggle, notably strikes. The Industrial Conciliation Act, like its predecessors, effectively prohibited strikes, not by formally proscribing them, but by creating so many preconditions that, in the words of one experienced participant, "a successful legal strike" became "almost an impossibility" (Andrews, 1941:37). The Pact regime, in administering the act, also administered these clauses. In part this involved state officials in a good deal of at least sometimes effective "moral suasion." When strikes were threatened state officials would intervene to persuade, cajole, or threaten trade union officials or strikers that their action was illegal and that they should instead rely on "proper channels." In certain cases too there were prosecutions for illegal strikes under the act. For example, in 1923 there were 109 such cases.

In addition to the greater level of actual state activity (the organization of concessions on the one hand and the impeding of strikes on the other), there was also, as mentioned earlier, the particular ideological effects of the party political relationship with the Labour Party. This factor should not be underestimated. There are numerous references in the contemporary labor press (both reformist and left wing) to ways in which either "loyalty to the Labour cause" or "hatred of Smuts" led, during the first two years of the Pact regime at least, to passivity and acceptance of state institutions. For all these reasons, plus the fact that a large section of the "white labor movement" consisted of organizations of new petty bourgeois rather than working class elements with a far greater degree of commitment to reformist solutions generally, the Pact period was the period in which the first really effective institutionalization of the struggles of white wage earners occurred. Some indication of this is given in Table 2, which shows both the sharp decline in the numbers of whites engaging in strike action and the increase in the numbers of white wage earners subject to institutionalized bargaining procedures.

Table 2. SELECTED STRIKE STATISTICS AND STATISTICS RELATING TO THE INSTITUTIONS SET UP UNDER THE TERMS OF THE INDUSTRIAL CONCILIATION ACT

	Strikes		Industrial Conciliation Act Machinery		
Year	Numbers of whites involved In strikes	Average number of man days lost per striker	Number of Industrial Councils in existence at June 30	Number of Conciliation Board agreements and awards	Number of "employees" covered
1910-1921 (avg.)	14,762*	14.3*	—	—	—
1925	—	—	2	7	na
1926	768	1.1*	14	5	na
1927	740	1.8*	22	3	na
1928	710	1.9*	29	5	43,000
1929	na	na	31	8	47,790
1930	387	5.8	38	7	45,049
1931	3,811	11.1	43	7	45,462
1932	2,387	8.6	41	9	46,252
1933	1,255	11.7	35	6	40,240

SOURCES: *Union Statistics for 50 Years* (Jubilee Issue, Pretoria, 1960) Table G18; *Social and Industrial Review* (Department of Labour publication) Dec. 1927:558-560 and Dec. 1929:1168-1171; *Department of Labour Reports* for 1933 and 1934.

* white and black

The institutionalization of the white labor movement had a significance beyond the fact that it succeeded in reducing the number of strikes at a particular conjuncture, however. Institutionalization within the apparatuses set up under the Industrial Conciliation Act had the effect of bureaucratizing the white trade unions (or at least increasing the level of bureaucratization already present). To appreciate the effects of this we have to understand something of the essential meaning of the phenomenon of bureaucratization. It is not, as Poulantzas has argued, simply a "technical" characteristic of organizations which reach a certain size, but rather (Poulantzas, 1975:274):

> in the only possible rigorous sense of the term bureaucratization is the effect in the social division of labour at the institutional level, of a combination of bourgeois (and petty bourgeois) ideology . . . and of an embellished and deformed reproduction of the bourgeois political relations of domination/subordination. Its characteristics . . . consist in an axiomatized system of rules and norms which distribute spheres of activity and competence; the impersonal character of its various functions; the payment of officials by fixed salaries; recruitment by appointment from above . . . ; specific forms of obscuring knowledge within the organization by bureaucratic secrecy; the specific forms in which the 'hierarchy' operates by way of successive stages of 'authority' . . . centralism, insofar as each level communicates with others by way of the higher level, which gives rise to a specific form of isolation of agents, etc.

The bureaucratization of the white trade unions essentially meant the "embellished and deformed" reproduction within them of the bourgeois political relations of domination/subordination through the creation and sustenance of hierarchical structures and the concomitant disorganizations and isolation of the lower echelons. In the specific case of the white trade unions in South Africa this took the form of the creation and sustenance of a distinct hierarchy of salaried trade union officials— numbering between 400 and 500 by the latter part of the Pact period— "professionally engaged" in the dual functions of negotiating compromises through the complex procedures laid down in the act and disciplining memberships to accept compromise concessions.

Although there were no doubt a considerable number of reformists and class collaborators in the white trade unions along these lines, this tendency toward bureaucratization was fundamentally the product of the institutional structures (and the conditions of class struggle which enabled this institutionalization to proceed) rather than the volition of particular agents. The negotiating procedures laid down in the act were complex, esoteric, and centralized—in a word bureaucratized—and participation within them therefore of itself imposed bureaucratization on the unions quite independently of the wishes of individual trade union officials. As a somewhat reluctant contemporary trade unionist explained (C. F. Glass of the Witwatersrand Tailors Association as quoted in *Forward,* Feb. 26, 1926):

> Trade union officials have an enormous amount of their time taken up in attending to the business of Conciliation Boards and Industrial Councils, with the result that the work of organization, which is the rock foundation of the trade union movement, is sadly neglected, thus rendering the various organizations incapable of fighting.

The inevitable result of institutionalization was thus bureaucratization, and the inevitable result of bureaucratization was the disorganization and isolation of the rank and file membership. For a short time this disorganization manifested itself in an actual decrease in union memberships. The official statistics show a fall in the membership of registered trade unions from 67,200 in 1926 to 58,400 in 1927, rising only slightly to 64,860 in 1928. Such extreme disorganization was shortlived, however (the statistics show a rise in membership to 69,900 in 1929), because capitalist employers began to see advantages in their white employees being members of bureaucratized trade unions, and they began to assist in the task of recruitment, in the main by collecting dues and entering into closed shop agreements. A government commission explained why (1935 Industrial Legislation Commission:90):

> In these days when the employees in a single workshop often number many hundreds, the arrangement of individual contracts of service would present many administrative difficulties and for this reason alone many employers have adopted the policy of encouraging their employees to link up with unions. . . . The better type of employer also appreciates the fact that well organized and disciplined trade unions can do much to reduce evasion of industrial legislation by . . . less reputable [competitors].

Except for the short initial period, therefore, disorganization and isolation manifested itself, not in reduced union membership, but in a widely recognized apathy and acquiescence on the part of rank and file membership.

This was the real "achievement" of the Pact in so far as its policies toward the white wage earning classes were concerned. At the cost of certain economic concessions (all well within capital's "capacity to pay"), and greatly assisted by the party political relationship with the Labour Party, as well as by the fact that a large proportion of the organized "white labor movement" consisted of petty bourgeois rather than working class elements, the Pact regime had succeeded in bringing about the almost complete political capitulation of the "white labor movement" to capital. By institutionalizing and bureaucratizing the white trade unions, it had ensured that these organizations no longer posed any political threat to capitalist political interests, but on the contrary functioned as apparatuses of the bourgeois state, acting along with other apparatuses of the state, to organize white wage earners as a supportive class for the form of state.

CONCLUSIONS

The changes in social relationships brought about as a consequence of the 1922 strike did not have any direct immediate effects on the structuring of relations between the dominant classes and the African, principal dominated, classes. Africans continued under the Pact regime to be subjected to various exploitative and repressive measures in much the same way as they had been under previous regimes: the only real change being the introduction of certain measures to prevent African labor flowing from capitalist agriculture to other sectors. But the changes in social relations which followed the 1922 strike did, by determining the specific configuration of class forces and class alliances in opposition to them, have important long-term effects on the African dominated classes. In the first place, the early achievement of hegemony by national capitalist interests, and the process of industrial and agricultural development which followed therefrom, laid the material foundations for a strenghtening of the position of the South African bourgeoisie both in its relationship to the African dominated classes and in its relationships within the imperialist chain. Secondly, the incorporation of the "white labor movement" into the state and the consequent disorganization of white wage earners as an independent and militant social force, marked their final emergence as a fully supportive class for the bourgeoisie. The changes brought about after the strike of 1922 thus had crucially important consequences: (a) in enabling a consolidation and strengthening of bourgeois rule, and (b) in determining that the polarization of class forces in the social formation proceeded, broadly speaking, along racial lines. This last point is not to suggest, of course, that there was ever more than a tiny minority of white wage earners polarized toward the African dominated classes in the period prior to 1922. There were a large number of factors which divided and isolated white from black wage earners from the outset—among them the different places occupied by white and black wage earners in the division of labor (in particular the fact that a large number of whites supervised blacks), and the fact that the major struggles involving white wage earners over the period (those over the powers of possession in the mining industry) created a form of competition and rivalry between white and black wage earners. Nevertheless, through the final subordination of the "white labor movement" and the emergence of white wage earners as a fully supportive class for the form of state, the racial polarization of class forces was made much firmer.

The class struggles characterizing the South African social formation at the present conjuncture are of course fundamentally different from those which characterized the social formation in the 1920s. The class contradictions dominating the field of political practices at the current conjuncture are the principal contradictions of the social formation—the contradictions between the dominant and African dominated classes. The issues at stake are therefore no longer simply related to the composition of the power bloc or the precise relationship of the power bloc to a supportive class, but to the fundamental questions of class domination and exploitation in the social formation. In at least one respect, however, the struggles of the 1920s and the struggles of today do bear certain similarities. Although the state's response to the struggles of the African dominated class has thus far been mainly repressive, the signs are that the dominant classes are moving toward a strategy involving the incorporation of certain categories of the black petty bourgeoisie and perhaps even certain categories of the black working class into various state structures. Whether such a strategy will in fact eventually emerge as state policy, and whether, if it does, it will succeed is of course still to be decided in the class struggle. What is clear, however, is that, if the state does succeed in incorporating significant numbers of blacks into stable relationships within the state structures, it will, as did the equivalent process with white wage earners, represent a strengthening of the position of the dominant classes to the ultimate detriment of the masses. For as Marx (1974:601) wrote: "The more a ruling class is able to assimilate the most prominent men of the dominated classes the more stable and dangerous is its rule."

NOTES

1. The role of supervisors in enforcing the control of capital at the point of production has led a number of Marxists to conclude that, although supervisors are wage earners, they are not members of the working class but rather of the new petty bourgeoisie (see Poulantzas, 1975:225-230).

2. See, inter alia, Doxey (1961); Hobart Houghton (1976); Hutt (1964); Horwitz (1967); and van der Horst (1971) for the "conventional wisdom" on this question. See Johnstone (1976) for a full critique.

3. The identification of capitalist fractions as "foreign" or "national" depends on the locus of the powers of economic ownership and not on juridical definitions. For the identification of mining capital as "foreign," and capitalist agriculture and industrial capital as "national," see Kaplan (1974, 1976).

REFERENCES

ANDREWS, W.H. (1941). Class struggles in South Africa. Cape Town: Stewart.

BROWNE, R. (1905). "Pamphlet on working costs of the Witwatersrand," reprinted as appendix to "Minutes of evidence mining industry commission." Pretoria: TG 2 1908.

BUNDY, C. (1972). "The emergence and decline of a South African Peasantry." African Affairs, 71(282):369-388.

DAVIES, R. (1976). "Mining capital, the state and unskilled white workers in South Africa 1901-1913." Journal of Southern African Studies, 3(1), October:41-69.

_____ (1976a). "The class character of South Africa's industrial conciliation legislation." South African Labour Bulletin, 2(6), January:6-20.

Department of Labour Annual Reports, 1933 and 1934.

Department of Mines and Industries: Labour Division Annual Reports.

DOXEY, G. V. (1961). The industrial colour bar in South Africa. London: Oxford University Press.

Forward: The Paper that Supports the Pact (Feb. 26, 1926).

FRANKEL, S.H. (1938). Capital investment in Africa: Its course and effects. London: Oxford University Press.

HOBART HOUGHTON, D. (1976). The South African economy. Oxford University Press.

HORWITZ, R. (1967). The political economy of South Africa. London: Weidenfeld.

HUTT, W. H. (1964). The economics of the colour bar. London: Oxford University Press.

JOHNSTONE, F. A. (1976). Class, race and gold: A study of class relations and racial discrimination in South Africa. London: Routledge and Kegan Paul.

KAPLAN, D. (1974). "Capitalist development in South Africa: Class conflict and the state." Sussex University, Institute of Development Studies seminar paper.

_____ (1976). "An analysis of the South African state in the 'fusion' period, 1932-1939." London University, Institute of Commonwealth Studies seminar paper.

_____ (1976a). "The politics of industrial protection in South Africa 1910-1939." Journal of Southern African Studies, 3(1):70-91.

LEGASSICK, M. (1974). "Capital accumulation and violence in South Africa." Economy and Society, 3(3):253-291.

_____ (1975). "The analysis of 'racism' in South Africa: The case of the mining economy." IDEP/UN seminar paper, Dar es Salaam.

MARX, K. (1974). Capital. London: Lawrence and Wishart.

Mining Industry Arbitration Board 1926/1927 (report and proceedings published by Chamber of Mines, Johannesburg, 1927).

Minutes of Evidence: Select Committee on European Employment and Labour Conditions (SC 9 1913).

MORRIS, M. (1976). "The development of capitalism in South African agriculture: Class struggle in the countryside." Economy and Society, 5(3):292-343.

POULANTZAS, N. (1973). Political power and social classes. London: New Left Books.

_____ (1975). Classes in contemporary capitalism. London: New Left Books.

Report of the Industrial Legislation Commission (UG 37 1935).

Report of the Martial Law Judicial Commission (UG 35 1922).

Report of the Mining Industry Board (UG 39 1922).

Report of the Native Grievances Inquiry 1914 (UG 37 1914).

Social and Industrial Review, 1927-1929.

Union Statistics for 50 Years (Jubilee Issue, Pretoria, 1960).

van der HORST, S. T. (1971). Native labour in South Africa. London: Cass.

WOLPE, H. (1972). "Capitalism and cheap labour power in South Africa: From segregation to apartheid." Economy and Society, 1(4):425-456.

_____ (1974). "The theory of internal colonialism — The South African case." Bulletin of the Conference of Socialist Economists, autumn.

_____ (1975). "Draft notes on (a) articulation of modes of production and the value of labour power, (b) periodization and the state." Sussex University seminar paper.

4

TRAGEDY AT THIAROYE:
The Senegalese Soldiers' Uprising of 1944

MYRON J. ECHENBERG
McGill University

> *Black prisoners, and I clearly mean French prisoners,*
> *is it true then that France is no longer France?[1]*

Thus Leopold Senghor began his poem entitled "Tyaroye," his moving lament over the martyrdom of African soldiers at the hands of their French officers. The event itself is so obscure in the scholarly literature, however, that few people outside French-speaking West Africa have been able to place it in historical perspective.[2] Yet to Senghor, a former soldier and prisoner of war himself, to thousands of West African veterans of the Second World War, and to an entire older generation of Francophone West Africans the name "Thiaroye" invokes the sort of bitter memory that "Sharpeville" brings forward for other Africans. This chapter describes the soldiers' uprising at Thiaroye and attempts to evaluate its significance in the context of workers' protest.

On December 1, 1944, at the barracks of Thiaroye on the outskirts of Dakar, French colonial troops and police brutally suppressed an uprising of some 1,280 African ex-prisoners of war who were awaiting demobilization and repatriation.[3] These men formed the first contingent to be repatriated of some 10,000 African prisoners held in German camps from the collapse of France in June 1940, until the Liberation in the summer and fall of 1944. Because the ex-POW were technically still soldiers in the Senegalese Rifles, the African branch of the French Colonial army, and because they were partially armed, uniformed, under military discipline, and had refused to obey officers' orders, the official French label of mutiny attached to the tragic events of Thiaroye applies. The actual numbers of casualties may never be known, but one official report made soon after the bloody event states that 35 Africans were killed, another 35 seriously wounded, and hundreds more less seriously injured. Some 34 ex-POWS were arrested to be tried on charges falling just short of mutiny. All were convicted and sentenced to terms ranging from one to ten years in prison. Before a general amnesty was issued on behalf of the Thiaroye victims in June 1947, some five prisoners had died in jail. On the colonial side, no lives were lost; one African soldier was wounded and three French officers suffered lacerations.

At first glance a soldiers' mutiny would seem an inappropriate case study to be found in a volume devoted to labor protest. Indeed, far too often in colonial and national instances, soldiers have constituted the state's main instrument of repression against labor. African conscripts in the French colonial army often found themselves utilized, as Senghor put it, as "black watchdogs of empire,"[4] whether to quell a rebellion in Indochina or Madagascar (see Buttinger, 1967, on Indochina; Tronchon, 1974, on Madagascar), as shock troops against militant workers (breaking up protests outside the Nice post office during the general strike of 1947), and even as scabs (unloading cargo during the Nice dockers' strike that same year. (Nice-Matin, Dec. 3-4, 1947; Réveil, Jan. 5, 1948)).

Approached in a different way, however, soldiers in colonial French West Africa were not only recruited virtually exclusively from the peasantry, but they also constituted perhaps the largest single group of men in state employ in the entire French empire in Africa.[5] Apart from the tiny handful of Africans engaged as so-called "native" officers, the bulk of these men, moreover, can be viewed as workers. Even their tasks conformed to this description. Apart from the common employment of colonial troops as combat infantry and as occupation forces, French colonialism often engaged African soldiers in a series of construction tasks, such as the building of posts, barracks, and other military infrastructure, and in various labor tasks required to maintain an occupation army of roughly 10,000 men posted permanently in the colony. In the First World War formally constituted labor brigades of colonial units were created. After the war, several thousand Africans were conscripted into the detested conscript labor brigades of the so-called "second portion" of the annual military draft. These units were turned over to private contractors for three-year stints under atrocious conditions on such projects as the Markala dam of the "Office du Niger" scheme, or as maintenance laborers on the Dakar-Niger railway. (Echenberg, 1975: 187). Indeed, the victims of Thiaroye were all men who had had direct experience not only as combat troops, but also as laborers in military dress.

If soldiers can be workers, then some mutinies at least can be seen as workers' protests. The term "mutiny" itself is a very crude analytical tool. At a minimum it involves defiance of or attack upon established military authority by subordinates. Some mutinies, such as the famous uprising against the British of the Bengal army in 1857, spread from the ranks of the military to become a generalized attack upon the political authority of the British conqueror (Spear, 1972; Sen, 1957). Others, like the major mutiny of 1917 among a significant fraction of the French army, were more like peasant jacqueries, explosions of rage and disgust at the widespread slaughter into which a cynical and incompetent French General Staff were leading their men like sheep (Pedroncini, 1967). Still other mutinies have been attributed to bad food and living conditions, tyrannical leaders, and internal conditions generally that push men under discipline past the breaking point (Pedroncini, 1967).

Two mutinies that help place the Thiaroye uprising in historical context are the Indian mutiny of the Bengal army in 1857, and the abortive mutiny of a few garrisons of Indochinese soldiers under French command in the town of Yen Bay, Tonkin, in 1930 (Buttinger, 1967). Each involved a colonial army, the first being one of the most famous and well documented events in British imperial history; Yen Bay is less well known, but more immediately relevant in that it describes an event in another section of the same French colonial army to which the Africans belonged.

The Indian mutiny was in essence a conservative phenomenon. The goal of the caste-proud Brahmin and Rajput officers in the Bengalia army who led the uprising was to restore the old Mogul order, thus bringing an end to British reforms which struck at the wealth and privileges of the old elite. Indeed, the tiny contemporary class of western-educated Indians opposed the mutiny as a reactionary movement. Nevertheless, as Marx himself observed, the mutiny had at least demonstrated that under the proper sort of leadership, colonial armies offered the potential for collective, national resistance to colonialism.[6]

Marx might have approved of the goals of the Yen Bay mutiny while deploring the plan. The uprising at Yen Bay together with one or two bombings in Hanoi and other towns during the night of February 9, 1930, were part of what was supposed to be a general military revolt against French rule planned by the Vietnam Nationalist Party (VNQDD), a revolutionary group of minor civil servants formed in the 1920s and closely modelled after the Kuomintang, with the same style of leadership and suffering from the same confused analysis (Buttinger, 1967). The VNQDD believed that it was possible to oust the French from control of Indochina by means of a vast military putsch, and concentrated its considerable efforts in politicizing the ranks of the French colonial army in an effort to persuade indigenous soldiers to overthrow their masters. On the appointed night, however, only one garrison, that at Yen Bay, rose up in revolt. The soldiers killed one French officer and held the camp for one day against a strong French counterattack before capitulating. The repression was terrible, but it had one positive consequence: the failure virtually eliminated a Kuomintang type of approach to revolution in Vietnam. This left the field open to Ho Chi Minh and the Viet Minh who could show the way to successful revolution against the French based on the far sounder and more careful building up of support among peasants and workers.

While soldiers' protests in French West Africa lacked the scale of the Indian example or the ambition of the Indochinese case, the tradition of protest was nevertheless real. Indeed, the strongest resistance of all came against inclusion into the army in the first place. Africans went to considerable lengths to thwart French efforts to conscript the annual levies of men that averaged over 10,000 per annum during the inter-war years and ten times that figure during the enormous mobilizations during both World Wars. Draft resistance in West Africa was characterized by techniques peasants had developed wherever undemocratic regimes have attempted to place the burden of military service on their backs. Flight, mutilation, and substitution were only some of the techniques involved. Although more rare, and ultimately disastrous, some communities even went as far as to take up armed resistance in opposition to conscription. Thus, the major uprising in large parts of Mali and Upper Volta in 1915 was in part a protest against the large First World War levies (Gnan-kambary, 1965). As late as 1931 Zinder, Maradi, and Tanout in Niger were the scenes of armed, though highly localized resistance to the draft.[7]

Once in the army itself, however, opportunity to resist grew smaller. As the socialization process that armies everywhere stress took effect, many impressionable young men began to view their reluctant occupation as something more than temporary. For the rest, a strict hierarchical structure and severe penalties for deviance combined to reduce the number of incidents. Nevertheless, what might be characterized as incidents of spontaneous rioting do appear in the colonial archives on certain patterned occasions. One such set of disturbances is the case of soldiers harassing civilian populations in Dakar, Kayes, and Dagana during November 1939, during a time of severe overcrowding in the garrisons as thousands of men were awaiting embarkation for France and the combat theater.[8] A similar increase in the number of incidents reported occurred during demobilization after the debacle of 1940, when groups of returning veterans are said to have been responsible for disturbances in Kankan, Dédougou, and Kindia.[9]

The Kindia incident in many ways anticipated the events of Thiaroye four years later.[10] At the signature of the Armistice in 1940, those African soldiers who had escaped the German encirclement were repatriated. Before leaving France they were told to wait until they arrived in Dakar to receive their demobilization bonus and their savings in metropolitan francs. In Dakar, the contingent from Guinea was informed that the money would be alloted in Conakry. When they arrived in the capital of Guinea, however, the Governor greeted them but did not pay them; instead he assured then that they would be paid eventually by the various commandants de cercle and that they should return home. By the time they reached Kindia barracks in the interior of Guinea, the men were furious. When it became clear that the commandant de cercle was not prepared to compensate them, they set upon him as well as the station master who happened to be present. Regular colonial troops and civilian police soon subdued the 31 men involved. They received sentences ranging from five to 20 years in prison for "outrages" against a superior officer.[11]

While individual circumstances may have varied considerably, every single one of the victims of Thiaroye had spent the better part of four years in one sort of German prisoner-of-war camp or another.[12] After a year or so in Germany, most African soldiers were transferred to so-called "Fronts-Stalags," workcamps located just inside occupied France. Here they were forced to work at tasks that contributed to the German war effort, particularly mining and armament-manufacturing that took place in the industrial northeast. In return they were paid minimal sums, and some men were even allowed contact with French civilian families. Some African soldiers occasionally received news from home in this and other ways,[13] and some even went as far as to serve clandestinely in the Resistance when the opportunity presented itself. A few soldiers apparently were pampered by the Germans in the hopes they would prove useful collaborators; but for most the incarceration, the forced labor, and the loneliness were sufficient to mark many men for life.

Then came liberation. While their French brothers-in-arms returned home immediately to tumultuous welcomes, African soldiers were less fortunate. Some, befriended by French families, shared vicariously in the joys of liberation. Others formed parts of newly formed French military units and resumed the fight against the Germans. Perhaps because they were reluctant to waste the opportunity, French officials even went as far as to put some of the African ex-POWs to work in military labor units. Within a short period of time after their liberation, however, all African servicemen were rounded up and grouped in six centers in central and southern France to await eventual embarkation home. Yet it was not until November of 1944, in some cases a full four or five months after liberation, that the first contingent of some 1,280 men set sail for Dakar. This shabby treatment in France was a severe disappointment to those soldiers who had anticipated heroes' welcomes. They found instead that they had exchanged stalags for French military camps; hard labor in the German war industry for construction work under French military supervision. The Germans, at least, under the terms of the Geneva convention, had been forced to pay the African workers minimum wages, whereas French authorities continued to delay back pay owing the soldiers as a result of their imprisonment.

The angry contingent of ex-POW arrived in Dakar on November 21, 1944, to yet another disappointing welcome. The men had complained bitterly to their understaffed escort of French officers during the voyage about the failure of the French army to issue back pay and other benefits. A few perhaps were mollified by assurances that the delay resulted from the fact that metropolitan francs were not valid in the colonies and that authorities preferred for this reason to regulate their salaries on arrival in French West Africa; but many disgruntled soldiers not only remained dissatisfied with this promise, they also refused categorically their officers' orders to clean the ship's decks before disembarking. In reply to the Governor-General's speech of welcome, to the inevitable music, dancing, and the distribution of biscuits, cigarettes, and kola nuts, a few angry soldiers were overheard to have remarked as they ostentatiously threw these tokens away, "It's not music we want, it's our money."[14]

The transfer of the men to the military barracks at Thiaroye, some 15 kilometers outside Dakar, was accompanied by "incessant" claims by the soldiers for their back pay, and for authorization to keep the metropolitan francs they held on their persons.[15] It is worth noting that the soldiers possessed substantial sums in some cases. Among the contingent of 1,280 men, a total of 18 million metropolitan francs was reported.[16] Averaging out at from 15 to 20 thousand francs per soldier, this sum was equivalent to the gross earnings a colonial laborer would obtain from ten years' labor at the notoriously low official rates set by the state. Even if this is an unreliable measure, there is no doubt that 20,000 francs in 1944 constituted a very substantial sum, A handful of soldiers, moreover, were said to be holding as much as 100,000 francs, capital sufficient to dramatically change their lives.[17]

These substantial sums no doubt added to the tensions between soldiers and their French officers. To paternalist officials, the existence of such substantial sums not only minimized the urgency to pay the soldiers what was due them in back pay and demobilization bonuses, but it also caused French officials to assume that the money had been gained by unlawful means, despite the evidence indicating that the men had received wages from their German captors. To the ex-POWs, the authoritarian manner in which they were being treated was a bitter reminder that they were returning home to an unchanged colonial system, unappreciative of the great sacrifices they perceived themselves to have made.

This heightened consciousness of themselves as men who had served the state well was an important change in attitude. Before the Second World War, Africans in their situation would have been forced to compromise, to accept, for example, the right to keep the funds they had accumulated in return for an agreement to return quietly to their villages to await an eventual and hypothetical settlement of their financial claims against the state. The men of Thiaroye were well aware that isolated in units of two or three as civilians in some remote rural district where they might encounter a minor French official once a year at best, their ability to obtain redress was severly limited. From this realization emerged a sense of solidarity among the men of Thiaroye, a determination not to allow themselves to be disbanded before being paid. Soldiers who came from urban districts, and who had somewhat easier access to the state, bureaucracy, as for example the men from western Senegal, were well aware of their advantage. Their determination to stick together in the interests of helping their rural comrades was an important measure of their solidarity as fellow workers in military uniform. The men of Thiaroye insisted upon a just settlement of their claims.

Indeed, the soldiers' claims for back pay and special bonuses were well founded. First, they had noted that their French comrades-in-arms had received combat pay for the entire period from the beinning of the war through to liberation. Also, a special hardship bonus of 5,000 francs was applied to these ex-POWs. On October 31, 1944, the minister of colonies had written Dakar authorizing a series of benefits to the ex-POWs soon to be demobilized.[18] They were to receive their back pay, only one quarter of which would be distributed in France; they would receive a demobilization pay of 500 francs upon their arrival in West Africa; and they would be issued a complete outfit of civilian clothes.

While these provisions fell short of the treatment afforded French ex-POWs, they were in any case simply not implemented. The African ex-POWs did not receive any back pay at all in France. Claiming a shortage of cloth, the colonial authorities planned on allowing the returning soldiers to keep their military uniforms in lieu of civilian clothes. Instead of invoking shortages a: d the administrative chaos of France in late 1944 as an excuse, colonial officials instinctively shifted responsibility to the colonial subjects. The men did not have clear proof of the number of days they had been in service. They had lost their identity cards and service records. Their claims could not be verified.

Hostility on money matters and especially toward the manner in which French colonial officials were treating them nearly spilled over into violence on November 26 as the French began to convert the soldiers' money into French West African currency. The conversion took place amid loud protests from the soldiers that they were being cheated out of their money. Some soldiers were said to have remarked, "Thieves! We earned our money; we won't leave this camp until we have killed these French pigs!"[19] Only with difficulty were the French able to restore order. So uneasy had the situation become that the military command decided two days later to dispatch some 500 men toward Bamako, and the Commanding General of Dakar and region, General Dagnan, made a personal visit to assure this departure in a calm manner. So angry had the men become that they went as far as to capture General Dagnan and hold him prisoner for a few hours. On his promise that the men would receive their money within three days, he was released.

The French had no intention of letting events deteriorate further. Upon learning of the mutinous state of the ex-POWs, the Commanding General for French West Africa, General de Boisboissel, ordered reinforcements of troops and police sent down from Saint Louis; these additional forces surrounded the camp of Thiaroye on November 30, the day the French had now decided upon for dispatching the 500 men to Bamako. For some reason, the dispatching was postponed once again, this time to the next day, December 1, 1944. The French effort to ship out these men that morning was the signal for the mutiny to begin. The soldiers began jostling their officers, most of whom were reservists from metropolitan rather than colonial units, that is, officers with little experience or rapport with their men. After the call to order failed, a first salvo was fired in the air. The men ran to the barracks to get their weapons. Now the order was to shoot to kill with the result that 35 men fell immediately and the same number lay seriously wounded.

Order was quickly restored. Some 34 men were arrested and marched through the streets of Dakar under machine gun escort, a decision deliberately taken in order to intimidate the local population.[20] The next day the detachment of 500 men was duly moved out toward Bamako, and several days after this, another large contingent of men was sent south by ship, all without incident.

The trial of the men of Thiaroye took place in February 1945. Lamine Guèye defended the men and pleaded for clemency on the basis of their outstanding service records, but all 34 were convicted (Guèye, 1966:124). On March 6, 1945, the Military Tribunal handed down sentences ranging from one to ten years in prison, with fines of 10,000 francs. Sixteen men received what might be called light sentences of three years or less. Among this group, one man died in prison, another 13 completed their sentences, and the remaining two were relieved of approximately one year of prison by the amnesty of November 1946. In the group having longer sentences, five men received the maximum of ten years, and the remaining 13 an average of five years. Of this group, four were to die in prison before the amnesty of 1946 freed the remaining 14.

Because the records of the Military Tribunal remain closed to research, very little is known about the men who were sentenced. What fragments that are available apply to those 18 men who received the stiffer sentences. It would seem that the men represented a typical cross-section of the Black Army: six men were from Guinea, four from Mali, three from Senegal, two each from Upper Volta and Ivory Coast, and one from Dahomey. Thus the majority of the men sentenced came from densely populated rural areas in the heartlands of the federation of French West Africa; only the colonies of Niger and Mauritania, where military recruitment was always light, were not represented. It is highly unlikely that more than four men, assuming that all the prisoners from Senegal and Dahomey were from large towns, could be said to have been from urban communities. The one man that a French report singled out as having been an especially militant mutineer was named Karimou Sylla. His patronym is Fulbe so it is likely that he came from either Guinea or Mali.[21]

French authorities put forward a variety of explanations as to the causes of the uprising at Thiaroye. Some opinions tended to reflect the concern of bureaucrats to shift responsibility to other shoulders. Thus, officials on the spot in French West Africa, while recognizing that the matter of pay was the leading grievance shared by the soldiers, attributed the poor discipline of the men generally to mistakes made in France.[22] Too many of the officers in command of the men were reservists, without previous experience in command of African units, and there were too few officers overall for the number of men involved. In short, the French officers did not know their men and could not hold their confidence. This same sort of failing was implied by the argument that, at the first signs of insubordination, which occurred well before the outbreak at Thiaroye, French leadership had failed to act decisively to restore order.[23] It followed that, after the uprising, advocates of this school would argue that only severe punishment of the mutineers would suffice to restore proper discipline and morale in the colonial troops.

Other French interpretations at least attempted to attribute the revolt to causes rooted in the harsh wartime experiences of the soldiers.[24] However, these positions were also often an attempt to shift responsibility elsewhere. Thus it was held, without much evidence, that German propaganda had been at work among the prisoners for their four years of incarceration, although precisely what form this had taken was never made clear. Because it is highly doubtful that Nazi ideologues would have held out honorary Aryan racial membership to Black soldiers, perhaps the allusion is to a generalized sort of anti-French or even African nationalist idea, although one French report explicitly discounted the presence of any such sentiment among the men.

Only a few Frenchmen were willing to consider the obvious possibility that African soldiers' wartime experiences had made them change their attitudes toward their colonial ideas. Invoking the time-worn cliche regarding class, race, and sexual relations between Africans and "a certain sort" of French woman, some concluded that African soldiers no longer respected French women and, by extension, French society.[25] Others, less subjective, recognized clearly the change that had taken place and the need of French colonial officials to do something about it:[26]

> Separated for many years from their homes, placed in exceptionally difficult circumstances, these natives have acquired habits and ways of thinking, indeed an entire mentality that tends to make them a very special element. At the moment of advance of the Allied armies in France, the native prisoners found themselves suddenly liberated. A good number of them, in keeping with the preparatory work of the Secret Army, were then incorporated into formations of the French Forces of the Interior or in the Partisans' units and they participated in military actions against the enemy. Others were taken in by honorable French families. Still others, and this is to be deplored, lived by more or less legal means and were sheltered by "godmothers" of doubtful morality. A veritable campaign of reorganization and recuperation had to be undertaken in order to put an end to this confused situation which did not always produce a favorable effect on the morale of these natives.

What French views, however perceptive, failed to recognize, of course, was the degree to which the men of Thiaroye had acquired a heightened consciousness of themselves as Africans united across lines of village, ethnicity, and region. Earlier incidents involving African soldiers returning from service overseas had demonstrated that some heightened awareness was the usual product of such service. Despite life in barracks under military discipline, many African soldiers experienced friendly contact with Europeans not marked by colonial prejudices. Often this amounted to nothing more than casual acquaintances with French families, for example, although in some cases more serious liaisons with French women did take place. In either instance, much less of colonial paternalism and alienation was involved in contacts between Africans and Europeans abroad than in colonies themselves. Return to the rigid, autocratic atmosphere of the colonies was then an unpleasant reminder for many soldiers that, despite any illusions they may have had about having served France, to the civilian administrators and Frenchmen in private life, the old colonial ways had not changed.

For prisoners of war, of course, all of these pressures were more intensely felt. Many had indeed served side by side with young French prisoners under German incarceration and had formed bonds in this way. Others had made important contacts with French members of the Resistance. In short, the Africans' sense of dignity and worth was significantly heightened by their long experience in suffering. The notion that they had served France above and beyond the call of duty was deeply imbedded in these men. Indeed, many must have shared a recurring African soldiers' sentiment that the colonial troops had been better defenders of France's sovereignty during the debacle of 1940 than had French officers and elisted men.

In these circumstances, the African soldiers' response to the shabby treatment they received from French officials from the moment of their liberation until the outbreak at Thiaroye must be understood. The demand for back pay was only a part of a generalized demand for equal treatment for equal sacrifices, as the political slogan of the African veterans after the war was to articulate it. Thiaroye reflected the determination of a group of African employees to be paid their due. It also demonstrated the consciousness of the men of Thiaroye of their dignity as Africans.

Whatever their interpretation of events, French officials all shared a deep concern as to the potential consequences of the uprising at Thiaroye. For Governor Cournarie, Thiaroye called into question not only the ability of France to restore order, but the entire issue of France's sovereignty in West Africa.[27] On the other hand, Cournarie had in mind the growing political awareness of West Africans, to what at this stage the French referred to as the "Parti Laministe" and the politics of ethnic nationalists like the Lebou leadership of the Dakar region. Indeed, because Thiaroye was so close to the federal capital, the French had felt it necessary to show the African public in the Cap Vert peninsula that they were clearly still in charge. On the other hand, they were also concerned about the spreading of this political awakening throughout the federation.

The Governor-General in Dakar issued instructions to all Lieutenants-Governor in the various colonial units making up the federation to subject the returning servicemen, and especially the ex-POWs, to particularly close serveillance, and to include as well in their political reports an indication of the African popular reaction to the events of Thiaroye.[28]

French anxieties about their sovereignty came also from a direction other than concern about potential African awakenings. The presence of significant numbers of Allied, and especially American troops in Dakar from 1943 until the end of the war against Hitler added a significant second dimension to French fears. In this view, it was held that the

Americans coveted France's West African empire and would welcome a convenient excuse to take over control.[29] A second troop mutiny, followed this time by linkages to the civilian population in the Dakar region, might very well have cost France her presence in West Africa, or so French officials had reason to fear.

With these pressures operating, the French lost very little time reasserting their control. At the same time they issued instructions for increased surveillance of ex-servicemen, and for the reporting of the political mood of the African population regarding Thiaroye, colonial officials set about diffusing the explosive situation. They dispersed the ex-POWs to the various colonies as soon after the first of December as possible, recognizing the importance of breaking large units of soldiers into smaller ones. They relied thereafter upon the ties of family and private life to continue the process of "detoxification" as they called it.[30] They did not at this stage feel it important to redress the original grievance that had sparked the Thiaroye rebellion. Increased pensions were not the answer, in their opinion. Thus there were no immediate benefits to the returning veterans. Only two years later, under the very different peacetime political climate of the Fourth Republic, did France begin to approach the veterans' issue in a new light.

Perhaps the only portent of a new political climate that was about to emerge was the French realization that the use of force could no longer be the patterned response to African opposition. As Governor Cournarie recognized, the use of force "could not be permitted to be repeated, under any pretext whatsoever."[31] It is unclear whether this is a reference to the growth of the African opposition or to the presence of the American threat. What is important is that the uprising at Thiaroye came as such a shock that it served effectively to delegitimize naked force as a political instrument. In its place, the new tactic of dividing Africans politically, and encouraging the growth of conservative political forces favorable to France emerged. In this context, the veterans came to be seen as an extremely important body, predisposed toward petit-bourgeois images of France's role and purpose in West Africa. Under these pressures, France began to pay much closer attention to veterans' benefits, as did the emerging African politicians.

There is no denying that Thiaroye sent shock waves throughout the French West African Federation. This was the sort of behavior the Free French had conditioned Africans to expect from Vichy, but surely not from a government that owed such an enormous debt to African men-in-arms. Indeed, despite Gaullist propaganda, the Vichy régime had never been responsible for such a blatant use of force. Its hold in West Africa was so fragile that it dared not risk situations of such direct confrontation

(Deschamps, 1975:Livre VI). News of the disaster spread like wildfire. It could not but do so. Not only did the French make a public example of the Thiaroye prisoners in Dakar, but the rapid dispersal of the rest of the 1,280 ex-POWs to their colonies of origin assured that this was so. Indeed, Thiaroye was on everyone's lips for months afterward. Friends wrote about it to African soldiers still in France and awaiting demobilization.[32] Others wrote to French families that had befriended African soldiers in the hopes of enlisting French public support for a pardon on the men held in prison (see, for example, Réveil, Aug. 26, 1946:2). Always the response was the same: shock and indignation, although a few conservative Africans had uncommon reactions. For the vast majority, of course, Thiaroye represented a brutal act of repression against soldiers whose only crime was to claim money that was rightfully theirs.

Thiaroye also served to bring out contradictions inherent in the African colonial situation. Thus, Seydou Nourou Tall and other conservative members of the Muslim heirarchy in Senegal supported the French repression on the grounds that men who had disobeyed and struck their officers could not escape punishment without producing severe troubles in the countryside.[33] Committed to collaboration with colonial authorities, the Muslim leadership was not prepared to make a political break with the French over Thiaroye, important an event though it might be. Seydou Nourou Tall, indeed, had been called in once before on the question of helping reintegrate African servicemen quietly into colonial society. In 1941, under the aegis of Vichy, he had produced a pamphlet in Arabic urging soldiers to respect their parents, their traditional chiefs, and French authority.[34] In the wake of Thiaroye, his immediate reaction was to criticize the French not for having acted repressively, but for having failed to call in traditional Islamic leaders earlier to help calm down the men and prevent the uprising in the first place.

The conservative Muslim leadership would change its attitude toward veterans only gradually. The real political initiative was about to pass to the new politicians about to achieve prominence in the postwar period. This was especially the case of the Senegalese politicians Lamine Guèye and Léopold Sédar Senghor, both of whom became directly involved in the aftermath of Thiaroye.

The victims of Thiaroye, determined to assert their innocence and their rights, turned for help to the incipient veterans' organizations that were beginning to spring up. Most prominent among the leaders of these groups was Papa Seck Douta, later to be head of the Federation of Veterans' Associations for all of French West Africa, who was in early 1945 President of the Senegalese veterans.[35] Indignant and shocked, Seck Douta saw in Thiaroye the undermining of all his efforts to promote the cause of veterans within the context of French assimilationist politics. A citizen himself, having been born in Dakar, Seck Douta was associated in French eyes with the new drive for political equality among African veterans who saw themselves as having been largely responsible for the Gaullist victory. Acting on instructions from the prisoners awaiting trial, Seck Douta contacted Maître Lamine Guèye, the best known African lawyer of the day, to lead the defense of the Thiaroye men. Guéye, about to launch his victorious campaign for mayor of Dakar, and with political ambitions to succeed earlier figures like Blaise Diagne and Galandou Diouf as the political spokesman of the Senegalese citizens, was pleased at the political opportunity inherent in an eloquent defense of the victims of Thiaroye.[36]

If Lamine Guèye benefitted from his association with the men of Thiaroye, the same is certainly true for Léopold Sédar Senghor. Indeed, the tragedy of Thiaroye had deep meaning for Senghor, because he himself had been a prisoner of war. As his moving poem entitled "Tyaroye" reveals, French brutality was part of a contradiction in Senghor's mind. France had acted in a deplorable manner, "a nation forgetful of its mission of yesterday," but the deaths of Thiaroye had not been in vain. The fallen men were martyrs to "a new world which will be tomorrow" (Senghor, 1964:90-91).

Senghor's emotional involvement with Thiaroye soon took on a political dimension. As the "deputy in khaki" and Lamine Guèye's lieutenant in the Socialist Party of Senegal (SFIO), Senghor actively solicited the veterans' vote in the first elections to the Constituent Assembly of the Fourth Republic in 1945 (Morganthau, 1964:136-138). The next year he remembered his debt to the veterans and to the victims of Thiaroye by lobbying actively for a general pardon for them.

The amnesty issue dragged on for months before it finally was resolved in a manner favorable to the men of Thiaroye. In April of 1946, the Constituent Assembly in Paris had passed a general amnesty law, pardoning all prisoners of war, deportees, political internees, and the like for offenses committed during the war. Senghor led a campaign among African representatives to the Constituent Assembly to have this law made applicable to West Africa, but was not until November of 1946 that this was done.[37] Even then this was less than satisfactory because the terms of the pardon required the prisoners themselves to make their request for amnesty within six months; in addition, the request then had to be endorsed by the appropriate military authority. Thus when first approached on this matter, the Commanding General of French West Africa and the Government Commissioner of the Military Tribunal both refused to recommend application of the amnesty law to the men of

Thiaroye because of the seriousness of the offenses in their view. [38] Only under continued political pressure from the French Ministry of Colonies, which itself was encountering persistent pressure of the African politicians, did the situation change. First, General de Boisboissel was recalled as Commanding General of French West Africa. Although to preserve appearances this recall was labelled a regular mutation, the African public was probably correct in viewing this as a belated repudiation of the repression at Thiaroye. De Boisboissel's successor, in January 1947, removed the veto against the application of the amnesty law in his words because of "political contingencies and the motion of the Association of Prisoners of War."[39] Not until June of 1947 did President Auriol of the Fourth Republic sign the bill bringing about an amnesty for the men of Thiaroye, which included those who had already completed their sentences (Réveil, June 23, 1947).

A pardon was not an acquittal. Because the men of Thiaroye continued to carry their convictions on their military records, certain jobs in the French colonial bureaucracy remained closed to them all their lives.

The amnesty debate during 1946 and 1947 helped make the uprising of Thiaroye, as well as incidents of lesser magnitude such as Kindia, publicly acknowledged events. Newpapers, silent due to censorship in 1944, could now profit from the changed climate to inform their readers of the events that had transpired and of the efforts of the politicians to set the record straight. L'AOF (June 23, 1947; Aug. 8,1947), the SFIO newspaper in Senegal, made it clear that Senghor and Lamine Guèye were playing a decisive role in the struggle for justice for the men of Thiaroye. The more militant RDA-backed paper, Réveil, while acknowledging Senghor's important role and publishing his correspondence on the subject, also reminded its readers that leading RDA politicians like Houphouet-Boigny and Hamani Diori were also playing an active part in the struggle (May 15,1947; June 12 and 23, 1947). Thus, Thiaroye, like the issue of equal pensions for African war veterans, entered the political domain.

Perhaps the last page in the Thiaroye story was written on February 19, 1950. Working in coordination with the French Communist Party, on that day the more militant Senegalese nationalist and communist groups attempted to keep Thiaroye before the public as a symbol of colonial oppression (Réveil, Feb. 13 and 27, 1950; Mar. 6, 1950). As part of an International Day of Struggle against Colonialism, the RDA, its youth wing, the newspaper Réveil, the Communist trade unions, and a series of veterans' associations combined to organize a public pilgrimage to the cemetery at Thiaroye where the fallen soldiers were buried. When the colonial officials banned the march and deployed armed European soldiers around the cemetery, the demonstrators were forced instead to direct themselves to the war memorial in the center of Dakar where they discreetly placed their wreaths at that spot "in homage to the massacred of Thiaroye, victims of Colonialism." Sporadically since that time, as in 1958 on the eve of independence, these ceremonies have been revived, but Thiaroye has not really become an annual event or the cemetery a martyrs' shrine. Instead, Senegalese veterans, like their compatriots all over French-speaking West Africa, continue to honor July 14 for their memorial services. To replace Bastille Day with Thiaroye would be a gesture of sovereignty not in keeping with the profoundly assimilationist attitudes of the African veterans' organizations.

The tragedy of Thiaroye burned deeply into the minds of Francophone West Africans of many social classes in the same manner, if not with the same force perhaps, as Sharpeville did elsewhere on the continent. It deserves recognition both as a watershed in modern West African history, and as a measure of the contradictions inherent among Africans themselves. At one extreme, the reaction of such conservative leaders as Saydou Nourou Tall was revealing. So devoted to the repressive social order of French colonialism had the conservative Muslim hierarchy become that they were prepared to justify and support the harshness of the Thiaroye repression.

For all returning soldiers and veterans Thiaroye produced a crystallization of their sense as a collective group, conscious of their need for unity just as the men of Thiaroye themselves had recognized. As one veteran was to remark, "We were not like the veterans of 1914-1918. We had our eyes open. We were not prepared to be treated like sheep."[40] Thiaroye provided a tremendous impetus for the growth of a whole series of veterans' associations,which emerged after the war in each colony, centrally coordinated through Dakar, and with significant links to veterans' groups in France. In the 1940s veterans were an important part of the legalist struggle waged by national bourgeois political parties and especially the RDA for equality before the law for "citizens of the French Union," as Africans and other colonial subjects were euphemistically labelled. The veterans' slogan, "equal sacrifices, equal rights," referred not only to pensions and benefits generally, but also could be and was applied to the struggle for justice for the condemned men of Thiaroye.

Yet there were also limits to which soldiers and veterans alike could be radicalized. Some did begin to look across their horizons of village, ethnic group, and colony and come to understand clearly the contradictions in the assimilationist position. Others could not so easily shed their military ties of discipline and institutional loyalty to France or to the kind of petit-bourgeois imperial patriotism inculcated in them by their officers. Even

Thiaroye was not enough of a shock to break this bond. When, after 1950, the French National Assembly voted to accept the principle of equal rights for equal sacrifices, that is, of parity with French metropolitan veterans, most African veterans reaffirmed their loyalties to the state that paid their pension.

For a minority of veterans, Thiaroye marked the beginning of a more militant consciousness. This was especially the case for those who had been prisoners of war and more closely touched by the long years of incarceration in Europe and by the subsequent ingratitude of the state. Some of these men were attracted to the more militant political parties and trade unions.

The events of Thiaroye have an indirect place in the history of Senegalese and French-speaking Western African workers. It is not that Thiaroye was itself a soldiers' strike, properly speaking. It was not a case of soldiers refusing to sell their labor by laying down their tools. Instead, it was a refusal to disband until the state as employer had fulfilled its contract, an act of military disobedience in the face of patently unjust treatment. It is technically labelled a mutiny insofar as the men were still under military discipline, but that is to obsure Thiaroye's nature, It was a premeditated, planned, coordinated piece of collective action taken by men who had achieved a high degree of consciousness of themselves a group.

Thiaroye by itself was also doomed to failure. It never succeeded in establishing political ties to the African population and could hardly have done so, given the isolation of the men. Also, the ex-POWs never established the crucial link with armed soldiers in regular service, all of whom remained loyal to the state in carrying out the repression. Indeed, the uprising at Thiaroye was a desperate act, successful symbolically only to the extent to which it generated a bloody repression.

Thiaroye's link with workers' history is however, more than symbolic in two respects. First, the state was delegitimized at a time when it had appeared to have generated considerable African support as a result of the recent liberation, the promises of the Brazzaville conference, and the triumph of De Gaulle. Thiaroye demonstrated that the Free French Government was as capable of acts of repression and injustice as its Vichy or Third Republic predecessors. Second, the widespread and significant public reaction, which so brutal an act of force provoked in France as well as in West Africa, was of considerable value to railway workers specifically, and for the emerging proletariat generally. During the prolonged and bitter rail strike of 1948, workers had at least the confidence that the state was extremely reluctant to repeat the naked use of force characterized by Thiaroye. Indeed, the belated recall of the

Commanding General, de Boisboissel, who had been responsible for the massacre at Thiaroye, and the awarding of amnesties in 1947 were interpreted by the African public as an admission by the French of their guilt.

Lastly, Thiaroye marked a turning point in the struggle of Africans in French West Africa to gain a dignity that the colonial system denied them. Earlier generations of returning soldiers had also expressed a distaste for the racism and paternalism that greeted them upon their return to the colony, but these men were unable to act collectively. The men of Thiaroye, through their actions, had given West Africans under French rule one of the most dramatic examples of resistance to oppression in the entire colonial period. To paraphrase Marx's analysis of the case of the Indian mutiny on a different continent a century earlier, Thiaroye offered the suggestion that the colonial army might under the proper circumstances provide "the first general centre of resistance which the [African] people were ever possessed of" (Marx and Engels, 1968).

NOTES

1. Senghor's poem was published in 1948 in a collection entitled *Hosties Noires,* in which the theme of Africans (including Senghor) performing military service for France is frequently invoked. The full text for "Tyaroye" may be found in French on pages 90 and 91 of his complete works of poetry (Senghor, 1964).

I wish to acknowledge the assistance of the Canada Council, whose Leave Fellowship has enable me to complete the research for this chapter, which forms part of my continuing inquiry into the social history of the Francophone African soldiers and veterans.

2. For example, in the works of Morganthau (1964), Suret-Canale (1964), and Crowder (1968). Even Lamine Guèye (1966) in his autobiography treats the uprising lightly.

3. There are significant problems of documentation with regard to the narrative account of the uprising at Thiaroye and especially its aftermath. The soldiers were under military discipline and were therefore brought before a military tribunal. The archives of French Military Justice, located at Meaux, are closed to the public, however, for 100 years after the trial in question.

The evidence upon which this chapter is based comes from the civilian archives of the Colonial Administration of French West Africa unless otherwise stated. The most relevant files are to be found in Archives de l'Afrique occidentale francaise (hereafter AAOF), Dakar, Senegal: series 4D, 2D, and 13G. While this governmental correspondence helps establish some of the basic facts regarding the uprising, it sheds little light on the personalities or backgrounds of the African soldiers who were involved. Such detail will only be available if the records of the military tribunal are opened to research.

I have also interviewed several veterans who vividly recall the events of Thiaroye, including one man who was a direct participant, and who received a prison sentence. In return for his willingness to be interviewed, I have agreed to respect his desire to remain anonymous. I can say that the interview took place in Dakar, Senegal, on May 18, 1973.

4. From Senghor's poem entitled "Prayer for Peace" (Senghor, 1976:136).

5. For specific studies of the recruitment and social organization of the Black Army, see Michel (1971); D'Almeida-Topor (1973); and Echenberg (1975). Earlier, more general works are those by Davis (1934) and Ly (1957).

6. Marx's original statement first appeared in his "Revolt in the Indian Army" (*New York Daily Tribune*, July 15, 1857), and has been collected in his essays, *On Colonialism* (Marx and Engels, 1968). He argued that the Indian army constituted "the first general centre of resistance which the Indian people was ever possessed of."

7. AAOF, 4D 70/81: General Freydenberg, Annual Report on Recruitment for 1932, Dakar, Sept. 15, 1932.

8. AAOF, 5D1/1: Chief of Police and Security Special Service to Director of General Security, Dakar, Nov. 27, 1939.

9. AAOF, 4D31/14: Governor-General of French West Africa, Circular letter to all Lieutenants-Governor of the Federation, Nov. 30, 1940.

10. AAOF, 13G69/17: High Commissioner for French West Africa to Minister of Overseas France, Sept. 18, 1947.

11. AAOF, 13G69/17: High Commissioner for French West Africa to Minister of Overseas France, Sept. 18, 1947.

12. French authorities obtained details on conditions ion German camps from the men of Thiaroye through interrogations held after the uprising. Excerpts of these inquiries were reported to senior officials under the rubric, "Renseignements." See, for example, AAOF, 4D31/14: "Renseignements," March 7, 1945.

13. Mail from West Africa could be channelled through the neutral offices of the neighboring colony of Portuguese Guinea to prisoners in Europe. It is doubtful if very much contact actually took place through such a cumbersome conduit. AAOF,4D31/14: Govenor-General of French West Africa to Minister of Colonies Feb. 26, 1944.

14. AAOF, 4D178/144: Department of Political Affairs, Government-General of French West Africa, undated report, "Sur les Incidents de Thiaroye du Premier Décembre 1944" (hereafter cited as "Sur les Incidents").

15. "Sur les Incidents."

16. "Sur les Incidents."

17. Based on United Nations Statistical Yearbook data giving increases in the cost of living, the French franc of 1944 has a coefficient of 28.46 in relation to the 1976 franc; thus, 20,000 francs of 1944 would have the purchasing power 1976 of 5,700 new francs, that is, roughly $1,150 U.S. United Nations figures indicate that official wages for laborers in French West Africa before 1945 were 160 francs per month, that is, 1920 francs annually.

18. AAOF, 4D31/14: Minister of Colonies to Governor-General of French West Africa, Oct. 31, 1944.

19. AAOF, 13G69/17: Report of Government Commissioner to the Permanent Military Tribunal of Dakar to the Minister of War, Jan. 27, 1947 (hereafter, "Report").

20. AAOF,2D3/1: "Reseignements," Dec. 2, 1944.

21. "Report."

22. "Sur les Incidents."

23. AAOF, 4D31/14: Administrator, District of Dakar and region to Governor-General of French West Africa, Dec. 4, 1944.

24. AAOF, 4D31/14: "Renseignements," Dec. 6, 1944.

25. AAOF, 4D31/14: "Reseignements," Nov. 15, 1946.

26. AAOF, 4D31/14: Minister of Colonies to Governor-General of French West Africa, Oct. 31, 1944.

27. AAOF, 4D31/14: Governor-General of French West Africa to Minister of Colonies, Dec. 7,1944.

28. AAOF, 4D31/14: Governor-General of French West Africa, circular letter to all Lieutenants-Governor, Dec. 14,1944.

29. AAOF, 4D31/14: "Bulletin de Renseignement" for French West Africa, Nov. 1944 to Feb. 1945.

30. "Sur les Incidents."

31. AAOF, 4D31/14: Governor-General of French West Africa to Minister of Colonies, Dec. 7, 1944.

32. AAOF, 4D31/14: "Reseignements," no date, contains a letter translated from Arabic and written by one Ibrahima of Dakar to his friend, Abdurahmane Traore, stationed in a military camp in the Bouches de Rhone district.

128   AFRICAN LABOR HISTORY

33. AAOF, 2D3/1: "Renseignements," reports of Dec. 2 and 6, 1944.
34. AAOF, 4D31/14: "Translation into French of Seydouw Nourou Tall's Statement to the Senegalese Rifles," June 25, 1941.
35. AAOF, 2D3/1: "Reseignements," Dec. 6, 1944.
36. For the earlier era of Senegalese politics, see Johnson (1971); for the postwar period, see Morganthau (1964) and Guèye (1966).
37. AAOF, 13G69/17: High Commissioner for French West Africa to Minister of Overseas France, June 10, 1947; *Journal Officiel* of the French Republic, Apr. 17, 1946: 3222-3223, for the debate on the amnesty issue..
38. AAOF, 13G69/17: Minister of Overseas France to High Comminssioner for French West Africa, May 20, 1947.
39. AAOF, 13G69/17: Minister of Overseas France to High Commissioner for French West Africa May 20, 1947.
40. Interview conducted by the author with a veteran of the uprising at Thiaroye, Dakar, Senegal, May 18, 1973.

REFERENCES

BUTTINGER, J.(1967). Vietnam: A dragon embattled: Vol.1, From colonialism to the Vietminh. New York: Praeger.
CROWDER, M. (1968). West Africa under colonial rule. London: Hutchinson.
D'ALEIDA-TOPOR, H. (1973). "Les populations dahoméennes et le recrutement militaire pendant la première guerre mondiale." Revue francaise d'histoire d'outre-mer, 60:196-241.
DAVIS, S.C. (1934, 1970). Reservoirs of men: A history of the black troops of French West Africa. Geneva: Chambery (orig. edn.); Westport, Conn.: Negro Universities Press (reprint).
DESCHAMPS, H. (1975). Roi de la brousse. Paris: Berger-Levrault.
ECHENBERG, M.J. (1975)."Paying the blood tax: Military conscription in French West Africa, 1914-1929." Canadian Journal of African Studies, 9:171-192.
GNANKAMBARY, B. (1965). "La révolte Bobo de 1916 dans le cercle de Dedougou." Unpublished mémoire, Ouagadougou, Ecole Nationale D'Administration.
GUEYE, L. (1966). Itenéraire Africain. Paris: Presence Africaine.
JOHNSON, G.W., JR. (1971). The emergence of black politics in Senegal. Stanford: Stanford University Press.
LY, A. (1957). Mercenaires noirs. Paris: Présence Africaine.
MARX, K., and ENGELS, F. (1968). On colonialism (4th ed.). Moscow: Progress Publishers.
MICHEL, M. (1971). "La genèse du recrutement du 1918 en Afrique noire francaise." Revue francaise d'histoire d'outre-mer, 58:433-450.
MORGANTHAU, R. S. (1964).Political parties in French-speaking West Africa. Oxford: Clarendon Press.
PEDRONCINI, G. (1967). Les mutineries de 1917. Paris: Presses Universitaires de France.
SEN, S. N.(1957). Eighteen fifty-seven. Delhi: Government of India, Ministry of Information and Broadcasting.
SENGHOR, L. S. (1964). Poèmes. Paris: Editions du Seuil.
_____ (1976). Senghor: Prose and poetry (J. Reed and C. Wake, trans. and eds.). London: Heinemann.
SPEAR, P. (1972). India, a modern history. Ann Arbor: University of Michigan Press.
SURET-CANALE, J. (1964). Afrique noire—l'Ère coloniale, 1900-1945. Paris: Editions Sociales.
TRONCHON, J. (1974). L'Insurrection malgache de 1947. Paris: Maspero.

5

THE FRENCH WEST AFRICAN RAILWAY WORKERS' STRIKE, 1947-1948

J. SURET-CANALE
University of Oran

From the end of the Second World War to the "loi-cadre" of 1956 two periods were marked by the rise of strikers' movements in French West Africa. From 1945 to 1946 two factors contributed to the rise: a deterioration in living conditions due to spiralling prices and the blocking of wage increases during the war, and the large political thrust concomitant with the victory over Nazism. From 1952 to 1953 strikes were held to push for the adoption, and subsequently the application, of the Overseas Territories Work Code.

Between these two periods the most important strike was that of the African railway workers. It was different from previous strikes in two ways: first, by its duration which was without parallel in the social history of French West Africa (it lasted over five months from October 10, 1947, to March 19, 1948); second, by its corporate character being limited to the personnel of the railroad company. The other strikes had not only been of shorter duration, but also of a more general character and had extended from the public sectors to the private sectors. Nevertheless, as we shall see, partisans as well as adversaries stressed that the thrust of this strike went well beyond the limits of occupational interests, in the narrow sense of the term. One must note here the relative importance of the number of strikers: nearly 20,000 employees in a French West Africa whose total number of wage earners in 1947 was estimated to be 241,700.[1]

Up to the present time this strike has not been subjected to a penetrating study. It has only been used as a backdrop for the novel of the great Senegalese writer, Ousmane Sembène, *God's Bits of Wood* (1960). The only general study, usually ignored by commentators, was published in

EDITORS' NOTE: This chapter was edited by Jean Copans and translated from the French by Alice E. Gutkind and Simon J. Copans, whose contributions to this volume, which includes the editing of other chapters, are gratefully acknowledged.

May 1948 in the CGT (Confédération Générale du Travail) review, *Servir la France*, by Pierre Morlet. Chris Allen examined this strike in detail in a more general study devoted to a critique of the notion of "political control" of French West African strikes. In essence he notes that academic studies repeat without further examination the thesis of "political" strikes influenced by the French communist party.[2]

One of the authors named by Allen is Franz Ansprenger. Nearly everything is false about the allegations made by Ansprenger: the African railway workers' strike began one month before the 1947 French strikes (November 12 to December 10, 1947), and it followed a warning strike which had taken place six months earlier on April 19, 1947. The Federation of African Railway Workers of the AOF, which comprised four unions, was autonomous: one of these unions, that of Bénin-Niger (Dahomey), was affiliated to the CFTC (Confédération française des travailleurs chrétiens). None were affiliated to the CGT. The strike, far from leading to a rupture with the CGT, led to an affiliation with the CGT in 1949 by the Dakar-Niger and Abidjan-Niger unions, and to the abandonment of previous links with the CFTC by the Bénin-Niger union, which became autonomous.[3]

The present study can thus be considered only as a first approach, relying on incomplete and fragmentary documentation. The basic sources are my personal memories as a witness, aided by personal archives, and an incomplete analysis of the press.[4]

THE FRENCH WEST AFRICA RAILWAYS IN 1947

In 1947 the economy of French West Africa was still wholly a trading economy. Collection and transport networks were necessary for gathering local products and distribution of merchandise, though carried on a very reduced volume. It was not an integrated network, but a series of lines leading from the ports. The railway networks reflected this function: there were four lines (or groups of lines) of penetration without interconnections, which were the Dakar-Niger (the two principal lines, Dakar-San Louis and Dakar-Bamako, met at Thiès) which was concerned with the collection of peanuts; Conakry-Niger (Guinea) which transported bananas; Abidjan-Niger (which at that time was being extended from Bobo-Dioulasso to Ouagadougou) which transported coffee and cocoa; and Bénin-Niger (Dahomey) which after transfer to trucks made the connection from Parakou to the Niger. The Dakar-Bamako line transported "navetanes" (occasional agricultural workers who migrated during the rainy period—"navet" in Wolof) from the Sudan to the peanut growing regions in Senegal. The Abidjan-Niger line transported Mossi manpower from Upper Volta to the plantations of the lower Ivory Coast.

Even taking into account the small volume of trade, this rail network was unbelievably decrepit and inadequate. In 1947 there existed a total of 3,772 kilometers of single track one meter wide, largely built before 1914 more for strategic purposes (troop transport) than for economic motives. The difficulties of communication with the metropole had made rotation of European personnel difficult. Their numbers were reduced in spite of important local recruitment of improvised European railwaymen hired more for their ability to "command" than for their professional competence. In order to make up for the drop in skilled metropolitan personnel, and the mediocrity of equipment, African workers were recruited on a massive scale.[5]

Ports and wharves were under the same administration as the railways and, in 1947, when the French West African railways were brought under state management, the port at Conakry, the wharves at Port-Bouët, Grand Bassam (Ivory Coast), and Cotonou (Dahomey) were put under the same management and their workers were affiliated to the same unions.[6]

Employees of the railways, ports, and wharves comprised nearly a tenth of the total wage earning population of French West Africa. Their relative concentration, and the facility for liaison inherent in their profession explains the early development and solidarity of their union bolstered by a tradition of conflict of many years duration (numerous strikes of which the one in 1938 on the Dakar-Niger line was studied by the Senegalese historian, Iba Der Thiam).[7] The blocking of the railway line by a strike certainly could not paralyze entirely the movement of goods because of the alternative of road transport; it could, however, delay movement and raise the cost of transport. In the southern colonies (the Ivory Coast and Dahomey), on the other hand, the blocking of wharves could completely paralyze commerce.

ORIGINS OF THE CONFLICT

The railway lines as well as ports and wharves were under the Department of Railways and Transport up to 1946 and this department was under the general jurisdiction of the Public Works Department. A ministerial decree of July 17, 1946, promulgated on December 6 of the same year by the governor-general of French West Africa transferred the administration of the railway network on January 1, 1947, to an agency of an industrial and commercial nature, which had legal status and financial autonomy, called the "Railway Administration of French West Africa" (Régie des chemins de fer de l'A.O.F.). This network comprised "supplementary and incorporated services" (that is to say ports and wharves) and connecting services on the Dahomey-Niger line managed by the Bénin-Niger line (which included automobile service from Parakou to Malanville and navigation of the Niger from Malanville to Niamey).

The change in status allowed the government to rid itself of the burden of the railway network and to justify the necessity for financial equilibrium which included tariff increases and simultaneous massive layoffs of workers. The change in status also involved revising the status of workers. Only a minority were integrated into the category of managerial personnel and had a status close to those of civil servants. The administration wanted to profit from the change in order to reconsider the acquired advantages (and to proceed more easily with projected layoffs). African workers, on the other hand, saw the change as an opportunity to call for an end to racial discrimination through the institution of a "cadre unique" (single staff system) (a demand also presented by all the civil servants) comprising a single hierarchical scale, which would give the same rights to all except for an expatriation indemnity for Europeans. At the same time they demanded that permanent auxiliaries (full time workers employed according to a revocable contract and therefore not enjoying civil service permanency) be integrated into the "single staff system." A single staff system and integration of auxiliaries were the two major demands brought out in 1946. One does not need to explain that these demands did not suit the administration because they would have entailed increased charges.

The climate of 1946 did not allow the administration to oppose the single staff system proposal. It had to admit this principle by convening a parity commission (a meeting of administration representatives and European and African workers with equal representation) in the last quarter of 1946 to discuss the creation of a single "federal staff system" and also the reduction of personnel (layoffs were presented as the price which had to be paid for the single staff system; the workers' delegates thus were forced to confirm the layoffs). But in the growing climate of reaction taking shape in the second half of 1946, the administration was able to play on the racism of European railway workers.

The unions, reconstituted in 1943-1944, had been formed with few exceptions on a racial basis, as in 1937. European unions, naturally, were affiliated to the French CGT which, since the unification secretly agreed upon by the Perreux agreement in 1943, was identified with French syndicalism. From 1944 to 1947 the CGT unified everyone, the former "unitaires" thrown out of the CGT in 1939 over their refusal to disavow the German-Soviet pact, and the former "reformists" with Léon Jouhaux at their head. But the latter, a majority in 1939, were from 1944 on in the minority because too many of their prewar leaders had compromised themselves with the Vichy regime. The CFTC played a marginal role, and the "social doctrine of the church" which it called for had a scent of corporatism and class collaboration not very attractive to supporters in the days following the liberation. According to C. Allen, who refers to G. Chaffard's (1967:355) and Pfefferman's (1967:216) data, the CFTC leader, Joseph Dumas, at the instigation of the deputy MRP (Mouvement Républicain Populaire) from the Cameroons, Aujoulat, had toured West Africa in 1946 to help establish CFTC unions. They only grew to some extent in the southern colonies (notably in Dahomey), in the African milieu, due to the influence of Catholic missions. The Bénin-Niger African union was affiliated to the CFTC even though in the same region the European railway workers' union was affiliated to the CGT (Morlet, 1948).

The first contacts with the French CGT were made in 1945-1946 through the intermediary of those belonging to the unitary faction, henceforth the majority. The CGT expressed its vigorous opposition to unions organized on a racial basis, demanded single unions, and attacked the corruption of some of the leaders of African unions who made union activities an enterprise, a racket, like some American unions (Suret-Canale, 1972:20-21). However, the presence in the CGT of purely Europeans unions, established by officials with whom they were in constant conflict, led the African railway workers staying out of the CGT.[8]

Nevertheless, a congress of railway workers was held at Dakar in October 1946 with the participation of a delegate, Prunault, from the Federation of French CGT Railway Workers. This congress (we have not been able to establish if it was a meeting of only delegates of European railway workers or both European and African railway workers) led to the formation of a "committee of *entente,* whose immediate aim was the establishment of a single staff system and afterwards a single union."[9] These decisions were able to be adopted because of the favorable political climate which still existed in October 1946, due in part to the insistence of the French Federation of Railway Workers and due also to the presence of some progressive European delegates, such as Tiberghien, secretary of the Abidjan-Niger European union and organizer of a communist study group in Abidjan, and Elzière, secretary of the Dakar-Niger European union.

In a letter of February 7, 1947, probably addressed to Bouvier, secretary of the Union des syndicats confédérés of Dakar, Tiberghien wrote:

>   We conducted things well until the meeting of the parity commission responsible
> for working on the single staff system. . . . The management has not openly attacked
> it, but at this time (by chance!) a dissident union was being formed by senior staff
> executives who in Dakar have taken the lead in killing the single staff system. . . . In
> reality, they do not want the single staff system, still less a single union. . . . In Dakar
> they have played on racist feelings and succeeded in separating the two elements,
> black and white.

In effect, as a first step, a dissident "cadre genéral" union was established (composed of higher ranking Europeans employees), led by Jourdan from the Bénin-Niger, who an article in the socialist journal *L'A.O.F.* (Karim Sow, Nov. 28, 1947) described as a "former air force officer from 1939-1945 based at airports in Thiès and Dakar" (which leads us to suppose that he was formerly a Vichyite).

In fact, a general assembly of the European union of the Conakry-Niger region on January 3, 1947, after regretting the division then in progress, aligned itself with the dissidents' position and laid the responsibility for this split at the feet of the secretary-general Elzière, "whose action has led to sharp criticism not only from senior agents but equally from many others," and asked for his resignation.

A motion proposed by Tiberghien was adopted in vain on the 4th of February by the general assembly of European railway workers of the Abidjan-Niger line by 32 votes to two, it "called again for a single staff system" and rejected the stand taken by the other European railway workers.[10] The "reconciliation" of the two European unions was brought about on the basis of racist positions directed against the African railway workers. This was facilitated by the elimination of Elzière, hospitalized at the time, and replaced as secretary of the Dakar-Niger line by his assistant Légé whom *L'A.O.F.* (Abdoul Karim Sow, 1947) characterized as Jourdan's "straw man." At the time of the African railway workers' strike in October 1947, the European union tried to play the role of strike breaker. Légé wrote an article in the ultra-colonial weekly *Climats* (Oct. 30, 1947) denouncing the "political" character of the strike. The union assembly held in Thiès on October 23, 1947 (bringing together the European agents from Nakar-Niger), unanimously voted for a rupture with the CGT, except for seven votes (which were those of SNCF (Société Nationale des Chemins de Fer) agents attached to the Dakar-Niger line).[11]

We have discussed at some length the attitude of the European unions, because it played a decisive role in the birth and development of the conflict.

THE STRIKE OF APRIL 1947

The position taken by Jourdan, on behalf of the senior agents and of the European union of Conakry-Niger, was communicated to the parity commission by its president on January 29, 1947. It provoked the indignation of African delegates and led to the immediate dispatch of a circular addressed to all African railway workers:[12]

> Today, after forty-five days of debate, some of our European comrades have asked for the suppression of the parity commission and others have declared that they are unable to subscribe to a single staff system. . . . The surprise for us, the African delegates, has been very great. It never occurred to us to think that in the same organization there could exist such racism and such egoism. . . . African workers, the time of colonialism is ended. We intend to cooperate, to cooperate with dignity and honesty, but we do not intend to remain forever exploited and ridiculed.

The African delegates left the commission as a protest against the attitude and declarations of the representatives of the European railway workers. After a futile exchange of correspondence with Governor-General Barthes and the federal director of the railways, Cunéo, the federal committee of the African railway workers' unions meeting at Thiès on April 11, decided to strike. The committee's motion states:[13]

> a) that from August 1946 to the present all means of conciliation have been exhausted.
> b) that the professional competence of African railway workers has been put in doubt by documents from directors as well as by European colleagues.
> c) that the obstruction encountered from directors only proves, in our view, the link with views of European comrades who have been hostile to the continuation of the parity commission's work along the lines of already accepted principles.
> d) that up to this date proposed layoffs are only applicable to African workers whereas a selection from the two sides (African and European) had been agreed upon between the high commissioner and the unions.
> decides:
> to use the only remaining means and cease work as a sign of protest beginning on the 19th April, 1947.

The strike took place on the stated date and was observed by all the African railway workers. It lasted only one day, ending on the evening of April 19 by a protocol of agreement signed in the presence of the French Overseas Minister, Marius Moutet, and the socialist deputies from Senegal.

The administration gained a point by having the unions accept the principle of layoffs and making them participate in the choice of victims. But the principle of the single staff system was admitted, and the parity commission undertook the formulation of a new statute which was adopted at the end of August and submitted to the administration's governing council (Morlet, 1948).

When the projected single staff system, established by the parity commission, was submitted to the governing council, the latter disavowed its own representatives and rejected it, in flagrant violation of the end of strike protocol.

This was proof that, for their immediate needs, federal administrators and the French Overseas Minister had unwillingly signed an agreement at the moment when it was absolutely necessary for them to settle the conflict, with the firm intention of violating it later.

The repudiation by the administration at this time after a year of discussion and delays provoked the exasperation of African railway workers. In a motion of the 8th of September addressed to federal and administration authorities, the managing committee of the Federation of African Railway Workers defined the different points in the dispute:

Unification of the cost of living and family charges [without which one could not evidently speak of a "single staff system." The African railway workers admitted an "expatriation indemnity" only for Europeans, exclusive of any other indemnity. J. S.-C.]

The granting of management bonuses to African personnel on scales three and four of the secondary rank before their integration into the single staff system (this bonus, given to European railway workers with the same qualifications, had been withheld from African workers).

Application of the single staff system from January 1, 1947 on, a principle accepted by the parity commission in December 1946.

The suppression of differences between African and European railway workers as to tests taken to pass from one set of pay scales to higher scales.

The motion indicated that, if these demands were not satisfied, the order for a general strike would be given for October 10 at midnight (Morlet, 1948; *Paris-Dakar,* Oct. 9, 1947).

On October 6 a letter from the administration's director, Cunéo, confronted the "railway workers with the consequences which would result from an illegal strike," conciliation and arbitration procedures not having been initiated. A decree of March 20, 1937, was invoked which made conciliation and arbitration mandatory in French West Africa at the risk of sanctions from the court of summary jurisdiction which would be applied to workers who did not carry out the decisions laid down by the administration's arbitrators. Thus the administration reverted to anti-strike legislation which had not been invoked since 1944 and which was considered no longer enforceable because, for all practical purposes, it led to the suppression of the right to strike. An attempt at conciliation having failed on the 9th of October, the administration sent a telegram to all workers on the 10th, threatening the strikers with legal action. In answer, traffic was stopped on all railway lines at midnight (Morlet, 1948).

THE DEVELOPMENT OF THE STRIKE

From the beginning the federal committee of the African railway workers' union was constituted as a strike committee. Its incontestable leader was its secretary general, Ibrahima Sarr,[14] who, with his executive committee, demonstrated his courage and capacity by resisting pressures and threats, thwarting provocations, and at all stages assuring the strike's cohesion.

In a circular of October 8, he gave the following instructions designed to avert provocation (see complete text in *Reveil,* Nov. 20, 1947, No. 261):

> In accordance with the decision of your federal committee, you will begin to strike on the 10th, at midnight.
>
> We intend that this strike, like the first one, be carried out within the framework of union laws. The utmost prudence is to be observed, every precaution taken. Many believe that striking is synonymous with acts of sabotage, demonstrations, battles, etc. . . . On the contrary, a strike should above all be calm, that is to say, *should avoid any demonstrations and all acts of sabotage.* It is recommended that all strikers do not leave their residences, stay at home as access to their work places will be forbidden to them.
>
> Train employees (engineers, firemen, conductors, ticket collectors, brakemen, etc. . . .) who are at work at the time the strike is declared will stop only at the first station. If, on the other hand, some trains are cancelled before arriving at the terminus and before the hour fixed for the strike (midnight), the train employees will stay at their posts until the agreed hour and will ensure that train fireboxes are kept lit. The surveillance of parcels will revert to the *alcati*[15] accompanying the train and exempted from the strike.
>
> Health personnel, personnel in charge of food (cooperatives) as well as personnel charged with the maintenance of public order (in short, police agents, that is *alcati*) will not participate in the strike.
>
> In each union sub-division of the line a strike committee will be set up, composed of the sector head and a representative from each service. This committee will act as a liaison between the administration and the strikers.
>
> An information meeting will be held once a day in an enclosed place and in the greatest calm.
>
> I am anxious that the present instructions be rigorously observed by all and that members of the directing committee as well as those of the union subdivisions personally watch over their strict application.

The African railway workers, by deliberately renouncing certain methods (strike pickets, occupation of local shops), counted on the cohesion of the movement to ensure its strength.

On November 1, 1947, the number of employees in the service of the railway was reduced to 525: 487 European railway workers and 38 African (out of nearly 20,000 including employees of wharves and shipyards; out of 17,300 if one includes only railway workers). On December 31, 1947, the 82nd day of the strike, only 838 strikers had returned to work. This number, together with 2,416 scabs recruited as strike breakers, provided an effective workforce of less than 4,000, although the administration estimated that 13,800 would be needed for normal functioning of the railway. In spite of the weakening of the movement on the Abidjan-Niger line (with a return to work of 60%), only 4,500 had returned to work on the other lines on the 160th day of the strike, that is 38% of the railway workers (excluding the Ivory Coast).[16]

Following the instructions cited above, general assemblies were held every day wherever the number of strikers permitted them. They kept the strikers up to date on the situation, kept up their morale, and transmitted directives. Members of the strike committee organized regular propaganda and information tours using whatever means they could find, trucks, private vehicles, and taxis. In regions outside of Dakar regional strike committees functioned in the same manner and transmitted directions and information from the federal committee.

The African railway workers' cooperative which only a short time previously had been freed from the tutelage of the administration (the importance of its role could be explained by the fact that food rationing was still in force) and had passed to union control, was responsible for feeding the strikers. In the Dakar-Niger region alone, 25 million French West African francs worth of rations were distributed by the cooperative (Morlet, 1948).

The hostile press *(Paris-Dakar)* was forced to admit that the strike was carried out calmly and did not give way to any disorder. Under these circumstances, attempts made to break the strike by repression failed.

PRESSURE AND REPRESSION

After the conciliation failure, the "High Commissioner Barthes, according to the law, informed the two parties that the conflict must be submitted to arbitration" *(Paris-Dakar,* Oct. 11, 1947). The two arbitrators, designated by the two parties according to procedure, were not able, as was predictable, to come to an agreement. The high commissioner then named a mediator, the president of the Court of the First Instance of Dakar. Naturally this mediator, chosen by the government, settled in favor of the railway administration.

From then on the strike was "illegal." The union, not having obeyed the arbitration decision to submit to the will of the administration, was given notice by the administration that workers who did not immediately return to work would be considered as having resigned and be immediately replaced. At the request of the ministry of public works, legal action was taken against Ibrahima Sarr, signer of the strike order. He was sentenced to one month in prison and fined 1,200 francs by the tribunal. In the *Paris-Dakar* edition of November 29, 1947, the governor-general published the following communique:

> It has recently been reported that negotiations were opened between the African railway workers' union and the High Commissioner. According to this report satisfaction was on the point of being reached regarding the demands whose rejection by the administration was the origin of the strike.
>
> The High Commissioner contradicts this assertion. No meeting has taken place since the 10th October between the High Commissioner and union leaders.
>
> The differences between the railway administration and its employees were settled by the judgement of the mediators' committee in executing the decree of March 20, 1937. It is not the High Commissioner's function to decide whether or not an enforceable jurisdictional and definite decision is carried out.

It is probable that this clarification was related to the steps taken by the SFIO (Section Française de l'Internationale Ouvrière) deputy, Fily Dabo Sissoko from the Sudan who, after having refused to be associated with a common approach by African parliamentarians proposed by Félix Houphouët-Boigny and Gabriel d'Arboussier, leaders of the RDA (Rassemblement Démocratique Africain), sent a telegram directly to strikers in the different regions asking them to return to work and affirming that he had obtained an agreement from the president of the administration's board of directors (Morlet, 1948).

Paralleling this, the MRP minister sent the ex-leader of the CFTC, Joseph Dumas, now a MRP deputy, on a semi-official mission. It was a so-called mission of reconciliation and in fact an attempt to obtain a return to work. It was hoped that his influence on the unions, which he had affiliated to the CFTC in 1946, would permit him to obtain some results (*Paris-Dakar,* Dec. 12, 1947).

The consequences of this step are known: the African union of Bénin-Niger left the CFTC,[17] and, after the end of the strike, publicly welcomed a delegate from the CGT in these terms: "We enthusiastically render homage to the great CGT which, without any ulterior motive, made our conflict their own" (*Reveil,* Sept. 30, 1948, No. 330).

The administration's management and the governor-general published numerous declarations describing a return to work, notably in the Ivory Coast, and repeatedly, but in vain, published the "return to work order." The first "order" was given for the 1st of December without results. Then, on the 31st of December the administrative "order of the day number nine" announced the return to work for the 1st of January, the strikers "moved by the love of their profession and their 'professional' responsibilities having finally understood their duty." This order of the day provoked a protest from the European union which was indignant that it had not rendered homage to the nonstrikers, and observed that "it is premature to speak of a return to work since up to this date returning workers comprise only about five percent of the striking employees" (*Echos Africains,* Jan. 10-11, 1948, No. 45).

Unable to make strikers return to work, the administration attempted to recruit workers elsewhere and to call upon the army for help. One fact is certain: much later, at the end of January 1948, 300 French railway workers were sent out and promised double the salary.[18] (Some had been candidates for a long time for an overseas assignment.) Some of them were aware of the role they were expected to play as strike breakers and refused the offer. From the moment of their arrival in Dakar, the secretary of the coordinating committee of the federated unions of French West Africa (CGT), Jean Blacas (a worker in the Dakar arsenal), succeeded in entering their restaurant and during a short talk he called on them to refuse the role of strike breakers. An appeal in the same vein by Blacas, in the name of the same committee, was published in the anticolonial press (*Reveil,* Feb. 2, 1948, No. 282; *L'A.O.F.,* Feb. 3, 1948, No. 2204).

Finally, workers were recruited locally. Former candidates for jobs who were previously refused because of incapacity or because of prison terms, and railway workers dismissed for professional faults or because of offenses under common law were hired: every little bit helped.

The results seem not to have been conclusive, if one judges by the lamentations in the right wing press about damage to the economy brought about by the strike. These complaints contrasted curiously with official news reports which announced repeatedly from November 1947 to the beginning of March 1948 that work was beginning again and traffic was returning to normal. On this point, as on the exact number of strike breakers, we will have to wait for access to the archives in order to know what to believe. A written note from the Dakar-Niger services shows the following figures for September 1947 (before the strike) and November 1947.

Table 3. TRAFFIC FIGURES FROM SEPTEMBER TO NOVEMBER 1947.

	Number of trains		Tonnage out (metric)		Tonnage in (metric)	
	Out	In	Gross	Live	Gross	Live
September	208	290	60,013	22,570	66,315	23,530
November	33	33	6,672	2,328	6,247	1,789

Afterward the administration partially restored the passenger traffic with the personnel it had at its disposal, but it could never do as well for goods traffic.

The failure of appeals for a return to work (except in the Ivory Coast) produced an increase in repression by judicial means at the end of January 1948. This method was certainly not applied in a "hit or miss" way as proved by the simultaneous and various pretexts for prosecution.

In Dahomey, two weeks after the "mission" of Joseph Dumas had miscarried, "strong action" also began to be used. Some railway workers, having returned to work on the 5th of January, had sent their resignations to the union on the following day. The union's executive committee let them know that the union's general assembly had been consulted and unanimously rejected their resignations: regarding their return to work, it added, "It is a matter of treachery which you will have to answer for to the union after the strike." On January 12 members of the executive committee were summoned by the prosecutor and arrested with the following accusations (of which this letter is produced as evidence):[19]

1) Flagrant offense against the right of liberty to work.
2) Threats of death or brutality (according to the prosecutor this was signified by the expression "you will have to account for your actions" in "local terminology") (sic).
3) An illegal strike which had as its aim a rise in wages, therefore a rise in the cost of living (sic).

The general assembly met immediately and voted for the continuance of the strike, and it:[20]

protested against this brutal arrest of the leaders which seemed to have as its aim the disorganization of the strikers and the breakdown of the strike movement. The assembly violently expressed its desire to have all its members taken into custody as they all had approved the terms of the incriminating letter (sic).

A provisional executive was elected immediately to replace the executive placed under arrest. The fact that the whole operation was one of intimidation was confirmed when the tribunal concluded there was no ground for prosecution (Morlet, 1948).[21]

In the Ivory Coast administrative pressure and also certain aspects of the local situation jeopardized the strike. The secretary general of the Abidjan-Niger regional union, Gaston Fiankan, was in Dakar (he was, with Sarr, one of the two African delegates to the parity commission and he ensured liaison with the federation). Two other members of the executive, Raphaël Konan and Léonard Koné, among the most solid, were on a mission in the north. The assistant secretary of the union, Benoît Djomand, and the treasurer, Joseph Coffie, took advantage of their absence to reverse the situation.

Some days after the departure of Fiankan, Djomand proposed at a strikers' meeting a departure for the wharf, insisting on the necessity of evacuating produce. (The exact date when this was done is not spelled out in the minutes, but possibly it occurred a month and a half after the beginning of the strike, therefore around November 25.) The strikers were opposed and asked that they first seek the opinion of the federal committee. In spite of this the leaders in favor of returning to work went to Port Bouët to appeal to the wharf workers to resume work. These leaders were called traitors but, under their pressure, some workers from the wharf went back to work only to stop again five days later. During the whole of December one witnessed this paradoxical situation: the union executive in meeting after meeting did the utmost to show union members the uselessness of continuing the strike without being followed by the majority, but not without having obtained, as can be easily understood, the defection of a certain number of railway workers.

The defaulting union leaders then had themselves accompanied by elected officials or politicians hostile to the strike, such as by Kakou Aoulou of the Parti progressiste (opposed to the RDA); then, in a meeting held on January 2, 1948, by Amadou Diop, grand councillor (SFIO); by the secretary general of the merchants' union of the Ivory Coast; and by an African engineer. After reading without commentary a letter from the secretary general, Fiankan, calling for the continuance of the strike, the assistant secretary, Djomand, called on the strikers to return to work on the 5th of January. The others spoke in turn to convince the strikers of the necessity of returning to work; Diop affirmed that he had a "guarantee" from the governor that strikers would be returned to their former jobs "up to the limit of available places." One striker emphasized the incompleteness of the guarantee and Diop was invited to return to the governor to obtain further assurances. The last meeting was held on January 4. Diop had not returned and the directing committee limited itself to ordering a return to work and declining to take any responsibility for those who continued to pursue the strike.[22] Paralleling this action, the head of the Abidjan-Niger region, Nicolas, distributed a tract which called for a return to work and ended with these words:[23]

> All former employees turning up for work will receive the best reception and will be rehired *as long as there are situations available* (emphasis added).
> *Therefore there is no longer any need to prolong the strike.*
> It is in the interest of railway workers, it is in the interest of the Ivory Coast, that the return to work takes place without delay.
> Let everybody be at work on the 2nd January.
>
> The regional head of Abidjan-Niger,
> Nicolas.

In fact, it was only on the 5th of January that the return took place, the same day that Fiankan returned from Dakar. He thus was confronted with an accomplished fact. It is difficult to say how important the return was (60% according to P. Morlet). What is certain is that it was not total.

THE PRESS, THE PARTIES, AND THE STRIKE

The governor-general and the administration, the formations of the right (the RPF [Rassemblement du Peuple français—the Gaullist party]), and also the MRP, the semi-official press *(Paris-Dakar)*, and that of the Dakar right *(Echos africans)*, the *Bulletin de Côte d'Ivoire*, or of the metropole *(Climats)* all used very nearly the same arguments. From the beginning of December 1947, *Paris-Dakar* began announcing the return to work:

> It seems that the strike of African railway workers is no longer very efficacious. Railway traffic has resumed a little everywhere, hiring is going on in all the territories of the Federation. Dahomey has returned to 80% of its normal traffic and Guinea to 60%. Moreover, the wharf at Cotonou has begun again to function (Dec. 13, 1947).
> Each day new returns to work are noted in all the French West African networks. Yesterday there was an important movement at Thiès when 120 strikers from Dakar-Niger presented themselves at work. Also we have learned that all Abidjan-Niger stations are functioning (Dec. 30, 1947).
> 'About the Abidjan-Niger strike' (from our correspondent): The wharf is now working at 50% of its capacity, a large number of new and former employees have been hired or rehired. At the RAN [Abidjan-Niger region] Mr. Nicolas, director of the network, has launched an appeal to all railway workers to return to work. It seems that this appeal is beginning to be heard. (Jan. 11-12, 1948).

Paris-Dakar deplored the economic consequences of the strike because the metropole urgently needed produce. It denounced the demagogic character of the railway workers' demands, pretended to commiserate with the misery of railway workers deceived by their "ringleaders" and called for authoritarian measures. Since the October 12-13 issue already cited, mention was made of the 50,000 tons of coffee blocked in the Ivory Coast and urgently needed by the metropole. Also, "it is feared that the peanut harvest of Senegal will not be able to be evacuated. Yet everyone knows the scarcity of butterfat threatens mankind with grave epidemics" (Dec. 20, 1947).

Wages of African workers, *Paris-Dakar* asserted, were superior to those of French workers: 48.93 francs hourly wages for skilled workers, compared to wages at Renault of 34 francs and 31.75 francs at the SNCF—Paris. "And don't fall over, dear reader, these gentlemen are asking for a base of 63.02 francs. And, as everyone knows, in French

West Africa the work is harder than in France" (Dec. 18, 1947). Also, "in order to satisfy the strikers' demands . . . the administration would have to double tariffs, for freight as well as for travellers" (Oct. 11, 1947). Of course, legal sanctions imposed on the strikers were duly reported. Nevertheless, at no time were the communists particularly implicated, or was the strike described as political.

The *Echos africains* and the *Bulletin de la Côte d'Ivoire* did not differ in their treatment of the strike. They were simply conspicuous by being more violent and, in the case of *Echos africains,* by invoking the "political" character of the strike (according to this newspaper, it was the anticolonial and antiwhite nature of the strike).

Climats, less embarrassed by local political considerations (vis-à-vis the socialists notably), addressed itself to an exclusively European clientele and was distinguishable by its violence and imbecile racism.

At the opposite end of the scale, the Rassemblement Démocratique Africain locally and the Communist Party in France were the only ones to sustain and defend a movement of which all the leaders (with the exception of Fiankan who was a member of the Democratic Party of the Ivory Coast) were unrelated to them. The leaders of the movement in Dahomey, as we have seen, were originally under the influence of the Catholic missions; the Senegalese leaders at Thiès and Dakar were or had been members of the Thiès Youth Movement (whose members had been persecuted by Governor Maestracci in 1945), and/or of the socialist party SFIO which had received its political heritage. Some were discouraged by the corruption of the leaders of this party and believed that their path lay in the direction of "pure" unionism or hoped for a renovation through the efforts of the young deputy, Senghor. Aynina Fall, a leader of the Dakar railway workers, was to become one of the supporters of the Bloc Démocratique Sénégalais created by Senghor after his rupture with the socialist party (Suret-Canale, 1972:22).

Réveil, which was willing to offer hospitality to the *Voix du Rassemblement Démocratique Africain* by ceding to it a portion of its columns, and which, during 1948, became the de facto organ of the RDA,[24] led an incessant campaign in support of the railway workers' cause, publishing documents dissimulated by their adversaries and leading the solidarity campaign with regard to the strikers. Three special issues were dedicated to the strike (261 of November 20, 1947; 264 of December 1; and 265 of December 4). The two latter issues were sold for ten francs instead of seven for the benefit of the striking railway workers.

Houphouët-Boigny and D'Arboussier, president and secretary general of the RDA respectively, spoke to all the African parliamentarians and suggested a joint meeting and joint intervention. Senghor responded positively, but the majority of the other socialist parliamentarians refused. The Grand Council of French West Africa, holding its first session, voted on a motion put forward by Houphouët in favor of a positive solution of the conflict and delegated some of its parliamentarian members to intervene with the high commissioner. This delegation ran into a flat refusal. "As for the High Commissioner, he declared it his duty to adhere to the mediator's decision taken in November."[25] A motion by the communist and RDA groups inviting the government to resolve the conflict was unanimously carried by the assembly of the French Union. (*Réveil,* Jan. 8, 1948, No. 275). A second resolution in the same vein was carried again by the same assembly on February 12, 1948 (L'Humanité, Feb. 13, 1948). The essential decision was carried out in the organization of political and material solidarity, of which we shall speak later.

When at the end of January the high commissioner was relieved of his official duties, the deputy from Dahomey, Apithy, brought into the Grand Council in the name of the RDA a motion inviting the permanent delegation to the Grand Council to contact immediately the new high commissioner in order to resolve the conflict. This proposal was objected to by the socialists.[26]

In this affair what was the position of elected socialists or those affiliated to the socialist group? The least one can say is that they were embarrassed. It was impossible, especially in Senegal, for African parliamentarians to declare themselves against the strike because they might be cut off from their own electoral base. On the other hand, they were "caught" by belonging to the minister's party who voluntarily created the conflict even if, in the interval, Moutet had to cede his position to the MRP minister, Coste-Floret (in compensation the post of high commissioner in French West Africa was given to the socialist mayor of Alès, Béchard, who took up his post on February 22, 1948). Desirous of losing neither the support of their electors nor the favors of the government, they equivocated.

The *Condition Humaine,* a bi-monthly review, was created by Senghor during the strike (No. 1 is dated February 11, 1948). He did not write a word on the strike. It was only after the end of the strike, in the issue of April 26, 1948 (No. 5), that Senghor devoted an article to this subject under the title "The Lessons of the Rail Strike." He presented himself as a man of compromise.

> One must render me this justice that during the five months the strike lasted, I did not write a single article on the question and that if I dealt with it at times in my speeches, I did so voluntarily, in measured terms. Although I affirmed the legitimacy of the principles supported by the strikers—their assimilation with civil servants and the suppression of racial discrimination—I advocated a compromise solution as the only one possible under the circumstances. The event proved us right.

In short, Senghor justified principles favorable to the strikers and an application (which was his own) favorable to the administration under the banner of "compromise."

The analysis of the *L'A.O.F.*, the organ of the Fédération socialiste de l'A.O.F., whose director was Lamine Gueye, reveals the ambiguous position of local socialists and their internal contradictions. One notices first the total silence of the two deputies who never expressed themselves on the strike. One can point to three major components in the newspaper which at that time coexisted in a contradictory manner. On the one hand, articles by metropolitan leaders (probably often reprinted from the French socialist press) from December on (the end of the strikes in France and the split of the "Force Ouvrière") took a more and more anti-communist and anti-confederation (anti-CGT) turn, to the point of hysteria. They never spoke of the French West African railway workers' strike. On the other hand, articles by local socialist leaders (Diop Boubacar Obeye, assistant to the major of Dakar; Sar Babacar, secretary of the Fédération socialiste) were visibly torn between national directives and the sentiments of the rank and file. Finally, articles by local militants, often friends of railway workers themselves or militant railway workers (like Abdul Karim Sow, founder of the Thiès Youth Movement and secretary of the young socialists of Thiès, Jacques Ibrahima Gaye of Thiès, Aynina Fall, militant railway worker of Dakar and close collaborator of Ibrahima Sarr), vigorously defended the strikers' cause and deplored polemics between the socialists and the RDA.

SOLIDARITY

Official propaganda attempted to isolate railway workers, to oppose them to France (whose food supplies they were said to jeopardize) and to the population (accusing them of hindering the supply of food and of being responsible for high prices).

On the French side, aside from political solidarity expressed only by the French communist party of which we have already spoken, it was especially through the intermediary of the CGT that this solidarity was affirmed. From October 16 on, the French Federation of CGT Railway Workers expressed its total solidarity with the demands of African railway workers and intervened along this line with the French Overseas Minister (*Réveil,* Nov. 20, 1947, No. 261). In his response Sarr wrote to the CGT Federation of Railway Workers (*Réveil,* Dec. 1, 1947, No. 264):

These two letters have been brought to the attention of all our militants in French West Africa. They have received widespread publicity in the local press. They have given us great moral support and still give us, once more, the assurance that French railway workers do not pay heed to racial considerations and are solidly behind their overseas comrades.

Locally, aside from the already mentined RDA, various sections of the CGT, the coordination committee of the Unions de Syndicats confédérés of French West Africa, the Union des Syndicats of Dakar, the Union des Syndicats of Senegal and Mauritania, etc. (*Réveil,* Nov. 20, 1947, No. 261), showed their solidarity through meetings, speeches, and collections. Among other messages of solidarity, let us mention that of the Union des syndicats confédérés of Guinea (in an article signed by Sékou Touré in *Réveil,* Dec. 4, 1947, No. 265), and that of the Union des syndicats of Togo (No. 265) against the attempts which were made to recruit "scab labor" from Togolese railway workers.[27]

Material solidarity was expressed through the dispatch of funds: 30,000 francs from the French Federation of Railway Workers; 50,000 francs from the CGT's federation bureau; 500,000 francs from the National Solidarity Committee set up by the CGT during the strikes of November and December 1947.[28] The RDA from the Ivory Coast contributed 350,000 francs. The CGT unions of French West Africa collected a total of about two million francs (Morlet, 1948).

These facts are significant: in general the strikers were sustained by the entire African population (and not only by wage earners). Their fight seemed to be that of all Africans against racial discrimination.

Yet there was an important and paradoxical exception. The RDA, whose bastion was then in the Ivory Coast, was the only African political movement that had clearly taken a stand in favor of the movement and had aided it financially. Yet it was precisely in the Ivory Coast where the strike's only break appeared with the return of a large number of employees at the beginning of January. It has been pointed out that here, contrary to what happened in Bamako, the secretary general of the merchants' union (these evidently were African) intervened on their side for the return to work. At that time a circular of Barbé, the leader of the overseas section of the French communist party, had seen in all this an indication that in the Ivory Coast the African bourgeoisie (and notably the planters), who with Houphouët had constituted the original basis of the RDA, had not supported the movement because it harmed their interests by blocking the movement of the crops. Barbé saw that this was the first deepening break between the bourgeois elements and the popular elements of the movement. History was to corroborate this judgments more amply than Barbé had foreseen.[29]

ECONOMIC CONSEQUENCES OF THE STRIKE

The effectiveness of the movement was due to the fact that it coincided with the period of transporting local products, of their commercialization, and of their evacuation to ports. Naturally, the timing was not deliberate (if it had been, it would have been more advantageous for the railway workers to have delayed the start of the strike by some weeks), but this coincidence explains the stiffening attitude of the administration and the colonial interests.

First of all, as one can imagine, the strike was very hard for the railway workers in spite of the solidarity, of which the collections already mentioned are only one aspect. The railway workers were able to hold on only because the surrounding population of parents, neighbors, etc., in the tradition of African solidarity, helped them to live. However, the anguished character of some appeals for solidarity, such as those from the Bénin-Niger railway workers at the end of December 1947,[30] shows that it was not without difficulty.

The appeal for solidarity from the Union des syndicats of Senegal did not hide the difficulties which people faced (*Réveil,* Nov. 20, 1947, No. 261):

> You can no longer travel except in a hazardous, inconvenient, onerous way, and not without danger. For over a month a good number of depots have not received supplies which means that their stocks will go on dwindling. Behind this perspective of painful restrictions, one can almost foresee the spectre of famine.

The dioulas (African middlemen) of the Sudan were without any doubt affected, even though solidly behind the strike, because the essentials of trade merchandise arrived in the Sudan on the Dakar-Niger line. The same was true of the planters of the Ivory Coast and the local African merchants whose reactions did not seem to be one of solidarity.

P. Morlet (1948) notes that for a long time a sizeable number of travellers as well as a great part of the foodstuffs and imports had gone by road.

> On the Dakar-Niger network, the main line used in the evacuation of peanuts which are non-perishable, the export trade attempted to "hold" on while waiting for the end of the strike, did not make firm purchases or establish stocks in warehouses in the interior. On the contrary, contract purchases were made at the producers' risk until there was a favorable occasion to evacuate produce to export ports.

He notes that on February 20, 1948, 409,000 tons of peanuts had already been sold by growers as contrasted with 326,000 tons in 1947 and 307,000 tons in 1946 on the same date. Morlet (1948) also noted that:

On the other hand, in Guinea where the banana is very perishable, transport by railway had to be replaced by expensive truck transport. The administration may even have been forced by the pressure of the small African and European planters, to buy a part of the crop.

In the Ivory Coast and Dahomey the question was complicated by the fact that the railway strike also included employees at the wharves which still are used in the absence of real ports at Grand-Bassam, Port-Bouët and Cotonou.

And if it is possible for road transport to substitute for the railway up to a certain point, there is no expedient to make up for the stoppage of port transport, not even the utilization of the navy.

The immobilization of produce—therefore of capital—had grave repercussions in exporters' accounts which explains why big business made very effort to ease the hold of the strike which was stifling them. We earlier saw how and why they partially succeeded.

For the railway administration, outside the loss of receipts, the strike had consequences due to the cessation of the maintenence of equipment as rail lines and buildings, already in a bad state because of the war, further deteriorated because of the employment of inexperienced employees. The administration had to increase rates massively at the end of the strike.

THE END OF THE STRIKE

After five months of conflict, although the majority of railway workers had "held on," the disintegration of the movement (notably in the Ivory Coast) and the exhaustion of strikers imposed a rapid solution. On the one hand, for reasons already noted, big business and the administration had an interest in putting an end to the conflict. They took advantage of the appointment of a new high commissioner, whose popularity it was useful to establish, to give him the merit of solving the conflict.

The end of strike protocol was signed by the Federation of African Railway Workers and the administration on March 16, 1948 (*Paris-Dakar*, Mar. 16, 1948). In an appeal dated March 17, Ibrahima Sarr, in the name of the federal committee, gave the order for the return to work and asked strikers to act in a way to preserve unity with those who had weakened (*Réveil*, Mar. 25, 1948, No. 297). The return to work was decided on for March 19, 1948.

The protocol was presented to the railway workers as a victory. In the context of that time and in the relationship of forces which had been established, it was in effect a partial victory. The administration was forced to recognize the legitimacy of the strike and renounce its pretense of considering striking employees as having resigned. "All administration employees who have returned to work by Friday, 19th March will be placed in their former jobs." (*Paris-Dakar,* Mar. 17, 1948, text of protocol.) All sanctions were cancelled, but the workers were not paid for the days they had been on strike.

As for the rest, save for some particulars, it was the administration's viewpoint (reflected in the mediator's decision) which prevailed. The principle of the single staff system was admitted, but in practice it was questioned through the maintenance of numerous privileges favoring European employees (refusal to unify the cost of living allowance and the allocation of management bonuses; refusal of the right of housing for African employees; refusal to permit complementary rest leaves, these only being granted up to 15 days under "exceptional circumstances," that is to say, dependent on the goodwill of the administration).

Integration was granted only to those auxiliaries "having the requisite qualities," thus permitting the firing of numerous unskilled auxiliaries. This integration was granted from January 1, 1947 (as the railway workers had asked), but only for seniority; as for remuneration, this was only to begin from June 1, 1947. These measures were applicable to ports and wharves until November 8, 1947, for the Cotonou wharf and until January 1, 1948, for the port of Conakry, "the dates on which these establishments ceased to be used by the administration" (*Paris-Dakar,* Mar. 17, 1948).

Finally, a 20% increase of wages and of most allowances was granted to take account of the high cost of living (*Marchés* coloniaux, Mar. 27, 1948, No. 124:491).

CONCLUSION

In a period of reflux of the popular movement and of offensive by the colonial reactionaries, the strike of African railway workers in 1947-1948 took on an incontestable significance. Even if the demands presented were not entirely satisfied, the determination of the colonial administration to question the right to strike and to shackle the union movement had been held in check. Let us note in passing that the strikes of November-December 1947 in France had ended without any demands being satisfied (at least immediately) and had led to massive layoffs of militants.

At the same time, the union scission had been started in France with the resignation on December 19, 1947, of five minority federal secretaries of the CGT, who created a short time after the dissident union "CGT Force-Ouvrière."

Far from resulting in the alienation of the movement of African railway workers from the CGT and the French working class, the circumstances of the conflict brought them closer. Responding to an address of solidarity from the coordination committee of the Unions de syndicats confédérés of French West Africa (CGT), Ibrahima Sarr, in the name of the French West African Federation of Railway Workers' Unions, expressed himself in these terms:[31]

> This having been said, let us now speak as unionists, that is to say, let us be precise and clear.
>
> Our strike which risked by its very duration the destruction of unionism in French West Africa and all democratic organizations, has finally ended. It is the victory of the working world over reaction and all its flunkeys. This victory for us, African railway workers, is due in large part to the active and generous solidarity of other workers. We will try, therefore, to never disappoint anyone, neither the reactionaries nor the workers.
>
> Moreover, the November-December strikes in France, the scission, a stab in the CGT's back and the repercussions of all that in French West Africa: these are serious questions which can only claim our attention.
>
> Our party is ready. We say now: 'No to scissionists.' Autonomy yes, if all free workers who want to remain free are for the creation of a large autonomous union affiliated to the FSM [Fédération Syndicale Mondiale]. But the comrades of the Unions de syndicats confédérés of French West Africa have renewed by a large majority their confidence in the great CGT. This attitude does not surprise us, the CGT being always on the side of those who suffer and who fight to weaken the foundations of imperialism. We cannot stay on the shore and watch other boats advance.

SOURCES

Article by P. Morlet (1948): "Une étape de la lutte anticolonialiste; la grève des cheminots africans d'A.O.F.," *Servir la France,* 37 (May): 36-42. Citations without page numbers have been made from the draft kept in our archives.

Personal archives: This is a dossier of which sections had been borrowed from the Union des syndicats confédérés of Dakar by Pierre Morlet for the drafting of his study. Pierre Morlet, teacher and secretary of the Union des syndicats confédérés of the Sudan, had been put by the governor of the Sudan at the disposition of its administration from the outset in July 1947. Refusing this arrangement, he had been sent to French West Africa at the beginning of 1948 by the CGT as a federation delegate. This dossier, left in my hands, was sent with my luggage when I was expelled in my turn from Dakar by the high commissioner, Béchard, in February 1949. It contains some correspondence held between the UD (Union départementale) of Dakar and the Federation of African Railway Workers, some notes and letters of Pierre Bouvier who, with Gueye Abbas, was until June 1948 one of the two general secretaries of the Dakar UD. Pierre Bouvier, who died a short time after in an airplane crash, was a French worker in the Dakar arsenal, a member of the Parti socialiste and councillor in the socialist municipality of Dakar. From the moment of the divisions he refused to join the "Force Ouvrière" and had worked for CGT unity.

Press: Besides some samples of journals and some press cuttings conserved in the previously cited dossier, we consulted collections of *Paris-Dakar, Réveil, Echos africains de l'A.O.F.,* and the *Condition Humaine* (appearing in Dakar), the weeklies *Climats* and *Marchés coloniaux* stored in the National Archives, overseas section (Rue Oudinot). Unhappily, these collections are incomplete and often in a bad state. We have not been able to consult the collections, better conserved and complete, which exist in Dakar at IFAN (Institut Fondamental d'Afrique noire).

NOTES

1. Rapport de l'Inspection générale du Travail en A.O.F. pour 1947.
2. C. Allen (1975:99-125) mentions Ansprenger (1961-85); Mortimer (1969:118); Pfefferman (1967:217); and November (1965:81-93).
3. See our review (Suret-Canale, 1962:60) of Ansprenger's book and C. Allen (1975:99-125).
4. The author of this chapter was at that time professor at the Lycée Van Vollenhoven in Dakar, secretary of the "groupe d'études communiste" (GEC) of Senegal, and rank and file member of the Union Démocratique Sénégalaise, a section of the RDA. In June 1948 he was elected to the secretariat of the Union des syndicats confédérés of Dakar (CGT).
5.

Table 1. FIGURES OF RAILWAY MANPOWER

	1938	1944	1946	Beginning 1947
Europeans	577	491	478	442
Africans	14,934	18,005	17,455	17,277
Managerial staff	1,105	1,567	1,729	1,691
Permanent auxiliaries	13,829	16,438	15,726	15,586

SOURCES: Gouvernement général de l'A.O.V. (1947). *Direction générale des travaus publics: Direction des chemins de fer et transports: Compte-rendu de gestion pour l'exercise 1946.* Thies: Imprimerie Dakar-Niger, p.12. Figures for 1947 in P. Morlet (1948:36-42).

6.

Table 2. MANPOWER FIGURES OF HARBORS AND WHARVES

	1942	1944	1946	
Europeans	37	43	52	
Africans	1,763	3,044	3,302	(Dakar port: 1,019)

SOURCE: Gouvernement général de l'A.O.F. (1947). Direction générale des travaux publics: Direction des chemins de fer et transports: Compte-rendu de gestion pour l'exercise 1946. Thies: Imprimerie Dakar-Niger, p. 45.

P. Morlet produced figures of 17 Europeans and 2,000 Africans at the wharves in 1947.
7. "La grève des cheminots du Sénégal de septembre 1938," Dakar, Dept. d'Histoire, 272 + 133 pp. (mimeo). See also Iba Der Thiam, 1976:300-338.
8. "The refusal to join the CGT was provoked by the attitude of various union branches composed of Europeans who had previously joined the union. This is why the African railway workers thought there was a common point of view between these branches and the CGT" (Morlet, 1948:38).
9. Personal archives. Letter from Tiberghien, secretary of the European Abidjan-Niger union, Feb. 7, 1947.
10. Manuscript and undated letter from Tiberghien, secretary of the railway workers' union in the Ivory Coast, and presumably sent to Bouvier. Mention "arrived March 10, 1947." Personal archives.
11. Report by Loubière from the Fédération française des cheminots CGT, no date (probably April or May 1948). Personal archives.

12. The delegates from the African railway worker unions to the parity commission in Dakar: to all African workers of the DN, AN, CN and BN regions. Dakar, Jan. 30, 1947, signed by Sarr (DN) and Fiankan (AN). Personal archives.

13. Motion presented by the "comité directeur" (managing committee) of the Federation of African Railway Workers' Unions, Thiès, Apr. 11, 1947. For the federal committee and the P.O. signed by Sarr. Personal archives.

14. Ibrahima Sarr was a union activist without any party affiliation up to the years before independence. He was a minister in the Senegalese government of that time. A partisan of Mamadou Dia, he was imprisoned with him and died a few months after his liberation by Senghor (in 1974).

15. A word of Portuguese origin. During the colonial period this word meant African policeman. The railway had its own police and its members were affiliated to the African railway workers' union.

16. Figures from *Rapport de l'Inspection générale du Travail en A.O.F.* for the year 1947.

17. *Inspection générale du travail de l'A.O.F. Rapport pour 1948*, p. 84.

18. Among them were 120 workers for repairs and maintenance. See *Climats*, Feb. 18, 1948, No. 114.

19. The African railway workers of the Bénin-Niger region's union committee to M. Ibrahima Sarr, general secretary of the Federation of the African Railway Workers' Unions of French West Africa in Thiès, Cotonou, Jan. 13, 1948. Signed D. Olivier. (general secretary elected in place of Sadeler who had been arrested). Personal archives.

20. Minutes of the general assembly of January 12, 1948, Cotonou, held at 6:40 p.m. Signed by the secretary, S. D'Almeida, and the president, M. Chadaré. Personal archives.

21. A letter signed by Sadeler, acting as general secretary, from Cotonou on February 20, 1948, proves that at this later date he was no longer in prison.

22. Minutes of the return to work in the Ivory Coast. Report unsigned, but dated at Treichville, January 24, 1948. Probably written by those who had refused to return to work for Fiankan. Personal archives.

23. Printed tract. Personal archives.

24. *Afrique Noire,* though representing the RDA, was not able to be published from its beginning. Firstly, the newspaper was refused the necessary paper allocation; then the only printer in Dakar capable of printing it, La Grande imprimerie africaine (belonging to the Delmas group), refused to do the job. It was through Charles-Guy Etcheverry, director of *Réveil,* former newspaper of the "France combattante" which had the right to be published since 1944, that the RDA received permission to use one or two pages of the paper under the title "La Voix du RDA."

25. *Paris-Dakar,* Dec. 26, 1947. Minutes of the first session of the Grand Council, Dec. 24, 1947.

26. *Réveil* attacked the socialist representatives in its issue of February 5, 1948 (No. 283) in an article entitled "Enough of Double Dealing":

You cannot pretend to defend the vital interests of Africa by voting on each occasion with the imperialists who live off the sweat, the efforts of its children. Stop putting a foot in both camps. Double dealing does not pay.

27. The railway network of Togo was independent from that of French West Africa and had not been involved in the strike.

28. *Réveil,* Jan. 8, 1948, No. 275. (Telegram from the National Solidarity Committee sent on January 2.)

29. We have reproduced the content of this memo from memory.

30. *Réveil,* Jan. 15, 1948, No. 277. Motion of African railway workers from Bénin-Niger, Dec. 27, 1947.

31. Letter from the Fédération des syndicats de cheminots africains de l'A.O.F. to the general secretary of the coordination committes of the Unions de syndicats confédéres d'A.O.F., Apr. 22, 1948. Personal archives.

REFERENCES

ALLEN, C. (1975). "Union-party relationships in Francophone West Africa: A critique of 'téléguidage' Interpretations." Pp. 99-125 in R. Sandbrook and R. Cohen (eds.), The development of an African working class. London: Longman.

ANSPRENGER, F. (1961). Politik im schwarzen Afrika. Koln and Opladen: West-deutscher Verlag.

CHAFFARD, G. (1967). Carnets secrets de la décolonisation, vol. II. Paris: Calmann-Levy.

IBA DER THIAM (1976). La tuerie de thiès de septembre 1938: Essai d'interpretation." Bulletin de l'IFAN, Serie B, 38(2, Apr.):300:338.

KARIM SOW, A. (Nov. 28, 1947). "Les trains fantomes: L'unanimité du pays contre Cunéo." L'A.O.F. (organ of the Fédération socialiste SFIO de l'A.O.F.), No. 2185.

MORLET, P. (1948). "Une étape de la lutte anticolonialists; La grève des cheminots africains d'A.O.F." Servir la France, 37 (May):36-42.

MORTIMER, E. (1969). France and the Africans. London: Faber and Faber.

NOVEMBER, A. (1965). L'évolution du mouvement syndical en Afrique occidentale. Paris: Mouton.

PFEFFERMAN, G. (1967). "Trade unions and politics in French West Africa during the Fourth Republic." African Affairs, 66.

SEMBENE, O. (1960). God's bits of wood. Paris: Le Livre contemporain; republished by Presse-Pocket (1971).

SURET-CANALE, J. (1962). Recherche Africaines. Paris: Editions Sociales.

———(1972). Afrique noire, vol. III: Paris: Editions Sociales.

6

TRADE UNIONISM IN KENYA, 1947-1952:
The Militant Phase

SHARON STICHTER
University of Massachusetts, Boston

In the years between the Second World War and the Mau Mau rebellion in Kenya, there took place a militant upsurge of labor protest in urban areas. The war had brought the beginnings of labor organizing among urban skilled manual workers and a great increase in strikes and labor unrest, culminating in the 11-day general strike in Mombasa in January 1947 and the formation of the short-lived African Workers' Federation, the first organization to represent the mass of urban African workers. After the war labor organizing grew by leaps and bounds, encompassing the Labour Trade Union of East Africa and the East African Trade Union Congress, both interracial organizations under the joint leadership of Africans and the left-wing Indian trade unionist, Makhan Singh. This singular period ends, however, with the movement of the main wing of African unionism into active participation in the Mau Mau rebellion, even while another faction moved into government collaboration and eventual industrial trade unionism.

Why did the main thrust of African labor organizing move from class-conscious interracial activity to nationalist rebellion? To answer this question, one must also examine two further questions, which are central to explaining both the fact of labor protest and its ideological character: (1) What were the connections between the socio-economic situation of wage earners at this moment and the timing and character of protest? and (2) What were the connections between colonial state labor policy and the pattern of protest? To explain the rise of militant trade unionism at this historical juncture, both kinds of forces, socio-economic and state policy decisions, must be taken into account. The one expresses the situation of workers directly within the mode of production, while the other refers to the state of the class struggle as it is played out in the political arena.

The two influences on the Kenyan labor movement operated in opposing political directions. In the period examined below, a peripheral capitalist economy based on part time migrant labor began to evolve into one based on full time wage labor. Increasingly dependent on wages, drawn into the modern capitalist economy but kept on the lower levels within it, the gradually forming urban African working class created a militant and nationalist labor movement.[1] Immigrant Indian workers, having been proletarianized for a greater length of time, created a kindred but more class-conscious and less nationalist version. Both were met, however, with an alternately repressive and paternalistic counterattack from the colonial government, and a struggle ensued over what kind of trade unionism would prevail in Kenya. On the one hand was the locally evolved militant "populist" conception of unionism held by the African and Indian workers, and on the other, a moderate "economist" conception imported from, and eventually imposed by, the colonial power.

THE ROOTS OF LABOR MILITANCE

A complex of socio-economic changes converged in the war and postwar years to make possible the beginnings of African labor organizing.[2] One important fact was the increasing numbers of Africans in employment; at the start of the war and through the postwar years levels of employment, particularly nonagricultural employment, rose rapidly. In addition, the workforce as a whole became increasingly concentrated in urban areas, making possible large scale strikes and labor organizations.

Even more fundamental for the rise of labor organizing was the changing pattern of African participation in wage-earning employment. By this time, following the slow expansion of the industrial and administrative sectors in Kenya in the late 1930s, the classic colonial pattern of part time participation in wage earning had begun to change for a small segment of African workers. For many though not all urban workers, the earlier pattern of a periodic one- or two-year stint at wage earning followed by an equally long return to peasant or tribal life began to give way to one in which wage earning occupied almost the whole of a worker's life. Simultaneously, the label of "target worker" became less and less applicable to these workers, and they became more and more dependent on their earnings from wages (see, for example, Kenya Colony and Protectorate, 1945:37,53).

It was in the main skilled and semi-skilled workers who experienced increasing stability/dependence. Expansion of secondary industry to serve the domestic market was an important result of the war, and led to increasing occupational specialization among Africans. Their movement into skilled and semi-skilled trades and their increased stabilization in wage earning made possible the rise of the first genuine African labor organizations.

It is important to understand the situation of these workers. Though their real incomes were increasing, the other side of this coin was frequently long hours of work (as in the domestic and tailoring trades), demanding physical labor (among dock and transport workers), and job insecurity coupled with decreasing access to land as an economic alternative. Also, rising incomes were barely able to keep up with inflation, with the new consumption desires stimulated by urban life, and the new demands made by less well-off family and kin.

The converse of increasing stability for one section of the wage-earning class was perpetuation of the pattern of low wages, low skill, and part-time labor for the bottom section. The majority of workers remained migrant, unskilled, and employed at statutory minimum wage rates (Kenya Colony and Protectorate, 1945: 37, passim). Thus, whereas on the one hand wages for skilled and semi-skilled African labor rose steadily after the war, a large number of workers remained at or near the statutory minimum wage rates. A 1950 survey of those near the minimum wage in Nairobi found that 58% of those employed in private industry and 30% of those in government service were in this category (East African High Commission, 1951). These workers spend about 72% of their income on food. They were nearly always in debt by the end of the month. Because the minimum wage barely kept pace with the cost of living in this period,[3] it appears that in real terms these workers experienced no gains at all.[4]

In effect, the contradictions inherent in the Kenyan colonial labor migration system were becoming acute, and they had not yet been resolved by a transition to the new pattern of labor utilization required by the limited industrialization of the postwar era. On the one hand, the crowded African reserves continued to supply large numbers of unskilled, partially proletarianized laborers whom the colonial economy could not absorb, even at the prevailing low wages—thus the labor surpluses in urban areas during these years. On the other hand, increasing capitalization, industrial investment, and imported technology were creating opportunities for higher paid skilled and semi-skilled employment, but only a relatively few Africans yet had access to the skills and training required for these jobs.[5] The bottleneck was not eased until government and industry took decisive steps toward labor stabilization in the mid-1950s.

Until then the underlying contradiction was expressed in industrial and political unrest. The persistence of low-wage migrant labor in the midst of postwar prosperity led to a heightened sense of discontent among unskilled urban masses. To this extent, the Carpenter Report was correct in attributing industrial unrest to the labor migration system. Although most of the urban poor were not actual members of trade unions, they formed a reservoir of discontent on which the trade union activists could draw when the need arose.

In social protest movements led by the relatively skilled, however, it is not so much the absolute level of income which engenders discontent, but the relative level in comparison to the visible and socially proximate classes. As I have suggested elsewhere (Strichter, 1975b), skilled and semi-skilled workers in the transport, building, domestic, and garment industries began labor organizing as much from a sense of relative deprivation in comparison to other races and classes, as from their undoubted absolute deprivation. Average annual money earnings for employed Africans increased steadily between 1946 and 1952 (Kenya Colony and Protectorate, 1955:Table 160, 1956-1957:Table 176), but average incomes for employed persons of other races also increased, so that the large racial differential did not appreciably decrease (see Parker, 1949:9-11, and especially diagram 23-24). Hence, in the labor movement there was a growing consciousness of racial barriers to economic advancement, and growing nationalistic feeling.

The fact that organized labor protest movements emerged in Kenya at the same time that wage rates for skilled labor were rising after wartime stagnation suggests that unlike food riots or social banditry, which are phenomena of economic downturn and the deprivation of the lowest classes, these movements in Kenya were born of economic upturn and rising expectations, and were led by a middle group motivated by relative deprivation. A somewhat similar outbreak had occurred in Kenya following the depression of the 1930s. In these cases it is the hope of amelioration of grievances as much as the consciousness of oppression that motivates protest.

Once formed, postwar labor organizations rapidly became increasingly radical in their actions and in their criticism of the status quo, a course which culminated in the involvement of some of them in the Mau Mau rebellion. This trajectory of development may be attributed to (1) the failure of labor leaders to achieve any marked change in the structure of racial economic domination; (2) the undercurrent of discontent among unskilled urban workers, stemming both from low wages and from unrest over land in Kikuyu rural areas; and (3) government repression.

LABOR POLICY IN KENYA

Much has been written on British colonial labor policy and its application in Kenya,[6] and in the space of this chapter only a summary account can be provided of the conceptions which underlay the specific labor policies followed in the years 1947-1952.

The Kenyan government, influenced by European settlers who strongly opposed any form of trade unionism for Indian or African workers, adopted until the 1930s a wholly repressive policy toward African trade unionism. However, pressure from the home government and from below in the form of Indian union organizing in the mid-1930s finally led to the legalization of trade unions in 1937. At the same time, however, they were to be closely regulated through compulsory registration, enabling government to refuse to "register" those unions of which it disapproved. By 1948, further legislation increased the powers of the Registrar of Trade Unions, making it possible to give or refuse registration to unions for a wide variety of reasons at the discretion of the Registrar and the Labor Department.

The growth of craft organizations among African skilled workers during the war, and wartime labor unrest in general, made the government aware of the imminence of African trade unionism. Its policy toward the newly forming associations among masons, tailors, painters, barbers, and taxi-cab drivers in Nairobi was to attempt to hold off their further development until the Trades Union Labor Officer, who would be in charge of guiding and controlling the associations, could be sent out to the colony after the war (Kenya National Archives, LAB 9/915/54,55, Sept. 12, 1944).[7]

By April 1947, a Trades Union Labor Officer, Mr. James Patrick, had arrived in Kenya attached to the Labor Department with the duty of fostering "responsible" African unionism. But because not all officials and very few settlers or employers were in favor of trade unions for Africans in the near future, priority was given to the development of works committees and staff associations as initial steps. As the Trades Union Labor Officer told a group of employers in 1947, (Kenyan National Archives, LAB 9/372/107):

> it was our policy in the Labour Department that every encouragement should be given to the development at the present moment of Whitley Councils or Workers Committees in view of the fact that the native was not yet far enough advanced to accept and operate the proper principles of trade unionism.

In theory, however, unions for Africans were acceptable. The central tenets of Labor Department policy toward full-fledged African unionism were that it must develop slowly and in such a way as to be (1) industrially organized, and (2) "non-political." Initially, unions organized on a craft basis were not discouraged, but by about 1953, when a colony-wide union structure was beginning to take shape, policy shifted to the setting up of unions solely on an industry-wide basis, partly under the influence, by this time, of a representative from the International Confederation of Free Trade Unions in the colony. This form was thought to be most appropriate for the new industries they hoped would be exported to Kenya from the industrial metropole.

From the beginning, general workers' unions open to all workers in a given area were explicitly opposed. This form of organization, however, is appropriate for the expression of populist or nationalist tendencies, and has been common in the early labor history of many societies undergoing the transition to wage labor. But in Kenya, at this point beginning an evolution toward a peripheral and dependent industrialism, administrators from the metropole perceived that such organizations would be conducive not to modern collective bargaining, but rather to political activism. Thus unions, it was preached, must be "economic" and not "political" organizations.

In attempting to enforce this nonpolitical structure, the colonial government showed its appreciation of an historical tendency for early labor movements to embrace radical criticism of the existing order. Whether this critique was a socialist one or an anticolonial nationalist one in one sense did not matter: the colonial government would be opposed to either tendency.[8]

The fast pace of African union organizing in Kenya, together with the social structural conditions predisposing unions toward radicalism, required that the government's conception of trade unionism be initially at least, imposed on African workers. The strategy required the direct suppresion of some sections of the movement and the carrot-and-stick tutoring of other section. We turn now to an examination of how this process worked in detail.

GOVERNMENT VERSUS AFRICAN UNIONS

It was in early 1947, with the arrival of the Trades Union Labor Officer in Kenya right after the January strike in Mombasa and the formation of the African Workers' Federation, that the two opposing conceptions of unionism, the evolving African one expressed in the African Workers' Federation and the government one, first came into direct conflict. As a general workers' union with a nationalist orientation, the Federation was precisely the kind of labor organization to which officials would be opposed. Formed by Chege Kibachia on the first day of the strike and aiming to represent all workers on strike, the African Workers' Federation eventually aspired to unite all African workers in one big union.[9] As the organization grew through mass meetings held throughout the strike and afterwards, it received support from nearly all sections of workers in Mombasa, and indeed from the unemployed. The most well-off white collar Africans apparently did not support it, while it appears that many clerical workers in lower-paid private employ did. The bulk of support seems to have come from urban manual workers throughout the city of Mombasa, including the large mass of workers in Mombasa port. Chege Kibachia, the Federation's leader, traveled throughout the colony urging workers to join; he received substantial support in many cities and on agricultural estates. In particular African Workers' Federation leaders met in Nairobi with representatives of the various associations of skilled manual workers already in existence there, and by July 1947 these associations had decided to form a branch of the Federation.

The fact that the African Workers' Federation took the form of a general workers' union may be at least partially explained by the concentrated yet relatively undifferentiated character of the workforce in Mombasa which formed its original social base; and, perhaps, such an organization might have been a suitable and effective agent in representing the claims of these African workers. In fact, it may have been potentially too effective; it is probable that it was the potential size and power of the Federation, as well as its initial militance in the use of the strike weapon, which induced the government to move against it. But a second equally important reason, both for the Federation's success and for its repression, was the racial (in addition to class) consciousness it exhibited, and its consequent links to African nationalism. In a letter to the press signed by Chege Kibachia, the Federation protested unequal pay scales under which Africans doing the same job as an Asian or European were paid substantially less. It also gave public support to the political goals of the Kenya African Union, the burgeoning postwar African nationalist movement led by Jomo Kenyatta. Chege Kibachia and other African Workers' Federation leaders were therefore arrested, and the resulting lack of leadership led to the organization's decline within the next few years.

With the gradual decline of the Federation, and because of the power Patrick wielded in recommending to the Registrar whether or not a union should be legally registered, he found in the years following 1947 some response among Africans to his activities promoting "proper" trade unions. The main center of his activities became Nairobi, where he counseled groups of white-collar, skilled and semi-skilled workers who were already forming small occupational or staff associations.

The Trade Union Labour Officer began in 1947 a series of lectures on trade unionism which many African labor leaders or aspiring labor leaders attended. He wrote and circulated booklets on trade unionism which emphasized that trade unions did not have political aims, and were formed not to call strikes, but to avoid them. Among the African workers' associations already in existence which the Trade Union Labour Officer counseled were the African Tailors and Button Hole Makers, the Kenya Houseboys Association, the Kenya Nightwatchmen Association, the African Painters' Union, and the African Masons' Association. All these were pressing to become legally registered organizations; the only African unions which had been registered up to this time were the Nairobi African Taxi Drivers' Union and the Thika Native Motor Drivers' Association. As Makhan Singh (1969:162) put it in reference to the Tailors Association:

> After Kibachia's arrest, when the functioning of the federation become impossible, they, like other trade unionists in Kenya, had no alternative but to form their separate unions, getting as much advice from the Trade Union Labour Officer as was possible and reasonable.

In almost all of these cases, however, the Trade Union Labour Officer told the leaders that they should aim to make their association a trade union, but that to do so they would first have to study his works on trade unionism and then demonstrate that they understood the principles of unionism and were in fact capable of leading a trade union. Only then could their organizations become registered as legal unions under the provisions of the Trade Union Ordinance.

The Kenya Houseboys Association, for example, a relatively large association under the enthusiastic leadership of Herbert Kaguma and Chege Kiburu and with a predominantly Kikuyu membership, found its application for union status opposed because "sufficient knowledge of the subject [proper trade union procedure] did not exist among the Domestic Workers" and because of the "difficulty of normal trade union negotiations" with a "multiplicity of employers" (Kenya National Archives, LAB 9/911/May 1949). The Department advocated instead a separate union for domestic workers in hotels and businesses only. The Painters' Union, one of the oldest associations, continuously active since 1944, was likewise held off from registration on grounds that its books and constitution were not in good order and that its leaders were not literate (Kenya National Archives, LAB 9/908/17-35). In both these cases the Department also appeared to have unspoken suspicions that these union leaders were potentially too militant. The Tailors' Association, on the other hand, found its application encouraged. Its leaders and membership were largely Luo, and the leaders had indicated a strong desire to work with the Trade Union Labour Officer and to follow his advice. The Union was registered in July 1948 (Kenya National Archives, LAB 9/925/July 1948).

This "go-slow" policy toward African unionism did not or could not head off the resurgence of "political unionism." Faced with this rebuff at the Labour Department, several of the African associations by late 1947 began moving into an alliance with the militant Asian general workers union, the Labour Trade Union of East Africa, whose leader, Mikhan Singh, had been attempting since the 1930s to organize Kenyan workers on an interracial, working class basis. Now Singh was beginning to have some success in this endeavor. The associations of nightwatchmen, painters, masons, stone workers, wood workers, shop workers and messengers became sections of the Labour Trade Union of East Africa and received organizing help. A clerks' section of the Labour Trade Union, of both Asians and Africans, was also formed.

In 1948 the domestic workers turned to Makhan Singh for help in drawing up a legal constitution and escalating their drive to become registered. By mid-1949 an application had been made over the head of the Labour Department to the Attorney General. The Labour Commissioner wrote to the Attorney General, "As you can well understand, I am not in favour of this registration which is being pressed for behind the scenes by Makhan Singh. The Trade Union Labour Officer has endeavored to convince them that to apply for trade union status at the moment is not in their interests. His advice has been rejected" (Kenya National Archives, LAB 9/911/Labour Commissioner to Attorney General, June 14, 1949). Although the Attorney General ruled that the application could not in principle be denied, the Department managed to get it further delayed.

But the African initiative continued to mount. The legally registered Kenya African Road Transport and Mechanics Union, formerly the Nairobi African Taxi Drivers' Association, began extending its influence and membership beyond its inital base, and organized branches in major cities all over Kenya. In 1948 the union claimed to have 14 branches and about 5,000 members (Singh, 1969:189). Its headquarters at Kiburi House in Nairobi served as a center for the whole of the African union movement. Up until about October 1949, when its General Secretary M.A.O. Ndisi left for Oxford on a T.U.C. scholarship to study trade unionism, this union enjoyed the support and encouragement of the Trade Union Labour Officer. After that time, however, Fred Kubai and John Mungai, more militant and politically nationalist leaders, took over the direction of the union, further expanding its membership and industrial activity and changing its name again to the Transport and Allied

Workers' Union. By January 1949, the transport workers had decided to ally with Makhan Singh's Labour Trade Union of East Africa.

The Labour Trade Union was campaigning at this time for "equal pay for equal work," nonracial pay scales, higher wages for all Asian and African workers in view of the rising cost of living, a "family minimum" wage for Africans, and an eight-hour day and 45-hour week (Singh, 1969:173-188). It also advocated a central organization of all trade unions to complete the alliance between Asian and African unions.

Two predominantly Asian unions followed Singh's nonracial lead. In 1948 the Typographical Union of Kenya opened its membership to all races, and the African Press Workers' Association merged with it. There were some 200 Asian and 50 African members in 1949 (Labour Department Annual Report, 1949). Demands were presented to the Indian Printers Association, inaugurating negotiations which culminated in a 1950 strike. The Shoemaker Workmen's Union, which had both Asian and African members, was also formed in 1948, and began a press campaign for an eight-hour day and 45-hour week in the shoemaking industry; the campaign led to a strike in April 1949 (Singh, 1969:199-200). An Asian and African sweetmeat workers section of the Labour Trade Union of East Africa was formed, and initiated negotiations with the Indian Confectioners Association aimed at higher wages and shorter hours. A bitter strike ensued in September 1949 (Kenya National Archives, LAB 9.947/1-84).

As an industrial strategy, Singh's nonracial policy worked well in those industries—printing, bakery and confectionery trades, tea shops and small commercial undertakings—where the number of African workers was relatively small and did not immediately threaten Indian workers, and where Indians as well as Africans were receiving very low wages. In these industries, employers were predominantly Indian, and an inter-racial union strengthened the position of all workers against employers. But in those industries where racial competition was strong and where large numbers of skilled Asians were employed—the railway, government services, building and construction—the interracial Labour Trade Union of the 1940s had little success. The rest of the Asian trade union movement, the Railway Asian Union, the Kenya Asian Civil Service Association, and the East African Ramgarhia Artisan Union, held aloof.

As a political strategy, Singh's alliance with African trade union and nationalist leaders was similar to those around the left-wing *Daily Chronicle*, who gave aid and publicity to African nationalism. Singh gave the same sort of assistance to early African unions in a host of vital matters such as constitutions, correspondence, negotiations and office work. The alliance with Singh served to strengthen the Africans' political position and to give increased and more articulate expression to African grievances.

Yet from the beginning there were some differences of political outlook between the African trade unionists and Makhan Singh. Although the union leaders took up the struggle to better the conditions of African workers, they were willing at critical points to subordinate the goal of workers improvement qua workers to the nationalistic goal of political independence under the rule of the African middle class. Improvement for workers seemed impossible until colonial rule was ended; thus, ending it tended to become the primary goal. The shift of emphasis becomes apparent when for example Fred Kubai, the foremost African labor leader, did not, after the suppression of his alliance with Makhan Singh, again return to specifically industrial issues, but instead decided to "bring the force of the African workers into KAU [Kenyan African Union]" (Rosberg and Nottingham, 1966:269).[10] The decision implied a wider consciousness of *African* grievances under colonial rule, rather than simply class ones. Yet even so, the unionists became more militant in pursuit of "uhuru" than the Kenya African Union leaders, advocating independence sooner, and using the unions as vehicles for oathing and other Mau Mau activities. Class differences thus tended to reappear within the nationalist movement.

Singh's campaigns, on the other hand, reflected since the 1930s a straightforward class-conscious, pro-labor philosophy. At the formation of the Labour Trade Union of East Africa in 1935, its president stressed that "the capitalists were enjoying upon the labour of the workers, and this was a great injustice" (Colonial Times, April 27, 1935; see also Singh, 1969:176). Singh was ideologically influenced by South African and Indian communist trade union leaders, although he seems to have had no actual organizational links to the Communist Party or other socialist movement. Although the Labour Trade Union had been loosely connected to African nationalism in Kenya before the war through overlap of leadership with the Kikuyu Central Association, its main concerns at that time were such reforms as workmen's compensation, the eight-hour day, abolition of child labor and rights of trade union organizing. (For example, see Singh, 1969:80.) It was not until after the war that the union began its campaigns for "equal pay for equal work" and for equal racial representation on the Legislative Council. It was also at this time that a concerted effort was made to bring Africans into the Union.

In the context of the postwar discussion of "multi-racialism" and political representation for non-Europeans, the Kenya African Union at first demanded greater African representation in the Legislative Council, while the East African Indian National Congress called for parity for Asians. By April 1950, the Kenya African Union and the East African Indian National Congress were jointly opposing European domination and advocating nonracial common roll elections. By then the trade unionists, including Singh, were already calling for immediate independence. But in the arguments supporting his political positions Singh went further than the Kenya Africa Union or the East African Indian National Congress or even many African unionists. To a government committee considering the form of Asian representation on the Legislative Council in 1948, he proposed (1969:178) the direct representation of labor through trade unions, because all other options before the committee "in one form or another, guarantee monopoly of all the elected seats to the commercial and higher sections, who are either ignorant of labour problems and needs of the labour, or totally opposed to the realization of its aspirations." In other contexts Singh also proposed full adult franchise for all, regardless of race, property or education, and trade union representation through proportional representation.

This and other stands indicate that Singh consistently refused to see colonial society, whether it was the composition of the legislature or the unequal pay scales for Asians and Africans, primarily in terms of racial domination. He saw it instead as the outcome of income inequalities operating in the interests of capitalists. His tendency to perceive colonial society in class rather than racial terms may seem surprising in the context of the actual colonial social structure. It represents, however, the outlook of the lower strata of Indian workers, who were the only group of workers to be placed in conflict with employers of their own race. Hence it was among this group that working class consciousness was likely to be most advanced and least mixed with ethnic loyalties. Singh's class outlook, however, had limited appeal to the rest of the Indian community.

The decision in January 1949 by the African leaders of the Transport and Allied Workers' Union to join the Labour Trade Union in a central organization came at a time of limited cooperation between the two chief political organs of the Indian and African communities in opposition to European domination, and was a parallel strategy in the trade union arena. It also came at a time of increasing frustration for the African nationalists, because their campaign of petitioning the government for redress of land and wage grievances seemed to be yielding no results. Militants like Kubai, therefore, were anxious to continue the struggle by other means. For several African unions, notably the Tailors, the Transport Workers and the still unregistered Domestic and Hotel Workers Union, the escalation also seemed necessary for industrial reasons: they had yet to achieve recognition from or satisfactory negotiation arrangements with employers despite continual attempts. For example, since its registration, the Tailors' Union had come into increasing conflict both with the Labour Department, which pressed them to moderate their demands, and with employers in their campaign against excessive working hours and poor wages. Thus they too moved into the central organization, after which their campaign culminated in a strike in January 1950, which led to lengthy negotiations with the Nairobi Master Tailors' Association (see (Kenya National Archives, LAB 9/925).

In May 1949, the East African Trade Union Congress was formally launched with Makhan Singh as General Secretary and Fred Kubai as President. Affiliated also were the Tailors and Garment Workers Union, the Typographical Union of Kenya and the Shoemaker Workmen's Union. The other Asian trade unions declined to affiliate. By 1950 the Domestic and Hotel Workers Union and the East African Painters and Decorators Union, both as yet unregistered, and the East African Seamen's Union, an Arab union in Mombasa, had affiliated. The East African Trade Union Congress received the official support of the Kenya African Union and Jomo Kenyatta, the British Trade Union Congress and the World Federation of Trade Unions.

The Labour Department's attitude toward these developments in the union movement was decidedly negative. From its point of view the Labour Trade Union and the East African Trade Union Congress were as "irresponsible" and "political" as the African Workers' Federation had been. The Labour Trade Union was, likewise, a general workers' union; even though it was composed of various occupational sections, the Department argued that it bore no clear relationship to employers in any one industry. Even though the various unions within the Trade Union Congress had all been engaged in attempts to begin negotiations with employers, the Department persisted in arguing that they were unsuited yet for bona fide collective bargaining. Finally, Singh's interracial policy was rejected by the Department, although never explicitly. The Department continued its policy of dealing with Asian and African unions separately, thereby strengthening the separation of union structures. Singh (1969:224), in turn, charged that this policy amounted to "divide and rule."

Officialdom regarded Singh as an agitator and made much of his supposed Communist affiliation. *Baráza*, the official government newspaper, said of the Trade Union Congress that "it was formed by a small group headed by an Indian who is known to be if not an actual Communist, ... It has sought and obtained recognition from the World Federation of Trade Unions which is a Communist dominated body" (see Singh, 1969:223). The Labour Department Annual Report referred in more threatening language to "the steady progress made in the field by the subversive and anti-British element developing in a part of the trade union movement" (1949:35). To the trade unionists, however, these seemed to be no way to genuinely ameliorate the conditions of workers without coming into conflict with the government.

The East African Trade Union Congress supported the large taxi-cab drivers' strike in Nairobi in October 1949, led by the Transport Workers as the last resort in their hitherto unsuccessful campaign against the new taxi-cab by-laws. It pressed the government to apply to Kenya the International Labor Organization conventions on the conditions of labor. It demanded workers' representation on government commissions and boards concerned with labor, and protested price increases, deportation of union leaders, trade testing schemes and a "forced labor" bill to provide a compulsory employment for "voluntarily unemployed" persons. It called again for the release of Chege Kibachia.

The Congress also took more "political" stands. In March 1950, with the support of a groundswell of African and Indian public opinion in Nairobi, it bitterly opposed the granting of a Royal Charter to the European-controlled Nairobi City Council. This act seemed to give a royal stamp of approval to European political domination. The Congress therefore decided to lead a mass boycott of the proposed Civic Week celebrations. How, it asked, could Indian and African workers take part in the celebration (Singh, 1969:253-254):

1. When the Municipal Council is dominated by a white majority and supported by other vested interests and nominated members;
2. When an overwhelming majority of workers in Nairobi have no right to elect the councillors;
3. When thousands of workers have to live in the dirty and unhealthy slums of Pumwani, Shauri Moyo, Marurani and River Road areas and when the roads in these areas are of the worst type in Nairobi;
4. When the workers already burdened by a high cost of living are further burdened by the Municipal Council with high rents, with meagre water and latrine facilities;
5. When the workers' children are not getting sufficient education and hospital facilities and when there is no future social security for workers;
6. When the capitalist-dominated Municipal Council ignores the representations made by the Transport and Allied Workers Union to repeal the repressive taxi-cab

by-laws, against which the heroic transport workers had to declare a big strike in October last year;

7. When plans are being secretly hatched to add to Nairobi more land of Africans.

At the same time, both Kubai and Makhan Singh were openly advocating immediate independence for Kenya under a democratic government "in which workers could have their own share" (1969:254).

Largely as a result of the successful boycott, the government moved directly against Singh and Kubai, arresting them in May 1950, on the charge of being officials of an unregistered trade union. The action resulted in the Congress calling the well-known general strike in Nairobi, the only one in that city's history. It lasted nine days, and although primarily a political strike, it also demanded an increase in the minimum wage. Some increase in the minimum wage did follow, but the strike did not secure the immediate release of Singh or Kubai, and East African Trade Union Congress declined through lack of leadership. The strike was also the occasion of some conflict between the trade union leaders . and the Kenya African Union, whose rather moderate leadership did not approve of the strike.

After the strike from late 1950 to mid-1952, the government and the Labour Department only clung more tenaciously to their gradualist and repressive policy. Immediately following the strike, the Labour Commissioner was quoted in the press (East African Standard, July 13, 1950):

There is obviously some doubt whether the Trade Union movement is applicable here. We are committed to foster it but obviously—our experience has already shown it—we must go about it another way and much more slowly.

In this spirit the Department continued to engage in delaying tactics, effectively discouraging various workers' associations—painters, night-watchmen, domestic workers—from becoming registered unions. The policy would continue until mid-1952, when oathing for the Mau Mau rebellion was already well underway in Nairobi.

The carrot-and-stick approach, however, had not yet succeeded in producing a trade union which was not nationalist in orientation or "excessive" in its demands; it had succeeded only in driving the unions into more political activism. In the next phase of labor organizing, beginning after the release of Kubai in February 1951, the cumulative effects of this policy, together with other social forces, would push many unions even further into underground rather than overt political activities; this time, into oath-taking and organizing for the Mau Mau rebellion (see Stichter, 1975b).

CONCLUSION

In the period of Kenyan labor history which has been examined above, it is apparent that socio-economic forces in the colony disposed urban wage-earners of all levels toward protest and labor organizing. The form and ideology which were eventually adopted by the emerging labor movement, however, were conditioned by other factors.

In these years, the principle of labor organizing on the basis of the whole working class, which in this context meant necessarily on the basis of Afro-Indian interracial cooperation, was introduced to African workers by local Indian trade unionists. For a brief time nonracial labor organization provided a vehicle for the articulation of African workers' grievances. In the long run, however, interracial organizing did not succeed, and the socialist rhetoric of the 1948-1950 period did not persist. The African trade union movement did continue to organize on a class basis among Africans only, but politically it associated itself with the goal of political independence under the rule of the embryonic African bourgeoisie. Workers saw in this option the only realistic hope for amelioration of their economic grievances. Thus for the African trade union movement, the years of flirtation with socialism can be seen as essentially a phase of militant escalation which, while perhaps not entirely without effect, was quickly superseded by the anticolonial voilence of Mau Mau.

One reason the movement assumed this character was that in colonial areas, and in particular in areas of white settlement in Africa, class and racial divisions largely but not completely overlapped. The fact that the employing class was almost wholly European or Asian, and the wage-earning class to a large extent African made it possible for African workers, unlike British ones for example, to see their struggle as much in racial terms as in class ones. Near monopoly by Indians of skilled positions within the work force made for two separate labor movements based on different racial sections of the workforce. In cases in which members of different races did occupy the same class position, for example among government clerks, remuneration was scaled according to race—Europeans receiving more than Asians and Asians more than Africans for the same job. The resulting wide income differentials between races in colonial society, wider than income differentials within any racial group, made the most salient contradiction in such a society appear to be the racial one.

In addition, fundamental economic factors tended to weaken the appeal of socialist ideology at this stage in the evolution of peripheral capitalism. The small scale of industrial development meant (1) that wage earners as a whole were only one of several social categories, the others being peasants and those in the subsistence economy; and (2) that a large section of wage earners were only part time or semiproletarianized workers. By contrast the labor movement during industrial development in England drew on a large and growing mass base, for whom wage earning was a lifetime condition. There it seemed more probable that the working class could be the agent of a major social transformation. In Kenya, however, it was Africans as a category, rather than workers, who constituted the overwhelming majority of the population.

Yet it is difficult to separate the structural and historical limitations on the emerging labor movement from the limitations posed by colonial government policy. It is clear that the government attempted to preempt certain organizational and ideological options for the movement. Organizationally, the colonial government did not simply delay the emergence of a strong African union movement in Kenya, it also effectively discouraged organization on a class-wide and/or interracial basis, even though these options may have been structurally possible only to a very limited extent. More importantly the colonial government banned general workers' unions of any kind, even those composed solely of Africans, thus ensuring that initial organization would be on smaller-scale occupational, and later industrial, bases.

Government policy was also in large part responsible for the weak state of the organized union movement in this early period in regard to its formal membership levels and its ability to initiate successful collective bargaining. The associations or unions which were pressing to become registered remained small in large part because of denial of registration. They could not, for example, legally collect dues from members, and so could not afford to pay a full time organizer. Also they could not claim to be a legal body with government backing; this status would have increased their membership. Finally, securing Labour Department support was essential if the union desired to begin negotiations with employers, because the majority of employers and employers' associations refused to recognize the unions unless prodded by the government.

Ideologically, government successfully set the boundaries of political dissent. Even though the socialist ideas introduced by Makhan Singh might never have had widespread appeal to African workers, still, whatever further appeal they might have had was effectively neutralized by the 11-year restriction of Singh and the suppression of the East African Trade Union Congress and the Labour Trade Union of East Africa. Thus censorship, aided by the racial social structure of colonial society, helped to determine that African unionists would continue to see their oppression as arising from colonialism rather than from capitalism.

The government's attempt to curb African nationalism within the unions, on the other hand, did not meet with the same success. The contextual forces supporting this tendency were too strong to be countered. The policy was effective only to the limited extent of restraining the more militant expression of nationalism. This effect becomes most apparent in the period of the Mau Mau rebellion, 1952-1955, when government policy succeeded in encouraging and widening a division along more militant/less militant lines, and in suppressing only the more militant pro-Mau Mau faction.

In sum, although the colonial government did not succeed in creating a "nonpolitical" union movement, it did reduce substantially the militance with which the movement pursued its nationalist and industrial aims. During the Mau Mau rebellion, the process begun in 1947-1952 was completed; cooperation with the Labour Department became a condition of survival for the union movement, and those union leaders who escaped detention were successfully steered in a "bread and butter" economist direction.

NOTES

1. An overview of class-forming tendencies and of the evolution of African labor movements up to 1947 can be found in Stichter (1975a).

2. The development summarized in this section are more fully described and documented in Stichter (1972, 1975a).

3. The cost of living for Africans as measured by the Mombasa African Retail Price Index rose by some 60% between 1947 and 1952 while the minimum wage in Nairobi rose by only some 50% (East African High Commission, 1948: Table F4; Labour Department Annual Reports, 1947-1952).

4. As the Carpenter Committee found in 1954, the minimum wage provided only the barest minimum income for a single man, and it was virtually impossible for a married man to support a family on such a wage (Kenya Colony and Protectorate, 1954:32).

5. On the persistent shortage of African skilled labor after the war, see the Labour Department Annual Reports, 1945-1948. On the origins of the small stratum of skilled laborers that did exist, see King (1975).

6. One of the most useful general accounts of British colonial labor policy is Roberts (1964). For Kenya, see especially Sandbrook (1970) and also Clayton and Savage (1974). This latter work, however, has the disadvantage of tending to portray administrative endeavors in excessively positive terms.

7. In 1944, for example, the Nairobi Municipal Native Affairs Officer wrote to Simeon Mutunga, of the nascent African Masons' Association: "Certainly there is no legal or other objection to you forming such an Association, but I advise you to wait until it is possible to form a proper legal trade-union." (Kenya National Archives, LAB 9/915/54, 55, Sept. 12, 1944.)

8. The problem with this policy was that even the labor movements in Great Britain and the United States were not "non-political." Thus the Kenya government was caught in an embarrassing situation in 1956, when labor leader Tom Mboya could successfully appeal to the British Trade Union congress and the House of Commons that he was not being given the same rights that British trade unionists enjoyed.

9. More complete accounts of the African Workers' Federation are found in Stichter (1975a), Rosberg and Nottingham (1966:208-210), Stren (1968), and Singh (1969:141-151).

10. J. Spencer's (1975) evidence indicates that this decision on the organizational level took place at least two years after the initial oathing of Kubai, J. Mungai, and some 24 other African trade union leaders in Nairobi. Oathing had been gradually spreading among Kikuyu workers in Nairobi as well, but it spread even more quickly in 1951 and 1952.

11. The East African Standard also reported that the East African Trade Union Congress had been recognized by the World Federation of Trade Unions, but noted that the Congress had not in fact actively sought this recognition.

REFERENCES

CLAYTON, A., and SAVAGE, D.C. (1974) Government and labour in Kenya, 1895-1963. London: Frank Cass.

East African High Commission, East African Statistical Department (1948). East African economic and statistical bulletin, No. 1, September.

———— (1951). The pattern of income, expenditure and consumption of African labourers in Nairobi, October-November, 1950.

Kenya Colony and Protectorate (1944-1952). Kenya National Archives, Labour Department files.

———— (1945). Report of the committee of inquiry into labour unrest in Mombasa (Phillips Report).

———— (1945-1952). Labour Department Annual Reports.

———— (1954). Report of the committee on African wages (Carpenter Report).

———— (1955). Statistical abstract.

———— (1956-1957). Statistical abstract.

KING, K. (1975). "The development of African skilled labour in Kenya: The white estate versus the Indian fundi." Paper presented at the Conference on the Political Economy of Kenya, 1929-1952, Cambridge, England, June 26-29.

PARKER, M. (1949). Political and social aspects of the development of municipal government in Kenya. London: Colonial Office.

ROBERTS, B.C. (1946). Labour in the tropical territories of the Commonwealth. London: G. Bell and Sons.

ROSBERG, C. and NOTTINGHAM, J. (1966). The myth of Mau Mau: Nationalism in Kenya. New York: Praeger.

SANDBROOK, R. (1970). "The state and the development of trade unionism." Pp. 252-295 in G. Hyden, R. Jackson, and J. Okumu (eds.), Development administration: The Kenyan experience. Nairobi: Oxford University Press.

SINGH, M. (1969). History of Kenya's trade union movement to 1952. Nairobi: East African Publishing House.

SPENCER, J. (1975). "KAU and 'Mau Mau': Some connections." Paper presented at the Conference on the Political Economy of Kenya, 1929-1952, Cambridge, England, June 26-29.

STICHTER, S. (1972). "Labor and national development in Kenya." Unpublished Ph.D dissertation, Columbia University.

———— (1975a). "The formation of a working class in Kenya." Pp. 21-48 in R. Sandbrook and R. Cohen (eds.), The development of an African working class: Studies in class formation and action. London and Toronto: Longmans and University of Toronto Press.

_____ (1975b). "Workers, trade unions, and the Mau Mau rebellion." Canadian Journal of African Studies, 9(2):259-275.

STREN, R. (1968). "Administration and the growth of African politics in Mombasa: 1945-1964." Kampala: University of East Africa, Social Sciences Council Conference Papers.

7

UNIONIZATION AND EMPLOYER STRATEGY:
The Tanganyikan Sisal Industry, 1958-1964

DIANNE BOLTON

Social scientists have placed too much reliance on the concept of trade union development as the main yardstick for measuring worker consciousness in colonial states. This has blurred the element of continuity present in the development of labor reaction to the different political and economic circumstances with which it has been confronted. This mistake has been made not only by writers and analysts of labor history, but also by certain sectors of colonial management in Tanganyika in the 1950s and 1960s who envisaged the domination and destruction of the nascent trade union movement as critical to the containment of worker militancy. The case study presented below deals with management reaction to the development of trade unionism in the sisal industry in Tanganyika. It describes the policy of the Tanganyika Sisal Growers Association (TSGA) to develop alternative institutions for consulting workers over specific work issues. The TSGA would not accept the inevitability of trade union development, as had the government. They still believed that they could find a substitute for it, which they could completely manipulate. The introduction of the Joint Consultative Councils (JCC) was an attempt to establish this alternative machinery.

In the period 1958-1964, the success of the policy of the TSGA varied considerably. One important determinant of its success or failure was the attitude of the state. In the initial stages of the campaign, during the Mazinde strike described below, many government officers expressed concern about the attitudes and actions of management. However, by the early 1960s, the aims and ideologies of organized labor and those of the nationalist politicians had become overtly divergent. The role of the state therefore changed from that of a controlling force on management activities, to that of an ally with management in the task of destroying the power of the newly established trade union movement. In the sisal industry, this alliance between state and private enterprise cemented an understanding which stretched farther than the confines of cooperation over labor issues. From this time onward the government began to accept, as relevant to its own development strategy, the standards adhered to in the realms of private enterprise. Increased rates of productivity and profitability were to be the main objectives in both private and, later on, in parastatal enterprises. A new participatory and more socialist vision of the role of the worker always took a less central priority in state and party strategy hereafter. This greatly influenced the role envisaged for the centralized trade union organization, National Union of Tanganyika Workers (NUTA), which replaced the Tanganyikan Federation of Labour (TFL) in 1964.

LABOR MILITANCY AMONG PLANTATION WORKERS PRIOR TO UNIONIZATION

The development of militant action among plantation workers was not synonymous with the growth of trade unionism. Since the 1930s there is evidence of a growing awareness among the sisal plantation labor force of specific facets of their exploitation by management. This consciousness manifested itself in such forms as absenteeism, strikes, property destruction and the organized evasion of taxes during periods when laborers were most discontented with their wages. In the Tanga region, the records show that industrial unrest occurred less over wage demands than it did over issues such as the arbitrary alteration of tasks by management or their maltreatment of the labor force. In the 1930s, district officers (DOs) were constantly reprimanding estate managers about their unnecessary antagonism of their employees by increasing work tasks without consultation, and by outright refusals to accompany task increases with wage increases. Many DOs forecasted that, if management continued to adopt these policies, labor simply would desert the plantations for better paid jobs.

From 1937 on, labor reports in the Tanga region comment on the frequency of strike action, and the increasingly economistic cause of the unrest. The DO observed in 1936 that certain changes had occurred "in the character of the wage earning class," which he found difficult to categorize. "A growing independence of spirit and a sturdier character are to be found amongst the wage earning classes, a development which may have some superficially unpleasant features; there can be no doubt that the working man is at last beginning to stand on his own feet." Another example of this new confidence on the part of labor was its growing willingness to try to take out quasi-legal action against employers who were breaking labor contracts or mistreating their workers.

During the 1940s, the use of the strike weapon by sisal plantation labor increased steadily, many of the strikes involving some degree of violence. Also, the poor wartime conditions in the camps aggravated the problems of desertion and absenteeism. A Reserved Occupations' Officer was appointed in 1943 to try to put an end to the industrial strife, and to ensure that war supplies were produced. Instant imprisonment was also introduced for desertion. Yet these measures did not deter the laborers from registering their protests in the only ways available to them. Nor did the stabilization of wages by the introduction of a fixed wage rate in January 1948, have any effect on the problem of stoppages. In 1949 strikes were just as great a problem to estate management, and on many occasions the police had to be called in to deal with cases of intimidation and unlawful assembly. Migrant labor from the Njombe and Mbeya districts of the Southern Highlands Province, particularly members of the Wabena and Wajika tribes, often provided emergent strike leaders. Once these ring leaders had been located and branded as agitators by management, they were generally dismissed unceremoniously with the tacit approval of the local labor officer. These early labor leaders had therefore to act in a clandestine manner because of the united policy of the TSGA to rid the area of potential labor militants showing leadership qualities. An office was opened to collect information on these leaders, who were then blacklisted from any type of employement on the sisal estates.

BACKGROUND TO THE MAZINDE DISPUTE

By the latter part of the 1940s, employers in general believed that there was enough evidence available for the discrediting of what they considered to be premature and irresponsible trade unionism.[1] Many employers saw this as an ideal opportunity to foster the development of substitute organizations such as staff associations and tribal councils. In the sisal industry there were further efforts made to establish trade unions, particularly along the Central Line at Kilosa and Kimamba; in retaliation the employers tried to usurp potential union functions by setting up Joint Consultative Councils (JCCs), through which selected workers could discuss specific issues with their employers. These councils were also used as means of gauging the mood of the working populations. TSGA records and JCC minutes suggest that workers were not keen to participate in either form of representation. The worker representatives who attended JCC meetings complained that the type of issues dealt with at these meetings were of little interest to the labor force in general. Increased wages was the major concern of the men whom they represented. When the workers could get no results over these issues, they not only lost interest in JCC meetings, but they also became directly antagonistic toward their representatives. Many of the representatives expressed fears about their own safety because "the labourers are suspicious that we are representing them in disguise for the benefit of the employers" (TSGA meeting at Tanga, Sept. 18, 1958). Sisal labor was not interested in sending delegates to meetings at which such issues as wage increases were put down in favor of sermons on the desirability of productivity increases and the need for worker education so that they might render a better return on task work.

From 1953 on, when registration of the African Commercial Employees Association (ACEA) was accepted by the government, small labor organizations began to spring up in various parts of Tanganyika. On July 10, 1955, a centralized trade union organization, the Tanganyikan Federation of Labour (TFL) was established. The TFL received many requests from plantation workers asking for help to organize themselves into a union. On March 26, 1956, the Tanganyikan Sisal Plantation Workers Union (TSPWU) was inaugurated. The government opposed its organization` on a national basis, so it was finally established on a provincial one. Although the TSGA used direct means to try to prevent the spread of unionization, it denied employing such tactics and stated that it was merely trying to establish its own consultative councils as an alternative form of conciliatory machinery. However, the trade union organizers claimed that the small response of the sisal workers to trade unionism was the result of specific management tactics to prevent the spread of unionization. Managers were accused of refusing to discuss important labor issues with any labor representatives, using excuses such as the sudden necessity of business "safaris." They were also in the habit of looking for excuses to sack employees who were union members, or who seemed to be emerging as spokesmen of their fellow employees. The naivety of the trade union organizers was illustrated by the way in which they tackled management over these issues. Some organizers approached the TSGA with the suggestion that it was still not too late for management to make restitution for their unworthy treatment of the trade union movement up to that time. In order to ensure future harmony in industrial relations, it was suggested that management now join the TSPWU in the promotion of a forced unionization scheme. Management should threaten their workers who refused to join a union with dismissal. This desire of some members of the trade union for complicity with management in such a scheme shows both their low level of organizational acumen and their lack of concern about the nature of their growing ties with their own rank and file numbers. Not surprisingly, the TSGA did not take up this offer of an alliance, but continued its efforts to play down the importance of union activities on its estates and to encourage the primary importance of Estate Consultative Committees. Official TSGA policy was that (TSGA memorandum, Feb. 28, 1957):

> Those estates with Consultative Committees are to continue with them. The ones without are to endeavour to dilute the union committee with persons of authority and responsibility such as headmen, clerks etc. That will then be recognized as the Estate Consultative Committee, as it is necessary at all costs to preserve the consultative machinery.

By 1958 it was evident that union organizers were beginning to consider that the only means by which the deadlock resulting from this joint representation could be surmounted was through militant strike action. By April 1958 the unions had only three representatives on Central Joint Council (CJC), a statutory industry-wide body, compared with 24 who were employer controlled. On the estates the unions were generally not represented on the councils; thus, the concept of joint consultation was developing a very one-sided reality. The resultant militant strike action was recognized by management as an outright attempt by the union to overthrow the status quo which they themselves were attempting to preserve at all costs. They fought the unions fiercely, resorting to police action whenever necessary to break up the strikes. One strike at Mjesani Estate, Tanga Region (a strike caused by workers' demands for the removal of a supervisor) resulted in a riot situation in which the police emptied two rounds of ammunition into the midst of the workers. A number of deaths and an ensuing panic resulted from this action. The antagonism between workers and management caused by this type of incident was further aggravated by the failure of the different sectors of labor to work together on the Central Joint Council (CJC). Later in the year (1958) the TSGA finally offered a 5% wage increase, which was rejected by the workers. When the offer was revised a split occurred among employees over whether this revised offer should be accepted. The management-selected employees accepted it, but the union representatives did not. Within three weeks of these discussions 24 strikes had occurred in the industry, though there was no official strike call. Against this background the significance of the Mazinde strike, described below, becomes very clear. The strike, which lasted for 68 days, became a confrontation between the old labor situation on estates and efforts to impose a new order by the trade union organizers.

THE STRIKE AT MAZINDE ESTATE

The owner/manager of Mazinde Estate in 1958 was Mr. David Lead. It is perhaps significant that during the period of the dispute he was also the chairman of the TSGA. His tough line of approach to the problems on his estate apparently implies that he was demonstrating the "correct line" for dealing with this particular form of trade union activity to the other managers in the organization. What started as a dispute on one sisal estate eventually ended as a united management front (including managers from other industrial sectors) against a form of trade union activity by which most managers in the area feared they might be victimized on some future occasion.

The Mazinde section of the Lead Estate came out on strike on November 25, 1958. According to David Lead's testimony, the strike was very strange in so far as no approach was made to management to present a list of grievances. Mr. Lead said that he was given to understand that workers insisted they had been given orders not to talk to estate management On the 28th of November, a Mr. Shehe, a delegate from the TSPWU, arrived from Muheza, the nearby district office, and expressed surprise that the employees were on strike. He denied that the union was responsible for the strike. Lead replied that, if this were the case, he would not require union assistance in settling it. Mr. Shehe obtained permission from the Commissioner and the Assistant Commissioner for Police to hold a public meeting on public land. At this meeting, attended by the Labour Officer, he questioned the workers as to why they were on strike and asked for representatives who would be willing to come and put their case before management.

The Labour Officer went to see Lead after the meeting and asked him who he was willing to meet to hear the claims of the estate workers. Lead replied that he was willing to see any person employed by the estate, regardless of their position, but he was not willing to have a union representative at the meeting. The Labour Officer informed the union representative of this; three members of the estate were then ushered into Lead's office while Mr. Shehe remained outside. Soon after the discussion had started Mr. Shehe went into the office to hear the proceedings, but Lead told him to go. Eventually he agreed to go, but he ordered the three representatives to leave with him. They complied with his wishes. From this time until December 6, 1958, no further meeting was held between management and workers, although Lead claimed that it was his daily practice to inform the employees of the estate that management would be willing to discuss any claims with any employee whether or not he was a union member. It seems that rather than settling the strike as quickly as possible, Lead had chosen to use it as a means of confronting the union with a challenge to their own conception of their right to represent workers in industrial disputes.

By December 6, David Lead had decided to settle the dispute according to his own prescription. He announced his intention of dismissing 100 workers each day until the employees returned to work. This procedure started on December 8 and continued until December 10, during which period 350 employees were laid off, some being repatriated. There is evidence that this action might have been prompted by Lead's receipt of a letter from Victor Mkello, the General Secretary of the TSPWU. In this letter the union declared its intention to support the strike fully because of the intransigent attitude Mr. Lead had taken. Mr. Mkello explained that workers on the estate had clearly and repeatedly stated they were prepared to work at any time provided that management would discuss matters with a combined representation of union and nonunion workers. However, management had refused and would only meet one or the other one at a time. Thus Mkello warned Lead that the strike would continue indefinitely with the full support of the TFL. On December 6 and 7 a meeting did take place between David Lead, the Labour Officer, Victor Mkello, Mr. Kamaliza (the TFL President) and Mr. Mpangala, a Plantation Workers International Federation(PWIF) organizer. At the meeting it was argued that there had been no proper machinery whatsoever through which the workers could air their grievances. The worker representatives at this meeting requested that management should allow the workers to elect their own representatives to sit on an estate committee, which would deal with all future disputes. The union added that, if this were granted, it would be prepared to advise the workers to return to work on December 8, but only after the eight alleged ringleaders who had been dismissed initially were allowed to return with the rest of the workers. The grievances of the labor force would then be put to management through the right channels, as soon as the estate committees were elected.

David Lead proceeded to ignore this possible solution and began to dismiss workers, as he had threatened, from December 8 onward. When the union saw him in action, it also took matters into its own hands and started transporting laborers away from the estate, the large majority of whom had not been paid off. The workers were taken initially to the offices of the TSPWU and to those of TANU, the nationalist political party. Nyerere, the leader of the nationalist political movement, appealed to all Africans in the Tanga Province to receive the strikers into their homes. Within a few days the workers had been moved to and housed in different parts of Morogoro and Tanga, although some were sent back to their homes as far away as Ruanda and Burundi. Some managed to get work on other sisal plantations in the Tanga area, despite the fact that the TSGA had sent circulars to all their members asking them not to allow any of the workers from Mazinde on their plantations.

In circulars to other TSGA members, Lead put out the following interpretation of the cause of the strike: it had been called by the TSPWU, through the branch committee on his estate, but it really had very little worker support. It was merely an example of the manipulation of ignorant workers by union organizers interested in their own ends. To back up this interpretation, he presented the following information to his fellow plantation managers. After he had tried to resume work on Mazinde Estate in a very small way, on December 11 he received a letter from one of his ex-headmen asking him to meet him, together with 14 other ex-employees at the union office at Korogwe. In this letter the workers stated they were part of a much larger number of workers who had been misled by the union, and who had left the estate under a false impression. Lead went to an estate at Ngombezi to collect these workers, and then on to the union branch office at Korogwe to collect their possessions. He said he was asked to return to collect more workers, but because the atmosphere around the office was getting rather ugly, he informed the police and the Labour Officer about his proposed return trip. Many of the workers asked him to return that night to collect them, but the police advised him against a trip of this sort at night. Lead concluded (Jan. 22, 1959):

> The intimidation in the area, caused by the body which organised the strike was on such a wide scale and of such an intensity, that the district officer from Korogwe had to spend several days endeavouring to persuade the locals in the area that there was no government order out to the effect that Mazinde Estate was closed down. There have been statements made by various employees returning to the estate that their belongings were held by the TSPWU and that they were hindered in every possible way from returning to the estate.

Lead also claimed that the TSPWU had been planning the strike for months before the strike actually began. He himself had known about the likelihood of its occurrence since November 20, 1958. He had received information from a watchman, who had come up from Makinyubi, that he had heard a union official informing some of Lead's employees that there would be a strike on the whole estate in the coming week. From then on workers who had been told to strike were intimidated from turning up to work mainly by Warundi gangs; anyone attempting to work was threatened with a beating. Lead therefore justified his rejection of dealings with the union by the fact that the union had organized this strike, even though the union continued to deny it when questioned.

Ignoring the question of further negotiations with striking workers,

Lead set about trying to rebuild his workforce. To combat his efforts the union spent more time publicizing their boycott of Mazinde Estate. Lead's correspondence shows that he also sent out various colleagues to spread the management interpretation of happenings at Mazinde. Some of these went as far south as Mbeya and Tukuyu. In the south, the traditional recruiting ground for sisal labor, there is evidence that the district commissioners generally supported Lead's case. They agreed to make sure that all chiefs and sub-chiefs understood that Mazinde Estate was still working; they stated that working for Lead had become a custom and tradition in certain southern areas, which would not be killed easily despite union efforts. However, Lead's colleagues also sent him word that in the south there existed areas which were suffering their own brands of disturbance at that time, very similar in nature to the happenings at Mazinde (letter from TSGA Mbeya district representative, Mar. 1959): "They have their troubles here too; a very large force of police have only just been withdrawn." They could not afford to add more fat to the fire of worker unrest by recruiting in these districts for the notorious Mazinde Estate. Yet overall Lead's colleagues usually managed to recruit on average about 80 to 90 laborers on short trips to the south. One feeling continually being relayed back to Lead was that the union question could be relegated to a minor issue if the TSGA built up better relations with the chiefs in the areas which had traditionally supplied labor. It was suggested that perhaps it might be wise for the TSGA to invite these chiefs up to spend some time on the plantations and, of course, pay their expenses for a trip of this nature. As one recruiter wrote:

> I find that trade unions cut no ice here. No one seems interested in them. What they are interested in is whether we are working or not. Village headmen and chiefs are very interested in working and housing conditions on our plantations. Housing conditions in villages here are amazingly high. It is probably due to the government's policy to 'build permanent houses or get out.'

Thus Lead and his colleagues were still clinging to the hope that a regeneration of benevolent, paternalistic policies on the estates, in league with the chiefs in the labor supplying areas, could prevent the influence of trade unionism from spreading on their estates.

According to the trade union accounts of the Mazinde affair, when Lead's efforts to rebuild his labor force were proving to be more difficult than anticipated, he took a more direct line in order to control the trade union leaders (Tandau, 1964).

> When the trade union boycott of the Estate was proving successful, and Mr. Lead's first attempts to recruit workers from other estates failed, he told the police that he was being threatened by the leaders of the union, who had said that they would kill him. In this way he got the protection of the police, and after pointing out the leaders who had threatened him, he got those union officials arrested.

The TSGA used the Mazinde strike as a pretext for breaking off the agreement it had made with the TFL, and would no longer recognize the TSPWU because of the way the strike had been handled. They also requested that the government establish an Industrial Relations Committee to investigate the labor situation on sisal estates. This request was granted by the Governor without even consulting the TFL. However, Mr. Barrett, a representative from the PWIF, was still in Tanganyika, and he approached the TSGA about the error in this policy. Negotiating machinery with the unions already existed on the plantation even though the TSGA chose to ignore it; also the government had already appointed one committee under Professor Jack to look into the situation. The TSGA therefore had to be satisfied with the findings of this Jack Report. It is obvious the TSGA had presupposed that an inquiry into the issue would not improve the position of the nascent movement on their estates. As Lead wrote to one of his managers on January 14, 1959:

> My impression of the attitude of the government as a whole is that they feel that, provided that an inquiry would not bounce back on the sisal industry as a whole, it would be a good thing to help them get a firm grip on the trade unions. I must say that these are merely my impressions gathered from meetings with various government officials. I have also gathered the impression that Mr. Barrett, the representative of PWIF is not at all happy at the moment with the manner in which his child is growing up.

It was therefore hoped that an inquiry would mark the end of the particular brand of trade unionism which had been giving management so many headaches.

Evidence therefore seems to point to the fact that this dispute at Mazinde developed more as a testing ground between management and unions, than as a genuine worker/management grievance with a capacity for being logically settled. Lead's correspondence shows that initially Muheza district managements, together with those of other estates in that area, had been debating for some time the value of a showdown with what they considered to be a totally irresponsible union. The challenge was readily taken up by the union which then concentrated its forces on this one test case estate. The ultimate threat which emanated from the union was that it would ensure that no one returned to the estate, and that the estate would be closed down for at least three years by trade union action. But despite the union's claims of being capable of effecting this type of result, Lead did not seem to find it too difficult to return to quasi-normal functioning. On Thursday, December 11, the 200 workers who had remained on his estate started working again. By means of an intense campaign against the unions in all the villages in which they had deposited labor, and by supplying transport to bring them back, the workforce was built up from 200 to 1,575 by the end of December, reaching 2,000 by mid-January. "One extremely good reaction is that the Africans themselves are fed up to their teeth with the unions and with anything to do with them, and they realise that the only benefits they received from their help were four to five weeks of no pay and extremely short rations, not to mention no housing." This statement directly contradicts the climate of the strike as described by the unions; nevertheless, there is very little doubt that Lead did not have much trouble in getting his workforce up to par again.

The Labour Office in the area greatly facilitated Lead's task, though claiming to "hold a fair and middle course." Yet Lead was still aware that the Labour Commissioner had one or two reservations about the way in which the affair had been conducted.

> His attitude is that I have taken a dirty advantage of inexperienced and ignorant trade unionists, who through their lack of training failed to follow the common sense, practical lines of running a trade union. He seems to be of the opinion that all nonsenses that trade unions make should be forgotten on the grounds that they are still learning. In this I am afraid that I am in disagreement; but confidentially I have been given to understand that his days with us are numbered.

One of the incidents which the Labour Commissioner probably regarded as part of this "dirty advantage" occurred immediately after the transportation of labor from the estates by the union. Lead wrote to many of his fellow employers in the area, whether in the sisal industry or not, explaining the significance of his stand against the unions for the rest of Tanganyikan employers. He also explained the urgency of his need to obtain labor, in order to demonstrate to the union the total impracticality of their threat to close down his estate. An example of the help he received in reply was that from a local company called Gypsum Products Ltd., which was owned by Colonel Dobie. The Colonel offered immediate aid to the extent of all his labor force for a period of six days. This shows clearly the solidarity of employers in and out of the sisal industry over the question of the development of trade unionism at this time. As a result of this kind of help, Lead was able to return to about 50% of normal production only a fortnight after the unions had issued the statement about their intention to close his estate. By January 6 production at Mazinde was back up to 80% of the predispute amount.

The unions continued to distribute circulars to the workers explaining what was happening at Mazinde. Circular no. 4 issued by the union expressed great disappointment with the workers who had returned to Mazinde, and also explained the inadequacy and falseness of the reforms which were then being attempted by David Lead in relation to worker organization and representation:

The employers have deceived the remaining few workers, and elected from them representatives of the estate council. The union had demanded a fresh election to be held as soon as the strikers returned to work, but the Mazinde employer had refused.

The union was very much against the functioning of this particular estate committee, because it represented to them yet another aspect of the duplicity of management dealings during these negotiations. At a meeting of the TSGA members and union delegates on December 22, it had been suggested by Mr. Markwalder, a TSGA member, that Mr. Lead should elect an estate committee and refer the matter concerning the dismissed workers at Mazinde to this committee for settlement before January 15, 1959. Mr. Lead agreed to this suggestion, and a date for it was set for December 29, 1958. The union requested the Senior Labour Officer to ask for postponement of the election until the workers had returned to Mazinde; otherwise a committee would have been elected which would be opposed to the interests of those workers who had not returned immediately. The union was then informed that Mr. Lead did not require any more workers, because he expected to carry on with the 1,700 workers which he had acquired by this time.

After creating this new estate consultative committee, Mr. Lead went on to try and solve the Mazinde upheaval "constitutionally" through this new institution. He attempted to do this at a meeting held on February 11, 1959. His idea of worker consultation is very clear when one looks at the minutes of the first meeting. He tried to wipe the slate clean at Mazinde by passing the following motion in a meeting which lasted 45 minutes.

(i) It is stated that up this present moment a dispute exists between employers and employees on the Mazinde Estate. It is unanimously agreed that this statement has no foundation and is quite untrue.

(ii) It is stated by the union that all employees of Mazinde Estate have been dismissed. The reality is that none have been dismissed; they have all gone on what they now realise was a foolish strike, and as a further point to emphasise this, all who returned to work did so on estate transport at the employer's request.

(iii) The union stated that the estate council had not been elected and was not representative of the workers on the estate. The truth is that all had been elected from their own groups. The election was witnessed by officers of the Labour Department, and at no time was any undue influence used as to the choice of representatives, which was done by the employees themselves with no employer present.

(iv) The union requested that all labour which had been removed from the estate either by themselves or by Mr. Lead, or which had left the estate as a consequence of the strike, should be reinstated. The answer is, the estate is now full. There are extremely few vacancies at present, and the committee cannot agree to these men returning to the detriment of those workers now happily employed. Everyone of those workers who left the estate had a chance to return, but that chance is now passed, and we cannot agree to the mass reinstatement of other personnel.

This declaration showed Lead's continuing determination to avoid any change in worker organization or attitudes as a result of the strike.

SETTLEMENT OF THE STRIKE AND ITS SIGNIFICANCE

Just when Lead appeared to have secured his organizational objectives, his strategy appeared to have suffered a dramatic reversal when the results of Professor Jack's report were published. The union comment on the results of the report and the outcome of the Mazinde strike was that they represented a complete triumph for the cause of trade unionism in Tanzania. The Jack report recommended the appointment of plantation worker representatives on the estates, and the drawing up of a new agreement between the TSGA and the TSPWU. At a meeting between TFL, TSGA and TSPWU delegates to discuss the report, it was decided that the old workers' committees on the plantations would be dissolved and new ones elected. Union members would be represented on these committees and the General Secretary of the union was recognized as the spokesman of the workers. Union leaders claimed that the value of these gains to the workers could be judged by the fact that these new committees imemdiately started collective bargaining negotiations with the TSGA, and for the first time these issues were given prompt attention by the employers. Lead also agreed to accept the return of the striking workers, including the eight ring leaders. (This was really no hardship for him in view of the high turnover figures and traditional labor shortages in the industry.) He also had to accept the checkoff system; the union raised 20,000 shs. in one day at Mazinde estate in subscriptions.

Yet this rather gushing appraisal of union gains by its leaders fails to take into account one or two key factors involved in the negotiations. Without government concern about the results of the intransigent and short-sighted attitude of small-scale management, which led to its intervention in the Mazinde affair and an inquiry being held, the union would have been helpless against the united action of the TSGA. The alleged union triumph was in no way a result of an increase in worker consciousness harnessed and directed by the union; the balance was tipped against Lead by the long-term objectives of the colonial state vis-à-vis labor policy. The outcome of the strike saw very little change in the attitudes of the TSGA or in the methods of representation and grievance settlement on the estates. The new constitutional framework for workers' representation perpetuated the procedure whereby management took the final unquestionable decisions on all major issues on the estates, but it was now specified that these decisions should be reached after consideration of views expressed in the consultative committees. This was exactly the type of passive consultative machinery which David Lead had tried to set up in the first three months of 1958, an action which had contributed to the growing union grievances. The union position on the Lead estates was therefore very similar to the one from which they had started. This is not surprising, because the union never really seemed in control of the direction which the negotiations were taking. By the time of the official inquiry, the union seemed willing to go along with the establishment of almost any type of industrial consultative machinery. Rather than the union having some say in the definition of its own role, it seemed content to be used by government as a convenient vehicle for negotiating the "desirable" aspects of the requisites of a stable labor force such as paid annual leave, hospitalization allowance and pensions. In the sisal industry the union did not develop as an organizational extension of workers' demands, culminating from a steady development of worker consciousness from the 1920s.

No particular brand of trade unionism was fully accepted by employers in the sisal industry. With the prospect of independence they reluctantly came to terms with the fact that they would have to accept some change in basic social and economic relationships on their estates. Yet rather than haggle about the scope of this change with a trade union organization which had very little grass roots support and no firm relationship with the nationalist party, the employers chose to negotiate directly with the politicians. Even though the TSGA had to pay lip service to the development of trade unionism after 1958, their acceptance of this development on many of their estates was tokenistic. The disorganization of the TSPWU and its lack of clear objectives gave support to the attitude of the TSGA, as did the deteriorating relationship between the trade union bureaucrats and the politicians after independence.

This case study of the Mazinde strike serves to highlight aspects of the relationship between labor, state and employer during the period when trade unions were gaining the right of free access to enterprises. Although industrial unrest did increase in the latter part of the 1950s (from 7,482 man days lost through stoppages in 1954 compared to 1,494,773 in 1960), this should not be equated with a situation whereby the nascent trade union organization was able to pressure government and employers into accepting its cause through the sheer strength of its position. By 1959, there were only seven small unions in existence, all suffering constant financial and leadership problems. Between 1957 and 1959, of all man days lost nationally through strikes, 71% were lost in the sisal industry. Yet, as illustrated by the TSPWU's marathon efforts at Mazinde, this union was not able to set the pace of negotiations after the confrontation. Without government intervention, Lead would have been able to return to normal production, setting his own terms and conditions for future estate organization. Government intervention proved vital to the outcome of the Mazinde strike. The essence of the intervention was that the government, wanting to rationalize and stabilize the labor situation in one of the main industries in the country, had to limit the paternalistic policies of the small family enterprise. The overall reaction of the government to the whole period of industrial unrest from 1958 to 1960 further illustrates its objectives. The 1958 government Labour Report spoke almost favorably of strike action which had resulted in the setting up of joint consultative committees, a measure which it thought had been put aside far too long by the small employer. The government tried to clear up the hazy conditions surrounding the state of industrial relations through legislation such as the new Employment Act to replace the old Master and Servant Act, through attempts to introduce minimum wage legislation for the Dar-es-Salaam area, and of course through the Trade Unions' Ordinance. Government initiatives in these fields put the early pioneers of trade unionism in Tanganyika in a difficult position. The lack of opposition by the government to trade union development was obviously a necessary precondition for its further entrenchment, but there were also disadvantages when the paternalism in government attitude veered toward an attempt to control the direction of union development. Debates of the Tanganyikan Legislative Council in the late 1950s contain many statements by union leaders showing that they resented government attempts to "advise" the labor movement on its chosen course.

The Mazinde strike and its aftermath also sheds some light on the debate about the cause of industrial unrest in the sisal industry during this period. There has been discussion about the degree of political motivation involved in these strikes as contrasted with basic economistic motivation, because of the alleged close relationship which existed between Tanu and the TFL. One cannot underrate the extent of anticolonial feeling which must have existed among the workers on these sisal estates owned and controlled by foreign capital and practices. However, a true representation of worker grievances must have been hampered to some extent by a trade union organization that tried to harness manifestations of worker unrest in a way which they felt would aid their own visions of stereotyped patterns of trade union development. These patterns of worker representation were very much influenced by imported standards of trade union behavior, and thus the directions in which they guided workers' actions at an organizational level rarely took into account the level of consciousness of the sisal workers or their unique work situation on the plantations. This accounts to a large extent for the failure of the union movement to demonstrate clearly to its members long-term objectives of its leadership and resulted in a lack of identity and support between the rank and file union members and their trade union organization. These points are further elucidated by another case study of a group of estates in the Tanga area on which the TSPWU also concentrated its attention during the 1958-1964 period.

COMPARATIVE UNION TACTICS AND MANAGEMENT RESPONSES ON NEIGHBORING ESTATES,1958–1964

The other group of estates that received much attention from the TSPWU was Swiss owned and called the Amboni Estates. This group had greatly expanded its sisal acreage in the Tanga region in the 1950s, particularly in the wake of the effect of the Korean War on sisal prices. Amboni Estates had been very confident about the prospects of their investments in relation to both their profit margin and the availability of plentiful and acquiescent labor supplies. Their annual reports in the early 1950s show that one of the factors leading to their expansion had been the success of their policy to reduce production costs. This had been achieved partly through the reduction of the wage rate. They did question the length of time during which they would be able to maintain this kind of policy and half expected some reaction from the workers demanding higher wages when sisal prices rose on the world market. Yet the type of industrial unrest which they did experience on their estates from 1957 on was not motivated by attempts to start collective bargaining negotiations. For example, a strike occurred at their Pongwe Estate on September 16-20 which took management very much by surprise. The workforce went on strike because it thought it had been denied the opportunity of presenting its grievances to a United Nations delegate visiting the estate. They accused management of using a stooge headman to represent the workers on this occasion. Violence among workers and threats to management characterized this disturbance, while some sisal fields were also set alight. Management was very alarmed at this new type of industrial unrest (strike report, Sept. 16-20, 1957):

> This type of incident cannot be called a harmless strike. In our eyes this is nothing more than a rebellion against good order, cleverly and deliberately brought to Pongwe Estate from the outside. No wage claims were put forward—no grievances aired. It is astonishing that a whole plantation can be roused by a small gang of subversive elements with the aid of a group of unruly Warundi.

Amboni Estates felt that one reason why they were more liable to be subjected to such treatment was the fact that they employed Victor Mkello, the TSPWU secretary. During 1958, Mkello's tactic of threatening Amboni with devastating union actions over relatively minor issues became more common. Cases which started off as straightforward matters, such as the question of unfair dismissal of one employee, were used to present management with a general list of grievances which the union would draw up about the estate. The complaints tended to be very general, but the threats used by the union were more specific. The most common threat seemed to be that the union would bring the whole force of its movement behind one estate if conditions on the estate did not improve (letter from Mkello to Amboni Estates General Manager, Feb. 11, 1958):

> Unfortunately we still have on Amboni European managers who regard Africans in general as semi-wild beasts which deserve any cruel treatment which can be found on earth. Indeed the position of the African employees on the estates is not short of slavery . . . we invite your prompt co-operation [in the matter of this unfair dismissal] for the simple reason that the force with which we intend to approach this matter will bring undesirable consequences affecting other estates in the Tanga and Pangani Districts.

The continual issuing of this type of ultimatum resulted in the dismissal of Mkello from his job with Amboni, because of "the use of threats in his union capacity." The TSGA expressed complete approval of the way Amboni had dealt with this issue; their attitudes toward TSPWU tactics were hardening. The intrusion of the factor of personal enmity obviously resulted in the worsening of relations between Amboni Estates and the TSPWU. Amboni Estates were determined to have no dealings with a union led by Mkello, and Mkello became more set on the idea of using Amboni Estates as an example to demonstrate the potential power of the nascent trade union movement, and the havoc which it could cause on estate which would not accept its rightful presence. From the time of this deterioration in relations with the union, Amboni Estates (which claimed to offer better camp conditions and working tasks than any other estate in the district), received far more severe treatment from the union than other estates in the area. Many Amboni estate managers thought that the General Manager at Amboni had courted this trouble somewhat, in so far as he had shown himself too willing to deal directly with the union leaders. They also resented the fact that union leaders were aware that individual estate managers did not have a free hand with labor conditions on their own estates; they felt the union was taking advantage of this "fair play" policy practiced by the Group Manager. This was a different situation from the one at Mazinde where the manager was refusing to deal with the union. However, both estates were having very similar union problems by the latter part of 1958; the concentration of union energies on Mazinde took the pressure off Amboni for a while.

Whereas David Lead tried to maintain the policy of refusing to deal with the union, the managers at Amboni decided that it was no longer a feasible policy to fight against the prospect of giving unions access to their estates. Management at Amboni was generally surprised at the outcome of this reluctant compromise with the unions. Although union recruiters tended to start their campaigns with inflammatory introductions about class differences and exploitation, their demands usually amounted to nothing more than the desire to see higher profits for management and higher wages for their workers. Workers were asked to work more and better, and to leave negotiations for increased remuneration to their trade union leaders. No basic questioning of economic structure and policy took place; a more benevolent version of the status quo was all they asked for. They provided more excuses for the wage freezes of the time than did management itself. In a period when nationalist politicians were uttering their most virulent condemnations of colonial and political practice, this type of appeal was hardly likely to generate much worker reaction. More than 100 men very rarely turned up at meetings, and only about 30% of these were willing to pay union dues. Lead's decision to prohibit the union's access to his estates led to far more inflammatory results.

The aftermath of the Mazinde dispute established the union's right of access to all estates. The year 1959-1960 saw a qualitative change in the nature of industrial disputes in the sisal industry. In March 1960 it was agreed by the CJC of the sisal industry to raise wages by 100% and labor productivity by an average of 30%. The sisal cutters' task was raised from 70 to 90 bundles of 30 leaves and other tasks were increased accordingly. Bonuses and rations were abolished. A cutter was now paid Shs. III/- per kipande; cultivation laborers were paid 84/-; and work was to be based on a 45-hour week. The 1960 wages agreement produced a comprehensive wage structure in which all types of employment in the sisal industry were classified under six separate classes and then divided into further categories depending on seniority and wage evaluation. Dissatisfaction with the implementation of this agreement was expressed by both workers and union officials. It was claimed that on some estates tasks were being increased by more than 30%, and this was on top of what was already considered excessive by some workers. Also as a result of this "rationalization" of the industry, wholesale dismissal of workers was taking place without consultation with the unions.

The TSPWU complained that, although it had done everything possible to effect a smooth implementation of the agreement, it was obvious that by abusing the clauses of this agreement the majority of the employers in the industry were trying to undermine the role of the union. Mkello claimed (letter to TSGA Executive Director, May 9, 1960):

> Union members are now no longer paying their dues as they have been made to believe that Mkello and his fellow representatives of the CJC have been heavily bribed by the TSGA to allow an increase in task. Employers have taken advantage of the structure to introduce unbearable conditions of service, to apply wholesale dismissals and all sorts of inhumanities, alleging that such conditions meet the approval of Mkello and his union.

He even suggested that the TSGA was sending African representatives in association with the criminal branch of the Tanganyikan police to the sisal estates to tell the workers not to accept the new wage structure and to ignore the unions. To combat this the unions had to send their own representatives to put out the correct line on the agreement. Accusations also continued that management was not consulting unions on important issues such as redundancies and that it was still getting rid of union members from labor forces whenever possible.

The union therefore saw itself in a very difficult position. Management was able to discredit it by surreptitiously making the workers aware of the less palatable aspects of the new agreement to which the union had commited workers without consultation or research among the grass roots of its organization. Yet simultaneously the union was under obligation to combat management attempts to over capitalize on the new agreement. On the one hand the unions had to support this move toward stabilization of labor in the industry, on the other it now had to oppose aspects of the agreement that it had already accepted. The management interpretation of the situation was very different. They thought the unions were trying to recapture the confidence of their members by manufacturing and high-lighting potential areas of grievance in the settlement. "It is our opinion that the majority of labour does not want to strike, but is being made to do so again by the union" (letter from Kilimangwido Estates Manager to Amboni Estates General Manager, Oct. 22, 1960).

At the same time rifts were occurring within the TSPWU. There was much fighting for the acquisition and retention of bureaucratic posts created by these new union functions, and when Mkello tended to reallocate these posts for different reasons (dishonesty of tenure being a leading one), he was accused of such malpractices as self-exaltation, attempting to develop rifts in the union, and adopting autocratic remedies against union members who did not go along with all his policies. Management gleefully circulated reports of these different currents of opinion developing within the union. These differences never, however, resulted in any direct opposition to Mkello's policies or leadership from within the union.

By the end of 1960 Mkello was again adopting the tactic of direct threats to estate managers in order that alleged breaches of the 1960 agreement might be remedied. Any slight problem of implementation relating to this wage agreement was used by the union to threaten management with strike action. The TSGA reported that, as before, Mkello had very little idea about the position into which he was getting himself and his union. He was very ill-informed about the actual situation on estates, and as usual was issuing advice and directives from a distance. Mr. Bryceson, the Labour Commissioner, was constrained to complain about Mkello's tactics.

But as usual Mkello's chief anxiety is to save his own face. His complaints about estate managements lack factual background, and his other complaints and lists of actions back to the wages committees carry little general substance, and certainly nothing to warrant the considerable damage which he is causing.

The TSGA felt that the TSPWU was merely playing with strikes and settlements to periodically demonstrate their own negotiating powers.

Thus immediately before independence, when TANU was in the process of assuming governmental responsibility, there was neither easing of tension between unions and employers in the sisal industry, nor any major breakthroughs in areas such as the establishment of consultative machinery acceptable to both sides. Estate consultative committees still existed and their functions still overlapped with those of the union. The TSGA was of the mind that it would tolerate but not aid the cause of trade unionism (particularly the brand Mkello was demonstrating), and the appeal of unionism to workers was very limited—Amboni Estates had only 35% unionized labor in 1960.

Very little changed with independence. Because political independence was in no way synonymous with a change of attitude or practice on the estates, labor struggles reached a new intensity in the 1962-1963 period rather than abating. As A. Tambile (1974:106) commented:

The continuity of colonial practice after independence was not to be found in the sisal industry alone, though the industry being one of the most conservative institutions in Tanganyika showed a marked resistance to change . . The workers had still to struggle for further changes in their wages and conditions of work, and most important of all, for a degree of participation in decision making or workers power.

But after independence one factor which greatly affected the significance of labor disputes for Amboni management was the widening of the split between TANU and the TFL at a national level. There had been signs of a split in the TFL for and against specific TANU policies even before independence. By 1962 the conflict between the TFL and TANU was coming out into the open. The TFL warned the government against interfering with the issue of free collective bargaining and pressed for a rapid Africanization policy. TANU's replies specified the limits to which the union could go in these demands (Tanganyika Standard, Jan. 23,1962).

When any group demands independence . . . to do anything, even to be destructive, then that sort of independence is not in the interests of the country. The government is not there for only one group, it is obliged to balance the demands of all groups within its jurisdiction. The trade union movement must realise that it has an obligation, a duty in the building of the country. If it forgets that duty it will destroy itself.

After Nyerere resigned the premiership on January 22, 1962, and Kanawa took his place, the TANU National Executive invited the TFL to form an opposition party with an alternative program. After accepting the trade union leadership as an alternative political power seeker, TANU than set about a major propaganda campaign to identify TFL leaders as opportunists wishing to usurp the colonial legacy for their own members. Many TANU politicians used the dock workers strike of 1961 as an example of unions holding the country to ransom, and they urged the government to curb strikes through legislative measures. It was against this different scenario that Amboni Estates faced their next spate of industrial unrest.

The beginning of 1961 witnessed a proliferation of small strikes on individual estates, culminating in a major strike in March. It started on Kilimangwido Estate on March 15 and soon involved 1,000 workers. The TSPWU put forward suggestions for a settlement to management five days later, but these were not accepted. By March 27 the strike had spread to more than 7,000 workers on all but two estates. Initially the TSPWU agreed with management that the cause of such a large scale strike was ridiculous and unjustified (the strike had been started by workers who were demanding a senior headman's dismissal). By March 25 the union was standing fully. behind the strikers. The union and management had clashed most strongly over the fact that management had issued offensive handbills urging the strikers to return to work. These bills said the union, by supporting the dismissal of this headman, was breaching its Africanization policy. On March 28 the Minister of Labour and Mr. Mkello (now president of the TFL) went to Tanga to try to settle the strike. It was decided that a government inquiry into the strike should be conducted. The TSPWU leaders now had the task of persuading the workers to return to work, but they asked the workers not to see this simply as a submission to the government. The union stated (handbill to workers, Mar. 27, 1962) that, if there was further cause for complaint on any estate:

> We shall resort to strike action again. Furthermore, if we do not get what we want . . . we shall repeat what we did with Mazinde. All workers will be taken from the estate.

Once again, the strike was settled by the establishment of a board of inquiry. Management saw the outcome as a complete victory for themselves. The union had demanded from the Board that the General Manager and Estate Manager at Kiligmangwido be expelled from the country because of their perpetuation of colonial management practices, and that the headman and field assistants at the estates who had fulfilled the role of management stooges be dismissed. The Board came out in favor of the TSGA's interpretation of the strike. The strike, which had lasted 16 days, was declared unconstitutional and contrary to the trade union's own dispute procedure. The union staff was criticized very much for ignorance of its own role, and for trying to interfere with certain management prerogatives (e.g., right of dismissal) that did not concern them. The union witnesses against management practices were declared "unreliable." Yet, after dismissing all evidence by the union, the Board concluded:

It is strongly felt that the workers did not trouble to cause this constant unrest on the estates if there were no real grievances to complain about. . . . In conclusion, it seems that this dispute and strike that followed was a result of the lack of appreciation and understanding between the rights of management and the duties of employees on the one hand, and the rights of management and union on the other. Until this division is appreciated and understood, industrial disputes will continue to bedevil the country.

This set a precedent for the government's attitude toward worker unrest. It admitted that legitimate worker grievances did exist. Yet because evidence of the situation was partial (on account of the workers'low communicative ability), and because productivity demands required constant and systematic application to work by the labor force, no real analysis was made as to the necessity for change in the basic economic and social structures. This might have involved some disruption which the private sector of industry was not prepared to accept.

The Board's report had very little long-term effect. The habit of striking over issues relating to supervisory malpractice continued for the rest of 1962. Work was usually resumed after a short period without any real gain for workers. Also there was constant haranguing of management over issues which had supposedly been brought up and settled at the Board of Inquiry. The district officer at Pangani was inundated with complaints about the Kilimangwido manager from employees and TSPWU representatives. These complaints included failure to give advances to workers, unwarranted dismissals, victimization, failure to cooperate with the trade unions and estate committees, wrong use of labor cards and failure to organize the check off system. The district officer begged the manager to cooperate more closely with the unions. The Amboni General Manager wrote to the Minister of Labour that these allegations were false and that this continued agitation was an attempt by trade unions to close their estates—the same tactic attempted at Mazinde.

During the 1962 disturbance the confused state of the workers' consciousness became very evident. Their grievances were acted upon and heightened by the trade union leaders when it was convenient to the leaders' own ends, and their causes were dropped just as abruptly when these ends had been served. Many of the sisal workers' grievances foreshadowed those which later came to the surface in 1971, i.e., complaints about the off-hand, elitist tactics of management, which failed to take into account any requisite social changes following independence. There was a dichotomy between union objectives and the tactics they employed. Because they found it difficult to rouse their workers over issues such as task readjustments and productivity deals, the TSPWU used more nationalistic types of grievances to threaten employers with potential strike activity over more basic economistic issues. One of the final areas of antagonism between union leaders and TSGA was over the terms of enforcement of the Marealle

Agreement of November 1962. This was another attempt at rationalization of tasks and wages in the sisal industry. It involved a further wage increase of 30% for task workers, who composed 80% of the labor force. This increase had been demanded by the TSPWU and then submitted for arbitration after employers had refused to agree to it. Increased productivity had not been a condition of the award, but estate management was now keen to enforce the 30% production increase demanded after the 1960 wage increase. This served as an excuse for renewed union activity on the estates. On Amboni Estates there were many stoppages over the issues of increased tasks and back pay allowances, despite the fact that strikes were now illegal.

On December 12, 1962, Mkello informed the chairman of the TSGA that the union was not in a position to consider their proposals to aid the employers' organization in the enforcement of the standardization of task increases on all estates. Not only did Mkello refuse to accept the increase productivity deals, but he also wanted to abolish the system by which the cutters' tasks were measured in bundles of 30 leaves. He favored the method by which cutters would produce as much as they could, and then their tasks would be weighed and they would be paid accordingly. He addressed the workers as follows (Notice to Workers, Dec. 13, 1962):

> Oh brothers, how can you manage to fulfill this new task. Even a donkey would not tolerate this. All cutters from this date should refuse to make bundles of 30 leaves. We are willing to work for the benefit of our country, but we shall never agree to be slaves to the employers of the sisal industry.

This declaration was followed by widespread strikes in the sisal industry in December 1962.

Again Amboni experienced what they considered to be more than their fair share of strike trouble, but this time they complained to the government that more definite action be taken to curb the activities of Mkello and company. In 1963 Mkello (leader of the TSPWU and President of the TFL) and Amin (organizing Secretary of the TSPWU) were "rusticated" to a remote part of Tanganyika; they were allowed to return only when the provision of the legislation had been implemented, and when industrial unrest had been curbed on the estates. By 1963 it was also being strongly rumored in management circles that plans were under way for the reorganizing of trade unions and their integration into a government agency. By this time the contradictions in the position of government in relation to the labor force were becoming very clear. On the one hand the government saw itself obliged to increase wages and stabilize the labor force. In return for this it wanted a guarantee of industrial peace, and for wage labor to maintain an image of investment worthiness for foreign investors. The failure of labor to live up to this latter demand meant that TANU had to find means of repressing these economistic tendencies of labor. At this time the politicians did not seem too concerned about achieving this through an alliance with foreign capitalist investment.

By 1963 there was evidence that the labor stabilization policies were having a positive effect in the sisal industry. This can be seen through the improved regularity of labor attendance; it increased from 69% in 1959 to an average turnout of 93% in 1963. This stabilization policy also warranted the dismissal of many workers. In 1961-1962 Amboni reduced its labor force by 637. The union complained that this opportunity was being used to get rid of militant trade unionists by employers who now felt they had government backing to curb union activities. Mkello was back in his role by 1963, and he tried to tackle Amboni Estates over these alleged victimizations; this time Amboni managers ignored the issue and reduced the labor force by a further 25% between 1962 and 1963. Generally they succeeded in justifying their dismissals and redundancies to the Labour Commissioner as being within the demands of the new labor laws. They were also extremely cautious about the provision of the right benefits for departing workers. This made no difference to Mkello's tactics and intentions. By April the General Manager was once more reporting to the Labour Commissioner that Mkello and his branch secretaries were causing more unrest through the continuation of their old tactics of "defending the undefendable." The general situation on estates was again deteriorating after satisfactory working relations had prevailed at the beginning of the year.

With the backing of the Ministry of Labour, Amboni was able to cope with the union activities this time. The industrial unrest of 1963 did not result in a new wave of strikes as it had before. On the contrary, production increased on the estates that year from 15,250 tons to 15,600 tons, a new production record for Amboni Estates. As the General Manager commented, "The labour laws introduced at the beginning of 1963 are working very well for us in combatting union initiatives: this year the union has been unable to hamper work." There is also evidence that the relationship between the government and Amboni Estates was improving. The collaboration over labor issues led to cooperation over other issues; consultation over joint enterprises such as the Handeni Nucleus settlement scheme started at this time.[3] Amboni management felt this was an appropriate means of repaying government for its aid in the settlement of their labor problems, and a token of the commitment of private enterprise to future national development plans.

CONCLUSIONS

January 1964 saw the completion of the political rift between the government and the trade union movement. It started with Nyerere's acceptance of the Citizenship Bill which thwarted the TFL's demands for immediate Africanization in the Civil Service. The unions' strong reaction to this issue, and the alleged involvement of trade union leaders in the attempted coup of January 1964, led to the arrest of 200 to 300 trade unionists. These included Mkello and many of the so-called militants in the TSPWU whose activities have been described above. It was followed by the disbanding of the TFL in February 1964 and the establishment of NUTA. The annual report of the General Manager of Amboni Estates for 1964 speaks for itself: "We are pleased to report that since the abandoning of the TSPWU in January 1964 not much has been seen or heard of the new NUTA."

Not only was management pleasantly surprised by the passivity of the new union organization, it was also relieved at the complete lack of response from the sisal labor force to the disbanding of their union (Bienefeld, 1972:24):

> No better illustration of the isolation of the trade union leadership from their members can be found than the bald fact that the arrest of the bulk of the trade union leadership brought forth no response, not even a work to rule. Such quiescence is difficult to explain simply as a result of intimidation, since that would be rarely so effective even when it was practised on a much larger scale.

The sisal workers failed to respond to the disbandonment of their union because militant action at an organizational level had very little correlation with the actual consciousness developed among the workers through their own experiences on the estates in the 1950s. As John Iliffe (1970:119) pointed out in his description of the various fortunes of the Dar-es-Salaam dockworkers in the 1950s:

> A labor movement has its roots in work. It grows out of the nature of that work, the economic and social position of the worker, and his response to that position. To view it solely 'from the top' is to miss the dynamic that powers the movement.

The sisal workers had developed their own methods of coping with labor problems and of registering their dissatisfation with conditions before the development of trade unionism. By the 1950s they were learning to act in solidarity with each other on individual estates, but they had not yet reached that level of consciousness whereby they were ready to act as a united labor force in opposition to the employer class. The TSPWU tried to force and quicken the development of this stage of consciousness of a group of workers who were not yet committed to national class action.

The reasons for these efforts by the new union movement were manifold. Firstly, trade unionism provided a new institutional form, supported and fostered by international trade union organization, which presented opportunities for economic and social advancement in administrative posts for the more literate and ambitious members of the labor force. The actual development of trade unions was therefore a more important consideration than the significance of these forms to many of the early trade union organizers. Rather than present workers with a developed and relevant socialist theory relating to their role, the early union organizers in the sisal industry merely tried to capitalize on various manifestations of worker consciouness. They tried to utilize these activities to develop a particular institutional form of worker representation which was seen as appropriate to the development of a stable labor force by themselves and by the colonial government. This resulted in disillusionment and confusion for the workforce because the success or failure of their militancy, channeled and led by the TFL, had end results which did not relate to the strength and weakness of their own position vis-à-vis the employer class. Rather, success depended on negotiations between trade union bureaucrats, employer federations and government administrators. The workers were presented with labor triumphs or failures as accomlished facts without having any means to participate in or influence the negotiations leading to these decisions. This was bound to hinder and blur the development of further worker consciousness. The relationship between group action and end result became unclear to the sisal workers; the union would often intervene at a late stage in their disputes and settle matters in an absentee capacity. After independence, when the nationalist politicians saw that the political and economic aims of the trade union movement were incompatible with their own desire to attract foreign investment, the worker regarded the situation as a dispute in which they had no vested interest between two sectors of the establishment.

In the sisal industry the domination of the trade union leaders by the government meant an implicit alliance between the TSGA and the politicians. The employers assumed this meant government acceptance of its whole attitude toward the political and economic role of labor, an attitude compatible with the philosophy of "progressive capitalism." This labor policy entailed the acceptance by the workers of the stabilization of the labor force, productivity agreements, wage freezes when necessary (dependent on the exigencies of the world market situation), and generally a passive role by the labor force directed by an elitist and commandist management class. Although these elements are contrary to many nationalist declarations, the Tanzanian government frequently felt it necessary to accept this brand of labor policy when advised to do so by certain sectors of private enterprises.

The leaders of NUTA did initially show some resistance to certain elements of labor policy practiced in the private sector. But the constant state backing for such policies dampened NUTA's concern about these breaches of nationalist ideology, and modified NUTA's conception of its own role. The influence of state policy in this context was more powerful because it was not counterbalanced by demands from a militant rank and file with a tradition of influencing trade union policy. After the reorganization of unionism under NUTA, employers in the sisal industry still complained about the disorganized, irresponsible organization of the union. It was alleged that many of the union's administrators did not understand their roles and confused and misled workers, but this situation was evaluated as being an improvement on the old relationship which they had had with the TFL.

The level of contact between the grass roots membership of the union and its leadership continued to decline in the sisal industry. As one TSGA branch secretary wrote (memorandum to Regional Secretary of NUTA, Jan. 18, 1966):

> I understand that the sisal industry employs 90% of the total union members in the agricultural section of the Dar es Salaam region. Yet up to the 20th of December 1965 only one estate has been visited by NUTA officials for the purpose of explaining recent tasks and wages.

Neither did NUTA's attempts at negotiating wage agreements endear it any more to its sisal plantation members. After the 1964 agreement between NUTA and the TSGA, which settled wage and task increases, many sisal workers complained that it actually resulted in their being paid less per task. Many of the new work loads were impossible to perform within the new 45-hour week, and overall many workers were experiencing a drop in wages when related to labor hours involved. The Presidential Commission of 1967 found many of these workers' complaints to be valid and criticized NUTA's performance, saying that they resulted from lack of contact between NUTA and its members.

After the severe criticism of NUTA's role by the Commission, NUTA attempted to play a more positive role as a pressure group trying to influence the political aspects of the government's labor policies. NUTA tried to approach the government over the matter of sisal companies failing to fulfill investment and maintenance responsibilities on estates because of their fears of the implications of future nationalization policies. However, even on the eve of the Arusha Declaration, which specified the party's commitment to the development of a socialist state, the government ignored NUTA's request for it to prevent employers from making workers suffer redundancies and wage freezes because of their reluctance to invest in industries threatened by nationalization. The government backed private enterprise totally in its labor policy at this time by accepting the fact that police action could be invited if NUTA pursued any militant action involving strikes and so forth on the plantations. After criticizing NUTA for its failure to be concerned about workers' interests, the government allied itself with the private sector when approached by the large, well established sectors in the sisal industry. As a result, even after the Arusha Declaration, a substantial sector of the sisal industry was allowed to remain in private hands, and to develop individual work and wage conditions to suit its own ends, different from those in the nationalized sector. This did not make NUTA's task as a negotiator for the whole workforce any easier. In theory NUTA performed the function of negotiating wage agreements on a national and industrial basis in accordance with the national wages policy. Yet up to the Arusha Declaration no such policy had been envisaged. As Bienefeld (1972:4) aptly commented: "The problems of NUTA have arisen in large measure out of the fact that the organization was made to play a role which inevitably forced it into a subordinate and ultimately collaborative role with capital."

The changeover from the TFL to NUTA did not mark any positive reorientation of worker goals along lines more conducive to a regime desiring the development of socialist goals. The workers were not presented with a clearer ideological perspective of their class position in Tanzanian society. Political pronouncements following the Arusha Declaration resulted in tokenistic, transient attempt to develop concepts and institutions associated with workers' participation. When these political pronouncements served to encourage workers to revive nationalist images of worker rights (which had been developed in the preindependence period), and resulted in a spate of militant worker action in the early 1970s, the state was ready once again to intervene and curb these activities, if necessary by force.

At this state one can only hypothesize about the likely impact on the labor force of the starkly contradictory elements in the state political ideology and propaganda, and of the prevention of the development of competitive, economistically geared trade unions in Tanzania. However, it is certain that, regardless of superstructural developments at a political level, the consciousness of the sisal plantation workers in Tanzania is still being shaped by the reality of their work experiences. These experiences are still being gained on plantations managed according to the dictates of capitalist production ethics.

NOTES

1. These attitudes were hardened by the February 1, 1950 strike by the dockworkers in Dar es-Salaam. Whereas the previous dock strikes had been very disciplined and controlled, this strike degenerated into being a very violent experience for the township. This was due to the open use of black-leg labor. On February 3 there was open confrontation between the police and a crowd of 500 to 600 people. The union lost control of the strike. Officially it was never called off, but on June 2 a High Court order dissolved the union. This marked a change in the attitude of the government toward trade union development in Tanganyika: Africans were no longer regarded as being ready for such organizational forms.

2. This refers to the increase of industrial disputes in Tanzania following the promulgation of "Mwongozo" in 1971. "Mwongozo" is the Swahili word for the "Tanu Guidelines in Guarding, Consolidating and Advancing the Revolution of Tanzania and Africa." Clause 15 set down a code of behavior for Tanzanian leaders, including management. It was said to have given the workers the political legitimacy they needed to question the behavior of the management class, which also led to strikes demanding more socialist attitudes in the organizational structure and functioning of the enterprise.

3. Amboni Estates Limited, together with its associates, signed a tripartite agreement with the government and the Rural Settlement Commission to develop two 4,000 hectare sisal estates in the Handeni area. One estate, Kwaraguru, was to remain part of Amboni Estates, while eventually Kabuku was to be fully owned by settlers in a cooperative. The families brought to Kabuku were mainly from the Kilimanjaro area. They had little or no experience as far as sisal growing was concerned, but they were very good farmers. This was very much in line with the "improvement approach" to development adopted during the period of the "village settlement schemes" of 1961-1966. Its objective was to achieve a "progressive improvement on present methods of crop and animal husbandry by working on the farmer on both psychological and technical planes, to induce an increase in his productivity without any radical changes in the social or legal systems." Capital would be fed into the two adjacent plots simultaneously, and it was expected that extension of areas would also progress at the same rate. This plan did not materialie; Kwaraguru, under the protection of Amboni Estates did progress appreciably, but the failure of Kabuku to keep pace was used by Amboni to demonstrate to the government the difficulties involved in transforming the structure of the sisal industry in the direction of small peasant production.

REFERENCES

AMBONI ESTATES LTD., Tanga, Tanzania (1958-1964). Annual labour reports 1957-1964 and correspondence between V. Mkello and the Amboni General Manger.

BECKFORD, G. (1972). Persistent poverty: Underdevelopment in plantation economies of the third world. London: Oxford University Press.

BIENEFELD, M. (1972). "A general theory of trade union development: Some lessons from Tanzania." Economic Research Bureau Paper (72.3), University of Dar es Salaam.

_____ (1976). "Trade unions and peripheral capitalism: The case of Tanzania." Unpublished manuscript.

BOLTON, D. (1976). 'The role of private enterprise in the Tanzania sisal industry 1964-1975." Unpublished manuscript, Centre of West African Studies, University of Birmingham (see for further details on the Kwarguru/Kabuku settlement scheme of 1964).

Central Joint Council of the Sisal Industry (1959). "Estate consultative committees—their duties and functions: An outline guide for the use of the committees." Issued by the Joint Secretaries to the Council at Tanga.

FRIEDLAND, W. (1969). Vuta Kamba. Stanford, Calif.: Hoover Institution Press.

ILIFFE, J. (1970). "A history of the dockworkers of Dar es Salaam." Tanzania Notes and Records, 71.

JACK, J. (1959). Report on the state of industrial relations in the sisal industry. Dar es Salaam: Government Printer.

MUSOKE, K. (1974). "Tanzanian politics at the cross-roads: Reflections on industrial disputes since 1971." Unpublished M.A. dissertation, Dar es Salaam University.

NUTA (1975). "The role of the National Union of Tanganyika Workers." Dar es Salaam: Nuta Press.

TAMBILE, A. (1974). "A history of the Tanga sisal labour force 1936-1964." Unpublished M.A. dissertation, University of Dar es Salaam.

TANDAU, A. (1964). A history of the TFL from 1955-1964. Dar es Salaam: Nuta Press.

Tanganyika Sisal Growers Association (1957-1964). Memoranda issued by the TSGA from 1957-1964.

_____ (1958-1960). Correspondence between David Lead and other TSGA members gathered from labor files on individual estates in the Tanga region.

Tanganyikan Labour Department Records in the Tanzanian National Archives. File numbers: "Labour—652/10," and "Labour-Essential Services—564."

Tanganyikan Sisal Plantation Workers Union (1958-1964). Correspondence from TSPWU Head Office to the TSGA from 1958-1964 collected from estate files.

The United Republic of Tanzania (1967a). Report of the Presidential Commission on the National Union of Tanganyika Workers. Dar es Salaam: Government Printer.

_____ (1967b) Proposals of the Tanzania government on recommendations of the Presidential Commission of Inquiry into Nuta. Dar es Salaam: Government Printer.

8

STRIKES, URBAN MASS ACTION AND POLITICAL CHANGE: Tananarive 1972

GERARD ALTHABE

The subject of this chapter is the analysis of the events in 1972[1] which were decisive in the recent history of Madagascar.[2] The regime set up in 1960 by the French, who had colonized the island after a military expedition in 1895, broke down under the pressure of popular demonstrations which at times were insurrections. The fall of the regime brought about a decline in French influence which, in spite of decolonization, had continued to occupy a dominant position in economic, military and political matters. This regime was replaced by a regime controlled by nationalist officers. They consolidated their power after smashing not only the politicians of the old regime, but also the attempts at popular power which had been born out of the street demonstrations. Tananarive was the theater of these events; the decisive struggles took place in the capital. The rest of the country only played an indirect role.

After a brief description of the city, this chapter will be divided into the following three chronological parts:

(1) A school crisis, which culminated in a general strike of secondary schools and universities, that began April 24 and 25. The seeds of this movement went back to mid-January.
(2) A week of insurrection, between May 13 and 20, during which the Tsiranana government fell and General Ramanantsoa initiated his attempt to establish a new regime.
(3) The new regime was installed after confrontation with elimination of the popular elements born in the streets of Tananarive, from May 20 to October 8 when a referendum legitimatized the new regime.

At the beginning of 1972 Tananarive (Antananarivo: the village of a thousand warriors) was a city of about 366,000 inhabitants.[3] Marked profoundly by history, it was the capital of a kingdom formed in the first year of the 19th century. It numbered 50,000 people when French troops

AUTHOR'S NOTE: This chapter was translated by Simon J. Copans and Jean Copans, and edited by Alice E. Gutkind.

occupied the country. Capital of the colony and residence of the governor general, Tananarive was a permanent center of resistance to French authority. Periodic crises were ended by repression. As early as 1915-1916, the French dismantled a secret society (the V.V.S: stone, steel, section) whose members came from the medical school and the school of administration and also from the Madagascan Protestant clergy. In May 1929, massive street demonstrations demanded equal rights for both the Malagasy and French languages. There was permanent repression of journalists who claimed the freedom to write articles in Malagasy. This was tolerated after 1936. This was the atmosphere in which the theme of independence was introduced. From 1944 on Tananarive was the center of a strong nationalist movement which flooded the whole country under the initials of MDRM (Mouvement démocratique de la Rénovation Malgache—Democratic Movement of Madagascan Renovation). Once again Tananarive was the scene of numerous massive street demonstrations as well as the principal center of repression.[4] In Tananarive thousands of people were arrested, tortured and deported to the convict prison of Nosy Lava (the Long Island, of the northwest coast). After 1956, though, most of the deportees were still imprisoned. Tananarive was the center of the reconstitution of the nationalist movement with the creation in 1958 of the AKFM (Party of the Congress for the Independence of Madagascar). When elections organized by the colonial authority within the framework of its strategy of decolonization were held, AKFM militants won control of the municipal council and the provincial assembly of Imerina.

The memory of the past, of an independent kingdom, was an important stimulus for the nationalist movement. The demand to annul the annexation law of 1897 by which the French parliament destroyed the kingdom (after a brief attempt at indirect government through a protectorate), was a constant slogan during all these years. The royal rulers and dignitaries who opposed the French conquest were celebrated in plays and poems. Hundreds of books and pamphlets produced by writers recounted over and over again the history of the kingdom. In spite of repression newspapers celebrated the important dates in the history of the kingdom. The Protestent parishes were an important link between nationalist resistance and the kingdom. Protestantism was the state religion after 1869 and was especially the religion of the ruling class. After that date the parishes were one of the three components of the state apparatus (the two others being the army and the administration. They were the only element of the past retained after the French conquest. During the entire colonial period they remained places of nationalist resistance where opposition to the French took the form of continuity with the royal past. Therefore it was not surprising for the AKFM leader to be a minister in one of the temples with the most glorious historical past. In 1962 the re-opening of the Palace Temple, which had been shut for 65 years, provided the opportunity for a gathering of several tens of thousands of people who prayed fervently for the restoration of the lost nation.

Two more factors must be pointed out:

(1) Almost the entire population of Tananarive adhered to this history. Ninety percent of its inhabitants were natives of the city or its region (the Imerina). This city cannot be compared to African cities where groups of many different ethnic origins co-exist. This identity of origin, this history shared by all, explains both the massive character of the demonstrations we are going to describe and how difficult it was for the internal contradictions present in Tananarive to emerge.

(2) This created a continuity between the city and the valley region of which it is the center: the rural Imerina with its 1.5 million inhabitants. These links between townsmen and their ancestral region remain deep-rooted even after several generations. These links explain why the regime, defeated in the streets of Tananarive, was never able to find a basis for a counter offensive in the countryside.

Tsiranana and his politicians first created the PADESM (Parti des desherités de Madagascar), and then the PSD (Parti Social Democrate), both of which were always opposed to the nationalists. Their ideology combined two elements: the maintenance of French authority (the refusal of independence was one of Tsiranana's favorite themes of propaganda; it was the Gaullist government which imposed upon him this new policy), and the unification of the coastal populations against Tananarive (and regionally Imerina). The maintenance of French authority was constantly shown to be the only defense against Imerina hegemony and royal despotism.

In 1972 the French still retained control over the strategic positions within the central state apparatus (the president's offices were controlled by a hundred French technical advisors!): two to three thousand technical assistants taught in the school system (secondary schools and the university), and the French "advised" the armed forces. Between 1960 and 1965 the opposition of the AKFM was eliminated from the positions it held in the provinces, then from those held in rural Imerina. But this process (accompanied by political repression) did not touch the capital where the government tolerated the rules of political democracy. Until 1972 the municipal council was controlled by an AKFM majority; three deputies (out of five representatives for Tananarive) also represented the city in parliament.

Colonization made Imerina a favored region for the formation of subordinate Malagasy bureaucrats (hence the high density of educational institutions). This process reinforced the bureaucratic bourgeoisie centered in Tananarive which formed the social basis of nationalists hostile to the regime. The regime defined a strategy to contain the thrust of Tananarive civil servants within the state apparatus. By delaying the departure of the French, the regime wanted to find time to place within the state apparatus bureaucrats from the coastal regions. By creating numerous schools in the peripheral coastal regions, the regime wished to furnish the new bureaucratic bourgeoisie with its own means of development and permanency. The Tsiranist regime, which in 1960 existed only thanks to the protection of the colonizers, now began creating its own social basis. The maintenance of the AKFM opposition in the capital can only be understood against this background. The regime's policy was to unite around it this newly created social class; a unity based on a mutual opposition to Tananarive and the plateaux population, the memory of royal despotism and the fear of Merina domination in the new state.

How did things evolve in the capital itself? The leaders and the rank and file of the ADFM realized and accepted their impotence. The city over which they had a type of hegemony was completely isolated from the other regions of the country. The governmental party was omnipresent even in rural Imerina which had been their fief only a few years before. In the city itself the governmental party seemed firmly rooted among the civil servants and among a special category of the urban population, the descendants of slaves who had been liberated by the French troops (the Andevo or Mainty: the black). There was an effort to introduce among the plateaux population the division Merina—peoples of the coast. The slaves were portrayed as having been taken away from the coastal population by the royal expeditions of the 19th century. The regime demonstrated the isolation and the helplessness of the opposition by organizing large parades several times a year. Thousands of Imerina peasants, civil servants and city dwellers of Andevo origin marched in the main streets of the capital holding placards asserting their loyalty to the party and the president. As we shall see this establishment of the governmental party in the Imerina and among the civil servants turned out to be completely artificial. It was the mere result of administrative and police coercion over the peasants, and of bureaucratic pressure on civil servants. This artificial force fell apart during the events of May. The direction of the AKFM, the associations and unions under its control, incapable of analyzing the fragility of the government, accepted the purely ideological role assigned to them. They continued to develop an essentially nationalistic opposition focusing on the denunciation of the

French presence and carefully limited to oral or written expression. They did negotiate, however, with the government in settling strikes of clerks in commercial companies or students.

The maintenance by the AKFM of its position in the opposition in Tananarive produced two effects: (1) A very strong nationalist trend persisted in the city and was encouraged through plays, poems, historical studies and essays about traditional culture. It was conveyed by the ten daily newspapers published in Tananarive (though they were not distributed outside the city). But this nationalism retained the characteristics acquired during the anticolonial struggles. (2) Government officials were still considered as French agents and had no possibility of recuperating this nationalism.

At the beginning of 1972 the regime seemed to have overcome an important crisis. During the night of April 1, 1971, in the extreme south of the country under the direction of the militants of a party everybody thought had disappeared, the MONIMA,[5] thousands of armed peasants occupied most of the small town of the region. They dispersed the next day. The repression conducted by the police and the government militia was brutal: 2,000 dead, 5,000 prisoners, widespread use of torture, destruction of villages and harvests. At Tananarive a dozen members of the MONIMA were imprisoned. During the same period, March and April 1971, the students were on strike, but their demonstrations took place on the university campus. The students protested against the automatic application in their examinations of decrees promulgated by the French government in their examinations. Their teaching programs, as a result of the agreements for cultural cooperation, represented only a fraction of those in France. The government succeeded in weakening the movement by setting up a negotiating committee which turned out to be completely ineffective. On June 1, at the conclusion of a meeting of the government, Tsiranana's right hand man, Resampa, was arrested. This, and the outcome of an internal fight between factions of the ruling class followed by tens of other arrests, was the starting point of a vast purge of the upper spheres of the party and of the followers of the former minister of the interior and executive secretary. In September and October the discovery of a secret organization with ambiguous tendencies brought about the imprisonment of a hundred peasants from the plateaux and about ten intellectuals of Tananarive, some of whom were leaders of Catholic societies. The alliance with South Africa, initiated in 1968, was reinforced. It was celebrated insistently on the radio and in official speeches. Tsiranana explained that this alliance would permit the dissolution of apartheid as Voerster and his friends could see by the example of Madagascar that "blacks are capable of self government." An extravagant campaign built up the cult of the president as the one chosen by God and the ancestors, a campaign which reached its highest point during the period preceding his re-election to the presidency by the quasi-totality of votes on January 30, 1972, three-and-a-half months before his fall.

These events of 1971 created in Tananarive the conditions which permitted the emergence of the revolutionary crisis of 1972. The break between the regime and the population of the city was accentuated in three principal ways.

(1) Thanks to the news spread by the militants of the newspaper *Ny Andry* (The Pillar), the extent of the repression in the south was known rapidly and was described as a continuation of the repression by the French colonial authority, especially that of 1947-1948 which resulted in about 100,000 casualties. Their assimilation with the foreign masters of the past was strengthened by the form given to the repression. The bodies of the peasants were left on the ground where some were devoured by dogs. Relatives were not allowed to approach them under penalty of arrest or death, and burial was forbidden.

(2) The South African alliance, more and more manifested by the arrival of numerous commissions, the granting of mining and territorial concessions to Johannesburg companies and the establishment of a regular air link, through the notorious land of apartheid, resulted in the fear of a new foreign domination founded on the same kind of discrimination Madagascar had known for 65 years.

(3) Finally, three successive waves of arrests in Tananarive were interpreted as a breakdown of the type of agreement which had allowed the maintenance of the AKFM opposition and which had protected the population of the city from this type of repression. These arrests, though they did not concern the AKFM itself, were taken as signs preceding the liquidation of the Tananarive enclave where political control had been relatively free.

At the same time, in the face of some of these events, the AKFM leaders abandoned their verbal opposition and affirmed their support of the regime. They publicly justified the repression in the south and blocked the timid attempts toward solidarity in Tananarive. Through the student union which they controlled, they intervened to put an end to the strike on the campus and joined in the pseudo-negotiations which ended the strike. They carried out an increasing campaign to prevent any repercussions among the angry students regarding the events in the south. Following the line of the government, they attacked the peasants as being blindly manipulated by adventurers in the pay of foreigners. During 1971, the AKFM leaders were forced to reveal more and more openly their collusion with a regime that was in the process of steadily losing its legitimacy. Therefore, it was not surprising that the attacks from the newspaper *Ny Andry,* which for some weeks had been denouncing vehemently this collusion, were listened to more and more.

THE SCHOOL CRISIS

It began in a small way and nobody, in the midst of a noisy presidential election, paid attention to the strike of the 210 students of the medical school of Befelatanana (the fan palm tree)[6] that started in the second half of January 1972. This school had been founded at the beginning of the century to train Malagasy doctors in an inferior way to serve as assistants to European doctors. This discrimination was maintained at the same time as numerous Malagasy doctors were being trained in medical schools in France. With the advent of decolonization, the first three years of the French medical degree began to be taught at the University of. Tananarive, but students continued to go to France to complete their studies. Yet the Befelatanana school still trained, as in the past, doctors at the lower level. The students of this school were recruited by a competitive examination among students of the ninth grade. Each province had a fixed quota, the result of which was to reduce the number of candidates from Tananarive. The majority of the students were thus of provincial origin and belonged to the new bourgeoisie of the coastal region which was the mainstay of the regime.

At first, the demands of the movement were limited in scope and concerned such problems as living conditions, the quality of food and insufficient number of scholarships. During the following weeks, these became more and more substantial. The students demanded the right to leave this inferior medical program, which they were obliged to follow because they did not possess the baccalaureate diploma, and be allowed access to the higher level program where fully qualified doctors were trained. They condemned the unjust distribution of doctors in the country. They pointed out the contrast between the urban situation where there was one doctor for 1,618 persons and the rural situation where the ratio was one to 21,784. They protested against their obligatory assignment to under-equipped rural medical posts while the highly trained doctors could open freely offices in the cities and build up a private clientele.

The strike began to stir more and more interest in the capital. The students held meetings outside of the school in the Protestant center and tracts were widely distributed, especially in secondary schools and at the university. When the government shut down the school and expelled boarders from the coast, families in Tananarive lodged them. In spite of ethnic differences, the student struggle activated the solidarity of the lower middle class bureaucracy who were confined to subordinate positions and whose children could not pass over the obstacle of the baccalaureate. The refusal of these students to accept their inferior educational channel was deeply felt by the entire social group.

Leaders of various organizations supported the strike: the union of university professors, the association of Befelatanana-trained doctors, the students' union. They formed, with members of the association representing the students (AEMEP, association of students in medicine and pharmacology), the decision-making center of the movement. For the first time in fifteen years, the AKFM had lost its hegemony over social groups it previously controlled completely. The AKFM militants were unable to assume the leadership of the movement and they could prevent neither the radicalization of the demands nor the growing popularity of the movement in the schools and university. They could not contain the strike within such limits as would have permitted them to end it through negotiations with the government.

For a long time the government remained inactive. It gave the legal opposition a free hand because the majority of the students belonged to its social base. The government thought the AKFM would continue to perform its role as a governmental transmission belt. The government was slow to realize the implications of the new movement and only took the decision to put an end to it three months after the beginning of the strike. The government announced its repressive measures and dissolved the AEMEP on April 22, but it was too late. On Monday, April 24, the strike began in the lycées and other secondary schools of Tananarive and the next day it spread to the universities.

Tuesday, April 25, and Wednesday, April 26, were important. On the 25th, the students came out of the schools and the university where the strike had begun. They succeeded in assembling in Ambohijatovo Park (Children's Hill) and began to march on Independence Avenue. On the 26th, they formed an executive committee composed of two delegates from each striking institution. More than 30,000 students marched from Ambohijatovo to Alarobia Stadium (Wednesday Stadium) where the Minister of National Education had agreed to meet them. The acceptance of this meeting place was a serious mistake on the government's part because it gave the students the opportunity of walking for more than four miles through most of the city. The spectators were mainly parents who manifested continually their solidarity during the student procession. The students, grouped together by schools, were preceded by placards giving the name of the school. They made known on placards and streamers their demands, which fell into three categories:

(1) those denouncing the arbitrary dissolution of the association of medical students and expressing solidarity with them;

(2) those of the AKFM opposition, recognizable by vocabulary and expressions, but expressing essentially the same demands; and

(3) those slogans already expressing what was to become future dominant tendencies: the denunciation of schools as a means of producing social classes, student refusal to be puppets of decisions taken elsewhere, and a proposal to organize a National School Congress to define the future of the schools.

These demands merged into a common massive denunciation of French cultural imperialism. The demonstrators called for the suppression of the cultural cooperation agreements that had made the Malagasy school system an appendage of France, and for the departure of the French "coopérants" who controlled the schools. This denunciation of foreign domination of education was the factor which profoundly united the demonstrators.

The events that took place in the stadium were very important. The minister was accompanied by several dozen militants of the governmental party. They wore hats of various shapes indicating their different ethnic origins. Others wore traditional costumes over their European attire for the same reason. This masquerade was intended to place the event within a framework of ethnic divisions. It was a visual interpretation of the minister's speech. He violently rejected the demands formulated on the placards and ordered the students to return to school. He accused them of being a privileged group and, to intimidate them, he threatened them with the intervention of the peasants and other peoples of the coast. His speech was interrupted by shouts and derisive songs in which the youthful crowd expressed its refusal to return to its schools. A spokesman for the lycée students then had the courage to stand up, despite the presence of numerous policemen armed with automatic weapons, and tell the minister that the strike would continue, because the minister had proposed nothing new concerning the transformation of the educational system. The government suffered an irreparable defeat. The students massively entered into a true movement of rebellion.

From then on, the strikers settled down on the university campus.[7] They established a collective organization which was capable of assembling tens of thousands of young people daily for three weeks. The central committee was constituted from the permanent council, numbering 400 members (two delegated from each educational establishment). Ten members of the council were chosen to function as the strike committee. These delegates' decisions could be revoked at two levels: by the general assembly of the school (meeting at the campus, since the schools in the city had been deserted) for members of the permanant council; or by the permanent council. As a matter of fact, during the three weeks of the strike, the turnover of delegates was considerable. There was a general tendency to radicalize the movement, and a parallel tendency to eliminate those suspected of representing the legal opposition. As happens often in similar situations, specialized groups tended to assume more and more influence and to break away from the control of the elected committees. This was the case of the group responsible for maintaining order and for the "animation-propaganda" group.

A typical day could be outlined as follows: In the morning, the students of each school formed various committees to discuss the educational system and make proposals, or they met in a general assembly, also on a school basis. During this meeting, their delegates to the permanent council gave reports of their actions, received new directives, had their mandates renewed or were replaced by new delegates. In the afternoon, all the students met in the campus stadium for a large general assembly with tens of thousands of participants. Reports were made, answers were given to the news broadcasts on the radio or articles published in the newspapers, and important decisions were adopted. The permanent council assembled in the evening.

During these enormous daily meetings, the leadership assumed by delegates was revokable at any time by the rank and file and corresponded to direct democracy. The intense and permanent refusal of delegated power was the chief characteristic of this strike. There was first of all the refusal to allow the government to define the educational system. Tracts and songs expressed in a thousand ways the desire to liquidate a situation in which students were considered only as children who should obey the "father and mother" state. Secondly, there was the refusal to allow the AKFM opposition to intervene in any way whatsoever in the movement. This refusal was permanent, violent and vigilant. It was both political (these politicians were denied any decision making in educational matters and above all any right to negotiate with the government concerning them) and material (every offer of financial assistance was vigorously rejected).

The refusal of any kind of delegation resulted in the breaking up of previously existing youth organizations linked with the parties, the churches or the unions. Through massive collections in the city, the movement was able to acquire financial independence, which made it possible to pay for more than 200 full time militants. The success of these collections also demonstrated increasing adult support. The search for an autonomous means of expression (in tracts, songs, poems) in strong opposition to the newspapers, in particular, was remarkable. This creative search for autonomy completely renovated the political language. This new language became the language of the polemics and engaged with the political language of the legal opposition which had developed over the past 15 years.

Faced by these thousands of young persons ensconced within the campus, the government hoped the strike would end through weariness and the gradual weakening of morale. Although on May 4th parents came in great numbers and offered support and financial assistance, the end seemed inevitable as the movement lost its momentum. However, it was restimulated by an incident that occurred on May 3rd in a small town on the border of the southern province, Ambalavao (at the new cattle pen). When the students tried to organize a street procession, they were violently attacked by the FRS. Two students were said to have been killed. This news was unconfirmed, but the militants of "animation-propaganda" communicated the report of the deaths to the general meeting on Friday afternoon in Tananarive and proposed holding a demonstration. In the evening, the permanent council, overriding the opinion of the strike committee, accepted this proposal and set the demonstration for the next day.

The march lasted from nine in the morning to three in the afternoon. Thirty to forty thousand young people walked in absolute silence through the streets of the center of Tananarive. As a sign of mourning they carried placards draped in black with a single slogan written on an enormous streamer at the head of the procession: "WE REFUSE DESPOTISM." A student leader, utilizing a loud speaker, explained to the watching crowd that the students were mourning their comrades killed in Ambalavao and that they were protesting against their murder. The next day, Sunday, these same thousands met in the campus stadium and participated in a Christian service in memory of the victims.

The government repeatedly denied this account of the events at Ambalavao. Then, the following week, it declared that young Modeste Randrianarisoa had died of fever in the police station of Ambalavao. Doctors even confirmed this version of his death. The young man's parents were prevented from recovering his body for burial in the ancestral tomb in Imerina. He was finally buried under police supervision in Ambalavao. The news of this ban was known rapidly everywhere and stirred up much excitement. By this action the government flouted the traditional customs as it had done the previous year by abandoning bodies to the dogs after repression in the small towns of the south. The government placed itself outside the Malagasy community and was revealed as the Malagasy reflection of foreigners.

The permanent council and the strike committee became increasingly radical as they definitively eliminated all moderate elements. On May 10, a tract was widely distributed calling workers to a meeting with the students on Saturday the 13th at two o'clock in the afternoon. This distribution was accompanied by direct contacts in front of plants and offices when workers and bureaucrats left work. The call for a common meeting, and these direct contacts, were carried out not only independently of the AKFM and government unions, but in an atmosphere of controversy. The latter violently denounced the proposed meeting, but by then they had lost all their influence. A very significant change was made in the choice of the meeting place. At first it was announced that it would be held on the campus, but after heated debates the permanent council decided to hold the meeting in the center of Independence Avenue. The strikers showed their determination to go beyond the questioning of the school system. Henceforth, the regime itself was contested.

For its part, the government launched a vast offensive and demanded that students return to school and leaders be punished. During the night of May 12, the campus was surrounded by police. The FRS entered the campus and arrested the 400 members of the permanent council who were preparing for the next day's meeting. They were sent, together with a dozen adults chosen at random, to the little island of Nosy Lava, the site of the colonial convict prison, where thousands of political prisoners had been sent since the beginning of the century. The government hoped to make good use of the terror associated with this legendary prison. In fact, the opposite effect was produced.

What triggered off this type of movement? The solidarity with the medical students threatened with repression was only an occasion which helped crystallize a more profound dissatisfaction. A few days earlier, on April 9, the vice president had announced on the radio that the government was abandoning the project, in the process of preparation since the beginning of the year in the administrative services, of a national competitive entrance examination for the class of "seconde" (more or less equivalent to 10th grade in the U.S.A.) in the state schools, in particular, the lycées. This examination had appeared as a means of challenging the existing monopoly of available places in this class (a monopoly for French students and children of the favored middle class). It had raised hopes that it would institute equality[8] in what was a very selective system. By officially rejecting this project, the government demonstrated that it was conducting itself as the protector of a privileged minority. In so doing, it broke its ties with the mass of minor bureaucrats whose children were the victims of this favoritism.

This event crystallized dissatisfaction and delineated the three main features of the school movement.

(1) In Tananarive the strike began in private schools and in the ninth grade of the CEG (Collèges d'Engeignement Général). Their students carried out the first demonstrations, especially that of April 25. The lycée students were not enthusiastic about joining the movement which they had not been instrumental in launching. The internal division of the bureaucratic middle class was therefore present from the start of the school strike. In effect, from the very start, the separation between top echelon bureaucrats and the mass of subordinate civil servants was a subject of discussion. This division was present during the three weeks the strike lasted and came into the open when the school system was accused of being a source of hierarchy, but it was constantly masked and dissimulated by the common denunciation of French cultural imperialism. The building up of a foreign enemy and the permanent heightening of its presence helped avoid any open manifestation of this fundamental cleavage within the student body.

(2) The rejection by the government of a national competitive entrance examination to the lycees created the conditions for the extension of the strike into the provinces. Most of the participants were students of the "troisieme" (9th grade) in the CEGs, who would be eliminated from school after that grade and for whom it was impossible to enter a lycée. By refusing to question the monopoly of admissions to the lycées, the government was going directly counter to the interests of the social groups which supported it, i.e., the lower middle class of the coastal region which the government helped develop during the previous 12 years. The government seemed to have betrayed these social groups.[9]

(3) The protest which centered around this examination excluded rural populations from any kind of participation. The core of the movement was the secondary schools. From 1960 these schools had been closed completely to the children of peasants. Thus the school movement was narrowly confined to the towns by both its participants and its purposes. The exculsion of the rural population from secondary schools was never raised. When the school crisis became a crisis of the regime, it was still limited to the towns.

THE WEEK OF INSURRECTION

May 13

The government believed that the school movement had been broken by the deportations during the night of May 12. The Minister of the Interior broadcast a particularly threatening speech denouncing the "communist plot," and proclaiming a state of siege and banning all meetings. In reply, an increasingly dense crowd gathered on Independence Avenue.[10] On the morning of May 13, this crowd, composed of several thousand young participants, both students and nonstudents, assembled in front of the city hall which was filled with FRS. At about ten-thirty the FRS received the order to clear the square; they proceeded to execute this order through heavy use of tear gas grenades, but without any success. Then at about eleven o'clock, they fired at the demonstrators. This was the turning point. The demonstrators scattered in the face of the use of automatic weapons and took shelter. Organized in commandos, they counterattacked and snatched weapons from the FRS. This encounter ended with dead and wounded on both sides. This was the decisive moment not because the FRS fired, but because the young demonstrators not only did not yield, but they counterattacked. The crowd grew in numbers with more and more adults present.

Then around eleven-thirty, the second decisive factor entered into play: police and soldiers of the national army took up positions on Independence Avenue, but remained with their arms at the ready. They watched the clash between the commandos of the demonstrators and the FRS without intervening. The crowd rapidly pushed against the troops from all sides, urging them not to fire on Malagasy like themselves, and asking them to protect the people from the FRS who were shedding blood of Malagasy on behalf of the French. They received no reply from these highly armed soldiers. The situation remained unchanged until three o'clock in the afternoon when the police and soldiers withdrew. The FRS evacuated the city hall, but some of them were killed during this operation. The crowd, now numbering tens of thousands, remained master of the square after having held the government in check. This victory was strengthened during the evening. The proclamation of a curfew and the threat to execute any person found in the streets after seven o'clock were not enforced and demonstrators remained on the avenue until a late hour.

About four o'clock in the afternoon, a column of demonstrators left the immense crowd on Independence Avenue and tried to advance in the direction of the Ministry of the Interior to demand the neutralization of the FRS. It ran into a powerful barrage of soldiers and police and fell back toward Independence Avenue. Another column of about 5,000, mainly made up of students, succeeded in reaching the section of the ministries (Anosy—on the island). Their objective was the radio building. They wanted to explain to the provinces what had happened in the capital. Unable to penetrate the well-guarded building, they contented themselves with attacking it with stones and setting some automobiles on fire.

On the way back to Independence Avenue, they set fire to the offices of the newspaper *Le Courrier de Madagascar*.[11] Their attempt to enter the radio building provoked conflicts between employees. Some of them asserted on the air their solidarity with the demonstrators and denounced the use of firearms by the FRS. Classical and Christian choral music was broadcast. It was seven o'clock in the evening before Tsiranana's speech and the proclamation of the curfew could be broadcast.

As soon as the clashes ceased on Independence Avenue (about three o'clock in the afternoon), commandos of young people dispersed throughout the city and fought against FRS units in numerous small street battles. In the evening, these commandos set themselves up as a police force and carried out a search for the FRS who, according to them, were disguised as civilians. They searched cars, sometimes homes. Numerous motorized patrols of police and soldiers did not interfere. This situation lasted all night and the following day. Forty demonstrators lost their lives.

The reaction of the government, after its defeat in the streets, was disorganized. Saturday evening Tsiranana made an incredibly violent speech in which he affirmed that order would be maintained even if it were necessary to kill "a thousand, ten thousand, one hundred thousand persons." This speech was one of the important factors that started off the movement again. Then a number of measures were announced that were interpreted as a retreat. The Minister of National Education was replaced by a professor at the university in Tananarive. The government thought that, in view of ethnic divisions, placing at the head of the education ministry a person of the same ethnic origin as the demonstrators would defuse the crisis. They also announced the setting up of a round table with an equal number of delegates from the strikers and from government supporters to negotiate seriously educational reforms. A gift of money was offered to families of the victims of May 13. It was presented as the traditional offering made at a funeral and organized according to ancestral traditions. Finally, a promise was made to free deportees under 18. Behind the scenes, dignitaries of the Christian churches (the Catholic cardinal, the ministers who directed the Protestant synod and the Anglican bishop) were solicited to serve as intermediaries.

The Attempt to Neutralize the Popular Movement (Monday, May 15 and Tuesday, May 16)

Unions and political organizations and the Christian associations launched a call for a general strike. An enormous crowd of 100,000 assembled on Independence Avenue and slowly marched toward the presidential palace.[12] This demonstration was carefully kept under control by a special policing force. Thousands of placards and streamers attacked the French presence and the cooperation agreements on the one hand, and demanded the liberation of the young deportees on the other. The use of violence was severely criticized. Some demonstrators called for nonviolent methods. The dissolution of the FRS was demanded. At no time was the regime questioned. The demonstrators were grouped according to factories, officer, and administrative services and each group asserted its identity by means of a placard designating the place of work and sometimes the exact address. Unsalaried demonstrators were grouped by neighborhood. Students continued to be separated according to their schools. This type of group identification was maintained in the big meetings on the following days.

The crowd stopped at the square just before the palace which had been transformed into a fortress. One of the three army generals of the Madagascan army, Andriamahazo (appointed military governor of Tananarive the following day by Tsiranana) served as spokesman for the president. He stated that the president was ready to talk to the delegates. He was told that the only delegates were the deportees at Nosy Lava. Within the palace, dignitaries of the Christian churches were negotiating. They obtained the promise that the deportees would be brought back and announced the news to the crowd at one-twenty in the afternoon. The crowd returned to Independence Avenue, but refused to disperse. Tens of thousands of people remained on the avenue and declared that they would await the return of the young deportees, because they had no confidence in the government's promise. The general and the Christian dignitaries mounted a podium facing the city hall and in various speeches appealed to their listeners to be patient and explained the technical difficulties of bringing back 400 deportees by air. At eight o'clock in the evening, as proof of their good faith, the government was able to present the first group of 12 deportees.

The next day, Tuesday May 16, a crowd just as large awaited the return of the deportees. The latter, assembled between noon and six p.m. at Ivato (at the stone) airport, marched in a procession to the city hall where they were presented from the podium to the demonstrators. In absolute silence each deportee greeted the crowd by raising his right arm. The ambiguity of these events is clear when one examines the personalities who welcomed the deportees at the airport and presented them solemnly to the crowd. There were two generals, two Tsiranist ministers, high level civil servants (selected, it seems, for their ethnic origin), ecclesiastical dignitaries who had played the principal role during the two days, as well as some leaders of the AKFM opposition. In the evening a badly organized Christian service was held in the same square in memory of the victims who had been the first to fall there.

The reasoning behind these events was clear. Those who took the initiative attempted to save the regime at the same time as they tried to escape from the impasse in which they found themselves after the first bloody defeat in the streets on May 13. By organizing a demonstration for the sole purpose of freeing the deportees, they permitted the government to remain in control. Although the government was weakened, its existence was not directly questioned. For two days the peacemakers, supported by most organized groups of Tananarive (the AKFM, its associations and unions, the churches, the army officers), pursued without respite this aim. They were the only ones found on the podium, the only ones who addressed the demonstrators.

They failed. Everything was to be decided at the beginning of Monday afternoon. After having announced the government's promise to liberate the deportees, they were unable to persuade the demonstrators to disperse. A growing number of the crowd that stood for many hours on Independence Avenue denounced the conciliation operation. They designated the government as the enemy to be overthrown. They set the city hall on fire and kept the fire lit for two days. This was a spectacular way of refusing the peacemaking intervention of the legal opposition whose existence had been part of this building for 14 years. This refusal was not merely implicit—it was inscribed on streamers displayed on the blackened walls of the city hall. The failure of the conciliators and the fact that a large majority in the crowd were determined to continue its actions against the regime were in part the consequences of events external to the mass demonstration. This demonstration, centered on the long wait for the return of the deportees, shifted between Independence Avenue, the presidential palace and the airport. Elsewhere in the city, the FRS carried out numerous raids. Some of them, concealed in an alley, fired on a group returning from the nonviolent demonstration in front of the palace and killed eight persons. Another group of FRS fired at people waiting in front of a hospital to donate blood for the wounded demonstrators. Young commandos and the FRS engaged in sporadic street battles throughout the city. It was not until Tuesday afternoon that army units and police put the FRS in their camp. Finally, on Tuesday, Tsiranana broadcast another threatening speech in which, among other things, he accused the demonstrators of being beasts incited by the smoking of hemp. This physical violence of the president gave a direct lie to the peacemakers. The demonstrators easily understood that repression would follow any retreat on their part.

General Ramanantsoa Comes on Stage

On Wednesday, May 17, a new phase was reached. Contrary to the hopes of the government and the conciliators, the return of the young deportees did not stop popular mobilization. In the early hours of the morning Independence Avenue was occupied by tens of thousands demonstrators. The ruins of the city hall were still smoking. The general strike was effective. With the return of the deportees, the students recovered their leaders, because on the night of May 12 all the members of the permanent council and the strike committee had been rounded up. But during the 17th, the students lost the leadership of the popular movement because it was assumed by a new organization, the central strike committee of workers. As we have pointed out, in these vast assemblies participants remained grouped according to their place of activities. In the morning each group on Independence Avenue elected its delegates who met in the afternoon in the Protestant center of Antsahamanitra (in the perfumed field). About 500 delegates were seated in an open air theater whose tiers had been dug into the side of the hill. Three conclusions were drawn from the discussions:

(1) There was a definite break with the two preceding days. The popular movement was no longer limited to the support of students, but was oriented directly against the regime.

(2) Any negotiations with a government whose legitimacy was no longer recognized would be refused. When General Andriamahaza came to say that Tsiranana was ready to receive a delegation from the assembly, he was rebuffed with catcalls.

(3) The participation of union organizations in the strike committee was violently rejected. Some of their leaders were prevented from speaking. This was in part the application of the principle of nondelegation and especially the rejection of the AKFM opposition which had been the dominating element in the organization of the school strike.

The delegates then rejoined the crowd on Independence Avenue. They explained the conclusions adopted at their meeting and had these approved. Their mandates were confirmed or new delegates were elected to participate in the meeting scheduled for the following morning.

Thursday morning, May 18, at nine o'clock, thousands of people had invaded the school center of Ampefiloha (at the dike) situated a mile and a half from the center of Tananarive. The delegates met in a hall surrounded by a vast crowd. Access to the hall was vigorously controlled and mandates scrupulously verified. This was to avoid the infiltration of union members, some of whom had been mandated by their fellow workers. This raised once again the question of the participation of union organizations in the committees, and the beginning of the meeting was devoted to debate on this subject. A decision was taken to continue to exclude union delegates. In the course of impassioned discussions, the following decisions emerged: The regime must disappear and its destruction be symbolized by the eviction of Tsiranana from the presidency. Power should be transferred to the generals, but only for a limited period until a National Popular Congress could meet. This congress would establish a new political regime founded only on legitimate power and the generals would stand aside.

These decisions reflected the views of the crowd which surrounded the meeting hall and of the demonstrators waiting on Independence Avenue. Most of the placards and streamers demanded the departure of Tsiranana and the assumption of power by the army. The assembly designated a limited group of 30 delegates to formulate the decisions and to serve as its spokesman. Finally, it was voted to march to the presidential palace to impose these decisions. The same morning the permanent school council met at the university campus, but was unable to take any clear-cut decisions. Its leaders ended by rallying, without any discussion, in support of the line of the workers' committee.

At the beginning of the afternoon, thousands of demonstrators crowded into Independence Avenue. There the decisions taken by the workers' committee were announced and approved. The delegates rejoined their comrades and explained the meaning of the morning debates. The march on the palace had begun when, at five o'clock, General Ramanantsoa, surrounded by high-ranking officers, presented himself on the podium. Half an hour previously, Tsiranana had announced on the radio that he was naming the general prime minister and entrusting him with full powers. The delegate of the workers' committee described the positions adopted that morning and insisted upon the temporary nature of the power which the people were handing over to him. He said that the general was only its representative responsible for organizing the National Popular Congress. The general's reply was ambiguous and evasive. But what difference did that make? The enthusiasm was indescribable. The general was carried in triumph to the broadcasting center where he addressed the entire country.

The End

A very uncertain situation had arisen on Thursday evening. The enthusiasm of the crowd was based on a misunderstanding. The people shouting with joy, embracing one another and dancing in the streets were celebrating a second independence. For them, the appearance of General Ramanantsoa signified implicitly the elimination of Tsiranana and consequently the destruction of the regime installed by the French in 1900. The reality was very different. Tsiranana remained president. It was from him that Ramanantsoa had received the post of prime minister and full powers. Gradually, in the course of the evening, the demonstrators became aware of this situation, which was made clear in the declarations broadcast by both Tsiranana and Ramanantsoa.

The entrance of the general on the scene did not appear to have solved the crisis. On Friday, May 19, a crowd just as immense as that of May 18 continued to occupy Independence Avenue. The limited committee of 30 appointed by the workers' committee had determined during the night the exact terms of the conditions which were to be imposed upon the general. These were the departure of Tsiranana, the renunciation of the cooperation agreements with France, the holding of a National Popular Congress because the generals' mandates were only temporary, the guarantee of liberty of expression for all political factions, and finally, the liberation of all political prisoners.

On the same day, however, the demonstrators were concerned with another theme taken up by the radio and elaborated by the ideologists of the most diverse views, including Catholic priests and Protestant ministers. They declared that the eviction of Tsiranana would start a civil war in which the Merina population would be opposed to that of the coastal region. This fear, which they attempted to spread among the mass of demonstrators, was strengthened by uncontrollable rumors announcing that columns of armed coastal inhabitants were marching on to the capital to liberate Tsiranana and restore his power.

Despite this rapidly increasing fear, the last mass ascent to the presidential palace took place on that same square where the demonstrators had been stopped on the preceding Monday. Ramanantsoa, surrounded by a large military force, awaited the crowd. In the midst of an icy silence, he rejected the demand that Tsiranana be removed from the presidency. He insistently repeated the theme of ethnic divisions and played upon the dread of civil war. He affirmed that the only rampart against the outbreak of such a war was the maintenance of Tsiranana as president, who he called the symbol of national unity. Open conflict was avoided. The demonstrators returned to the lower section of the city without trying to penetrate the spectacular military protection which separated them from the palace.

That evening, in the barracks where staff headquarters were located, the delegates of the three committees (teachers, students and workers) met with Ramanantsoa and high-ranking army officers. The general was inflexible in his refusal to accept the eviction of Tsiranana and he rejected also the immediate renunciation of the French cooperation agreements. On the other hand, he accepted the other positions of the committees: a meeting of the National Popular Congress, freedom of political expression, the liberation of all political prisoners and the payment of wages during the strike. The terms of this agreement only reflected the failure of the demonstration that had taken place a few hours before. The balance of forces henceforth favored the new master of power, Ramanantsoa and the other generals.

The week of insurrection ended on Saturday, May 20, and the situation was basically the same as on the previous day. The city continued to be agitated by fear of civil war. A tract of unknown origin, widely distributed, threatened the Merina population with massacre if they touched Tsiranana, a native of the coastal region. Numerous rumors gave substance to this menace of terror. The radio played an essential role in this effort to smash popular mobilization. Tsiranana asserted on the air that he was remaining as president. Ramanantsoa in another broadcast threatened the "troublemakers" who wanted to continue an objectless agitation. Union leaders, speaking in relays in the studios, took revenge and appealed for a return to work. The leaders of the AKFM intervened in the same sense by distributing a text which highlighted the risk of ethnic conflict.

All these heterogeneous elements brought terrific pressure on the committee in session since the beginning of the morning (the workers' committee at Ampefilhoa, that of the students at the campus) as well as on the numerous demonstrators still occupying Independence Avenue. In great confusion, in spite of the opposition of a large minority, the agreements reached with Ramanantsoa the day before were accepted. The workers' committee, in particular, very reluctantly approved what it called "the suspension of the strike." These decisions were announced on Independence Avenue that afternoon accompanied by the jeers and protests of some of the demonstrators. The same afternoon an ecumenical Christian service in which thousands participated was held in Mahamasima.[13] Church dignitaries who had retired backstage on Tuesday evening yielded their places to the generals. Ramanantsoa, who attended the service with Tsiranana, received at it a sort of legitimization. The unanimity of the great popular mobilization had been broken up. Some demonstrators in front of the city hall hoped for a revival of the struggle. Others were at the ceremony at Mahamasina and crowded around the general. Henceforth the city was divided into two.

Despite the powerful conciliation offensive, on May 15 and 16, the dominant thrust of the events was the popular will to eliminate those who held the central state power. Their demand for elimination was limited to the actors alone, the governmental team of Tsiranana. The power of the state itself was not directly affected. The week of massive popular demonstrations ended with a mere change of actors, and not even that was complete because Ramanantsoa successfully imposed on the people the maintenance of Tsiranana as the fictive president of the republic. Those who attempted to utilize the events in order to challenge the power of the state were forced to postpone the realization of their objectives until a future and problematical National Popular Congress. The holding of this congress would depend on those very generals who restricted the popular movement within the limits we have just described.

What was the basis of this internal limit to the movement? The way in which the enemy was portrayed, the mode of existence given to him was decisive. The Tsiranist government team remained defined throughout these days of insurrection as an agent of the French, as a puppet power behind which was the power of foreigners. The Tsiranist government signed and guaranteed the execution of those cooperation agreements which were stigmatized as "agreements for establishing slavery." Thousands of streamers, slogans and speeches tirelessly demanded their renunciation. The government group thus remained the captives of their origins, and the memory of the last colonial governor general who had imposed it was still present. Nationalist feeling and the history of anticolonial struggles which permeated the city weighed heavily in producing this feeling about the adversary. These events were to a large degree part of a movement of national liberation in which the entire population of the city, all social classes united, imposed the realization of decolonization which had so far been only fictitious (the theme of the second independence appeared on May 18).

This position did not designate the government group as an adversary because of the place it occupied in the center of a system of domination and exploitation. State power in itself was protected from turmoil as long as the holders of its power were replaced in the unique struggle against foreign domination. Moreover, this orientation made it possible to maintain the unity of the demonstration. By attacking the foreigners hidden behind the government, it was possible to mask the class divisions which would have inevitably appeared if, through this same government, the state itself had been put into question. The analysis of the government as an adversary assumed that the former government was only a subordinate agent and that the French were the principal enemy. This enemy, omnipresent during all the events and attacked in a thousand ways, played an ideological role. At no time was it implicated in any form of conflict. It was noteworthy that the French embassy, situated near Independence Avenue, was not the object of a single demonstration. Yet for the demonstrators it was there the real power resided against which they had risen. Not one of the 20,000 Frenchmen living in Tananarive had been threatened. The demonstrators never attempted to transform the ideological enemy into a actual one. To understand this, one must recall the constant threat that hung over the city—the presence of 2,000 French paratroopers based about six miles from the city center and commanded by General Bigeard, legendary for his repressive action in Algeria. His presence in Tananarive seems to have been motivated by the terror-inspiring reputation attached to his name. The French made it clear that these troops would intervene only to protect property and lives of French citizens. The slightest provocation organized by followers of the regime could at any moment furnish a pretext for the entrance of the foreign paratroopers into the city. This military threat explains why the French played an ideological role in a confrontation in which demonstrators and the government, as French agents, were opposed. The outcome of the confrontation was the continuance of the French presence.

General Ramanantsoa was able to assume powers because the popular movement was contained within the limits we have just described. Moreover, this operation had been decided by the passive role which the army and police played. Ramanantsoa took over the power as supreme commander of the armed forces, but only because the armed forces did not participate in the battles in the streets of the capital.[14] Everything was decided on May 13 when the soldiers and police remained passive during the fighting between the FRS and the young demonstrators. They dissociated themselves from the FRS by their nonintervention. They seemed to reply in a positive fashion to the demonstrators who crowded about them and shouted statements such as: "Don't fire on Malagasy like yourselves. Don't resemble those FRS who are shedding Madagascan blood because they are the dogs of the French. The government composed of Malagasy has been unable to give the order to fire upon other Malagasy only because it is the slave of the French." Their passivity that day made it possible to implicate the army in the nationalist movement of unification. They were not driven back toward the government and its foreign masters. Thus the military leaders were able to present themselves as the bearers of the nationalist aspirations of the crowd.

The passivity of the soldiers and police was the result of the situation within the armed forces. The decision not to fire had been taken by the general staff itself. The generals did not wish to run the risk of being disobeyed by the troops and their decision was the only way they could maintain the unity of the army and preserve their control over it. In effect, the officer corps, especially the lower echelons composed of young officers formed in the local military academies, were strongly nationalistic. As in the case of the teachers, their principal incentive was a revolt against the rigid control exercised over the soldiers and police by the French military of the cooperation agreement. The French hierarchy occupied the most responsible positions. The real "boss" of the armed forces was a French general, head of the Presidential Defense Bureau. His name often appeared with that of Tsiranana on the accusatory posters and streamers.

One of the essential points of these events was the continuation of Tsiranana as president. Ramanantsoa won a decisive victory when he imposed this situation at the time of the May 19th demonstration, because at that time the popular movement was directed against Tsiranana himself. The retention of the former president must be analyzed from two perspectives:

(1)The situation in Tananarive. Ramanantsoa risked open conflict with the demonstrators when he imposed Tsiranana in this fictitious presidency and he was staking the legitimization of his own power by this move. By presenting himself as having been invested by Tsiranana, he refused the legitimization of his power by the popular movement, which only granted him temporary and precarious power. The only role this movement offered him was that of preparing the meeting of the National Popular Congress which could codify a state power reflecting the aspirations of the people. The movement was restricted to attacks against the government team as agents of the French, instead of the power of the state itself, and was the determining factor in Ramanantsoa's victory. The continuation of this tendency explains why the fear of a civil war with ethnic overtones was so effective on May 19 and 20 in paralyzing the final offensive against Tsiranana. Nationalism during the history of Madagascar was linked with ethnic divisions: pro-French coastal people against Merina nationalists. As long as the demonstrators continued to be caught up in this type of nationalism, their fears appeared in such guises as armed coastal inhabitants coming to liberate Tsiranana.

(2) The situation in the rest of Madagascar. The maintenance of Tsiranana as president did not concern only the Tananarive demonstrators. It was consistently broadcast on the radio which addressed the provincial population. This demonstrated the fact that the permanency of the central state authority was identified with the president and thus avoided doubts about the local state authority. The agents in each local center of power based their legitimacy on their relationship with the central power in Tananarive, which was ultimately the president. At all levels, the local centers were based on the articulation between the administration and the governmental party and on the alliance with Tsiranist bureaucrats and politicians. The elimination of Tsiranana would destroy the vital ideological base of these local centers of state authority as well as state power throughout the country. The generals, it seems, feared two dangers of differing trends:

(1) In the provincial towns where they possessed a solid social base, Tsiranist politicians and functionaries might have tried to establish local authorities opposed to those of Tananarive and continued to base their legitimacy on a Tsiranana-held prisoner. These attempts would have led to conflicts within each town.

(2) In the countryside the destruction of the central state authority, which would have followed the elimination of Tsiranana, would have resulted in violent dislocation in villages and counties. This violence would have been a reaction to oppression and coercion imposed on villagers by Tsiranist agents. The armed demonstrators of 1971 and the rural insurrection of 1948 were not forgotten. A power vacuum would have been created in the countryside which could have provided an opportunity for the Tananarive popular movement.

Thus, by keeping Tsiranana as a fictitious president, Ramanantsoa succeeded in maintaining a state power based on an administration and a party faithful to the overthrown regime throughout the country. During the following weeks the new government established its control over local and regional authorities of the state apparatus. It dispensed with Tsiranana only when its control had become effective.

DISSOLUTION OF POPULAR POWER AND THE FOUNDING OF THE RANAMANTSOA REGIME (MAY 20 -OCTOBER 10, 1972)

During the last week of May and throughout June the struggle remained the same as at the end of the week of insurrection. On the one hand, Ramanantsoa and his government were linked to Tsiranana who was powerless and confined in his presidential palace. This was the new regime's way of asserting its refusal to be captive to the popular movement. On the other hand, committees brought together workers' delegates, students and teachers and assured the direction of the mobilization during the insurrection. Thanks to the compromise reached during the negotiations of May 19 and 20, these committees gained permanent status in the prospective meeting of the National Popular Congress which the generals had accepted.

In the period after May 20, a complex organization whose core was created from the committees instituted during the school strike and the week of insurrection was set up. It maintained the division initially into three distinct groups calling themselves "seminars" (students, teachers, workers), but very soon a fourth group was added, the ZOAM[15] seminar. Each of these seminars chose a "standing committee" and the assembly of these four standing committees formed the Common Committee of Struggle (KIM). This organization, the only one qualified to enter into contact with the government, played a central role in the following weeks. The seminars met in two places: the workers and the teachers in the Ampefiloha school center and the students and ZOAM at the university campus. Every Saturday afternoon a general meeting was held in one of the two places and tens of thousands of participants assembled in May and June.

It is impossible to analyse the considerable production of these seminars and committees. In practice, the work was divided up into precise tasks. The seminars, formed into committees, had as their principal activity the preparation of the National Popular Congress (they prepared documents, elaborated proposals). The KIM, composed of about 60 members, set itself up as a center of power vis-à-vis the government, sent militants into the provinces to spread the movement there, and attempted to encircle the government in the precarious position which the committees of May 18 had tried to create.[16] The question of power was decided during these crises between the KIM and the government.

The first difference arose as a direct result of the conflict which had ended with the compromise arrived at during the negotiations of May 19 and 20. Its terms were expressed in an identical manner. The KIM asserted that Ramanantsoa had received his power from the popular movement. He was, therefore, a captive of the conditions established on May 18 and his power was subordinate to that of the KIM. Because the general asserted that his independence from the popular movement was due to the fact that he had received his power from the president of the republic, still in office, the KIM directed its offensive against Tsiranana, and against the different elements of the political system (the constitution, parliament) in an attempt to destroy the source of Ramanantsoa's legitimization. This was the political orientation around which a vast meeting was organized at the university campus as early as May 27. The opposing views of the participants prevented the organization of a demonstration in the center of the city. A large number of them refused to run the risk of a direct confrontation with the government. The defeat of May 19 was thus repeated on May 27. That same afternoon, Ramanantsoa announced the composition of his government and officially appointed his ministers by presenting them solemnly to Tsiranana, who was thus confirmed in his role as the source of legitimization. Such was the reply made to KIM. The situation remained deadlocked during the following two weeks. The big meetings of June 3 and 10 continued to reiterate the denunciation of Tsiranana and the affirmation that the KIM was the sole legitimate source of power, but tens of thousands of participants remained at Ampefiloha and the university campus. KIM showed itself incapable of imposing its claims in the streets of Tananarive.

KIM made an attempt to escape from its impasse by exploiting to the utmost an error of its adversary. The government authorized the French ambassador to organize a special session of the baccalaureate examination for the French students from the Tananarive lycees. It was to be held at the military base where 2,000 French paratroopers were stationed. An immense uproar spread throughout the city. On the afternoon of June 17 the university campus was the scene of a tremendous meeting. Placards, streamers and speeches demanded the banning of the examination. Above all, the presence of foreign military bases was widely denounced; the main objective of the crowd was the departure of the French soldiers. It was decided that on the morning of June 19, the date selected for the examinations, a meeting would be held on Independence Avenue and a march undertaken to the military base in opposition to the exams. The government was completely panic stricken and on the evening of June 17 opened negotiations with the KIM. At three o'clock in the morning, the government capitulated. The French ambassador was informed that permission for the examination had been cancelled. The next day, on June 18 at a big meeting at Ampefiloha, which was originally called to plan the march, the victory was celebrated instead and it was asserted that the struggle would continue to make the French troops leave.

Why did the organization of this examination in a French military base arouse so much excitement? Why did the KIM consider it an opportunity to give a boost to the popular movement? In this one spectacular event were linked together the two factors on which the continuation of French domination was based: education and military forces. This conjucture highlighted the presence of the principal enemy who, until then, had only performed an ideological role. The KIM attempted to give new life to the movement by directing the mobilization of the popular forces toward direct opposition to the French. The government preferred to yield rather than face KIM on this terrain. It did not desire, in any way whatsoever, to appear as the ally of the French. Otherwise it would have found itself in the same position as the overthrown government in May, with all nationalist groups lined up against it.

KIM tried to exploit its victory of June 18 in the arena of the legitimization of power. It offensive was formulated on two levels.

(1) It demanded the suppression of the celebration of the proclamation of independence on June 26 which it stigmatized as establishing the perpetuation of colonial slavery; it also demanded the suppression of the flag because it symbolized this perpetuation. It proclaimed May 18 the new date for the national holiday, as the day when the people won their real independence. This was a new approach in destroying legitimization

that the government had used in making itself independent of the popular movement. However, the denunciation of Tsiranana continued as previously.

(2) KIM also made an effort to open up a front in the countryside. On Friday, June 23, a telegram was sent throughout the country proclaiming the dismissal of minor state officials, village and county chiefs and mayors. Seminars replaced them and established popular power in the hands of prefects and sub-prefects.

The assembly on Saturday, June 24, was dominated by these two positions. A decision was taken to organize a mass meeting on Independence Day in opposition to the ceremony the government was preparing at Mahamasina. The government's response was rapid and violent. A state of siege was proclaimed, soldiers and police patrolled the city and on the radio Ramanantsoa employed threatening language:

At the present time a minority of agitators are going to exploit the spirit and struggle of the people to further their own personal ambition. Their objective is simple—they wish to seize power and to install a regime which will suppress dialogue and liberty.

Nonetheless, on Sunday negotiations were held between KIM and the government, and a compromise was reached which marked the defeat of KIM. On Sunday afternoon the general assembly had no choice but to accept it. On the morning of June 26 the Independence Day commemoration took place at Mahamasina. The military parade was presided over by both Tsiranana and Ramanantsoa. At the same time, KIM held a meeting at Ampefiloha and the themes developed over the previous month were debated, but the participants were confined to the perimeter of the school center. The streets were closed off to them by soldiers and police. The government was clearly the winner of the conflict.

The events of June 24–26 were decisive. The government had successfully solved the problem of dual power in the capital. In July the big weekly meetings of KIM were less regular and less well attended. The final reaction by KIM took place at the end of the month when leaders of the Tsiranist party announced their intention of holding a congress at Tamatave at the beginning of August for the purpose of rebuilding their party. On July 26 KIM announced that it would oppose by every possible means this resurrection of the PSD, and on July 29 succeeded in assembling several thousand demonstrators at the university campus. Tsiranana was again vigorously attacked and a decision was taken to denounce, by a street demonstration, the holding of the PSD congress. In order not to appear too openly as the protector of the politicians of the old regime, the government immediately backed this move and prohibited the congress. Once the situation of dual power had disappeared, the seminars and committees devoted themselves exclusively to the preparation of the debates for the future National Popular Congress. A new draft for a constitution was drawn up, the new organization of the state was worked out, and relations with the former metropole were redefined. At the end of July, an organization was established, comprised of delegates from all the sub-prefectures, that was responsible for organizing the meetings of the National Congress scheduled for the beginning of September. The KIM of Tananarive had only a theoretical existence.

The epilogue of these events took place in September. The date of the opening of the congress was set for September 4. Ten thousand provincial delegates had already arrived in Tananarive when a state of siege was proclaimed on August 29, justified, according to the authorities, by the risk of disorders. The city was again controlled by soldiers and police. The next day Ramanantsoa solemnly announced that a new constitution would be proposed to the people in the form of a referendum and the date was fixed for October 8. The referendum, brutally announced in this atmosphere, must be understood as an act of opposition to the National Popular Congress due to open on September 4. The congress was thus denied any possibility of setting itself up as a center of power in opposition to the government. The legitimization of power was not to be centered in the congress, but in the referendum of October 8. The government merely drew these conclusions from its June victory and the referendum consolidated its independence vis-à-vis the popular movement.

The National Popular Congress met from September 4 to September 19. Its opening and closing sessions were marked by large meetings, but it ended without having accomplished any significant results. Its participants reduced it to a simple series of meetings where recommendations were drawn up to be presented to the government who would do whatever it pleased with them. At no time did the occasion bring forth a revival of the popular movement.

Outside the popular movement, the Catholic and AKFM ideologists launched a violent campaign denouncing any political significance of the congress. Almost unanimously, the newspapers reduced the congress to a forum without any power. Moreover, while the congress pursued its discussions, the campaign for the referendum became more and more active and began to set up the oposition between Ramanantsoa and Tsiranana. The latter broadcasted vehement appeals for a negative vote. During the second part of September, the entire political scene was occupied by this false duel. (On September 30th Ramanantsoa brought together 50,000 people at Mahamasina.) The National Popular Congress ended in general indifference.

The congress was dominated by the defeat of the Tananarive committees (that of the workers and especially the ZOAM committee), which attempted in vain to rekindle the flame. They ran into the hostility of the provincial delegates who submerged them by their numbers; most were unconditional allies of the government. Focusing on the referendum campaign, and on the opposition between Ramanantsoa and Tsiranana strengthened the provincial delegates in their position. They had been chosen on the basis of their hostility to the old regime and took part in the struggle which seemed to be going on outside of the congress.

After its victory on October 8, legitimatized and separated from the preceding regime, the government completed the destruction of the popular movement in the domain where everything had begun—education. The National Popular Congress had succeeded in taking only one clear decision: the refusal to let the schools reopen before a serious reform of the school system was undertaken. In the midst of the favorable atmosphere created by the newspapers, the government announced on October 13 that the schools would reopen on October 23. When a meeting was held on October 21 to attempt to plan a way to oppose reopening, it became clear that the groups which had made up the framework of the popular movement had disappeared. Only a handful of students, and practically no workers, attended. Only the ZOAM participated in large numbers, thus revealing that it was the only remaining organized force. The reopening took place with the schools spectacularly protected by soldiers and police in battle dress. The ZOAM alone demonstrated in front of the principal lycées. Some of them managed to install themselves in the classrooms of one of the finest lycées, thus asserting their right to an education. These were the last manifestations of the popular movement.

These events, of which the capital was the theater, were only part of the total picture. The situation in the rest of the country played an essential role in the failure of KIM and in the dissolution of the popular movement. As soon as it had been formed at the end of May, KIM sent numerous militants into the provinces to set organizations similar to those in Tananarive. In a few days each chief town of a sub-prefecture actually had its own KIM. In July when the KIM in Tananarive was only a shadow of its former self, the *Ny Andry* group and the ZOAM committees sent a new wave of militants to the provinces with objectives much more radical than those of the preceding wave; but at no time did they succeed in finding in the provinces support for their opposition to Ramanantsoa.

The Provincial Towns

The struggle against the Tsiranist regime in Tananarive was followed by varying reactions in provincial towns. The school strike was widespread; significant street demonstrations took place. At Majunga on May 13 physical violence between police and demonstrators resulted in eight deaths. The Ramanantsoa regime gave a free hand to the politicians of the old regime who withdrew to the provincial towns where they had strong roots. By maintaining Tsiranana as president, the government left these politicians an ideological base for their power and they conserved their positions as mayors or deputies. In each of these towns KIM set itself up in opposition to them. The militants sent from Tananarive spent all their efforts in polemics with these politicians of the past. The administration appeared to dissociate itself from this struggle. The KIM was established and the seminars met under its protection. The prefects often presided over the opening sessions. At no time was the power of the administration contested and in no provincial town did the question of dual power arise with the KIM as it had in Tananarive. In general, the leaders of these provincial KIMs saw the government as their sole protector against the politicians of the old regime who had more or less reconstructed their local power. This explains why the provincial delegates to the National Congress adopted a position that was unanimously favorable to the government—a position which smashed the efforts of the militants of Tananarive.

The Countryside

The mass of the peasants remained outside of the movement. This was the principal weakness of the movement. We have already pointed out that the rural population was excluded from the schooling crisis which concerned secondary education and was therefore an urban problem. Protests against the regime during the week of insurrection were weakened by this situation. During the following weeks, events in Tananarive had reprecussions only in those rural regions where actions by the state technical organizations were particularly intensive. In the development societies, the peasants, under the strict orders of technicians, had been reduced to the condition of unskilled laborers without a regular salary. In the rice growing regions of the plateaux, which for several years had been placed under the careful control of technicians who imposed new production methods, the peasants had been forced into increasing indebtedness to the state bank. In both cases, peasant committees were created which attacked the technical intervention of the state and demanded the return to the previously existing situation. Paradoxically, the peasants who engaged in these actions remained under the thumb of the minor officials from those very same technical organizations they were attacking. They were led by the very people responsible for applying the new techniques against which they were revolting. These committees disappeared during the September referendum campaign. The participation in the National Popular Congress by peasants was nil. The hastily selected delegates from the country were not representative and remained under the control of minor agricultural technicians who treated rural problems in their name.

The government ensured that the peasants remained outside of the urban turmoil through a particularly clever maneuver. By retaining Tsiranana as president, it avoided the violent and immediate destruction of authority exercised by the state over the villages. On June 26, Ramanantsoa solemnly announced the supression of the personal income tax which, under the Tsiranana regime followed the tradition of the colonial authority, was the principal instrument by which the despotic state power had victimized peasants. On the one hand, the government kept in place the custodians of the authority of the state and avoided a power vacuum. On the other hand, it removed from these same custodians their principal means of exercising their domination. In so doing, the government took away from the militants of the capital the support which would have enabled them to mobilize the peasants against the state authority.

Let us attempt to explain the internal development of the governmental position at Tananarive. The former legal opposition immediately joined with the government. The AKFM reaffirmed its existence in the course of a congress held at Tananarive on June 19-22, and reconstituted its organization despite the attacks of KIM and the seminars. Its satellite associations and its numerous newspapers were placed at the service of the new regime. The Catholic newspapers adopted a similar line of conduct. The quasi-totality of the media in the capital, including the radio, were thus under the control of the government. KIM had at its disposal only two newspapers, but it also had very large quantities of tracts produced by the seminars. During the entire period, the line developed by the government partisans did not vary. They denounced KIM's and also the National Popular Congress's claim that any power whatsoever should be devolved on them and presented the Ramanantsoa government as the sole repository of power. They justified this double line (attacks on the popular organizations and the unconditional rallying to the new regime) by making use of their two "enemies," the PSD politicians and the French, to whose omnipresent intervention they pointed. The collusion of these two was exemplified by a thousand plots aimed at the restoration of the old regime. Ramanantsoa and his government were described as the only rampart against the return of the past and against the reestablishment of the Tsiranists and the French in their previous dominant position.

At the beginning, the actions of the government contradicted the line elaborated by its followers in the capital. As a matter of fact, throughout its combat with the KIM in Tananarive, it built up its legitimacy by the maintenance of Tsiranana as president. To avoid repetition in the provinces of the conditions of struggle in Tananarive, the PSD provincial politicians were granted freedom of action, and the government protected them from any possible repression. It was only when the KIM in the capital had been crushed that the government was able to detach itself gradually from the old regime. Then it moved away from the PSD politicians by protecting the provincial KIM's from their hostile acts, and it even prohibited the congress they were preparing to hold at the beginning of August. Tsiranana, who had shown himself regularly in public in June, completely disappeared. At the end of August Ramanantsoa made his first tour of the provinces during which he conducted himself and was received like the head of state. Independence from the former metropole was marked by a series of minor but significant acts. The expulsion of the five principal technical advisors of Tsiranana was highly publicized. No official representative attended the reception given by the French ambassador on July 14. A policy of alliance with the African Liberation Forces was announced. Thus, progressively, government action became unified with the line expressed by its partisans in Tananarive. This line became increasingly effective in rallying the different social classes of the capital to the regime. Finally, the following situation emerged during the referendum campaign. The government turned against the politicians of the old regime. Ramanantsoa transformed Tsiranana into an adversary and made the referendum a choice between himself and the former president, between the new and the old. In this situation, the AKFM was strengthened and took over the referendum campaign in Tananarive and Imerina. Henceforth the regime and its followers appeared as the leaders of the struggle against foreign domination and its local agents, the politicians of the old regime.

CONCLUSION

We are going to attempt to present concisely the political force which, during the first phase of these events, radicalized the movement (the school strike, the first days of the week of insurrection) and then tried in vain to oppose the establishment of the regime headed by General Ramanantsoa. Until October 8 this force was the principal adversary of the new government, and the strategy of the government was directed against it. It was practically the sole target of the attacks by the 20 to 30 AKFM, Catholic and Protestant newspapers.

A relatively limited group of about 30 militants formed the center around which this political force, whose composition varied, was concentrated. From 1969-1970, these militants had been united with the weekly newpaper *Ny Andry*. One of the themes they had elaborated was the denunciation of the alliance between the Tsiranist regime and the legal opposition. This denunciation was more and more widely approved after the support given by the AKFM leadership to the repression of the peasant demonstrations in April 1971. In Tananarive they spread and diffused the news about the repression. These militants were present at every important event in 1972. During the school strike they directed the "animation-propaganda" group which, through the use of leaflets, played a determining role in the orientation of the movement. The spread of this movement beyond the schooling problem was largely due to their action. They were responsible for the May 6 demonstration, and they were the ónes who utilized the murder of Ambalavao to instill new life into a movement that seemed doomed to fall apart. During the week of insurrection, on May 17 and 18, they proposed the formation of a workers' strike committee to take the place of the students in the leadership of the popular movement. They played an important part in this respect and it was a militant of this group (Manandafy) who, on the afternoon of May 18, acted as the committees' spokesman before Ramanantsoa on the podium on Independence Avenue. After May 18, during the fading away of the unanimity which had characterized the prededing period, they gathered about them those forces which, through the KIM in particular, tried in vain to oppose the establishment of new regime.

The Political Line

In the struggle against the Tsiranist regime, this militant group developed a strategy based on a type of direct democracy. Because the government and the legal opposition made the emergence of responsible delegates impossible, any negotiation was out of the question. It was through this mechanism of direct democracy that the radicalization of the school movement was encouraged. The same process as applied in establishing the workers' committee.

Ramanantsoa's accession to power on May 18 created a new situation. Nonetheless the same line was maintained. KIM was named as the sole legitimate source of power and all its hopes were placed in the meeting of the National Popular Congress. In this way, they exercised pressure in the realization of the objectives which had been expressed during the struggle against the Tsiranist regime. In their opposition to the Ramanantsoa government, these militants lost the initiative. By retrieving the nationalist aspirations which had dominated the May days, Rananantsoa and his new regime succeeded in taking the place of the old regime without the power of the state being questioned.

In the face of this reinforcement of the government's position, the militants of *Ny Andry* adopted a defensive policy. They denounced the continuity of state power; above all they stigmatized the hierarchies it created and the society based on rank it produced. They presented this society as perpetuating the caste system of the past. They called for the destruction of hierarchies and for the establishment of equality for everyone. They designated as their objective the setting up of "the state of little people" (fanjakan'ny madinika) in the form of a National Popular Congress which would realize their dream of direct democracy. This utopian construction was to be produced by the simple inversion of the hierarchical society and despotic power they were attacking. Equality for everyone was to reign in "the state of little people"; no one was to have authority over anyone else.

The Political Force Crystallized Around this Political Line

In the course of the struggle against the Tsiranist regime, this line unified the majority of students and teachers during the first days of the week of insurrection, most of the workers and almost all minor civil servants. However, in the struggle against the Ramanantsoa government, they could only bring together a fraction of these social classes. As the new masters of power moved toward a rupture with the old regime, this fraction dwindled away and disappeared in September and October. On the other hand, during the same period the *Ny Andry* militants assembled around a ZOAM movement. This movement grew in strength and constituted an autonomous force which, in October at the time of the attempt to prevent the reopening of the schools, appeared as the only remaining organized popular force.

It is essential to answer the following question: Why was this strategy, based on the practice of direct democracy, with its tremendous debating assemblies, its refusal to delegate power, its rejection of would-be spokemen for the demonstrators, so effective when the adversary was the Tsiranists, and why did it fail so badly against Ramanantsoa and his government? In approving this strategy, the demonstrators were following Fokonolona, a term which had considerable significance. Fokonolona designated the type of relationship which was said to have existed in some indeterminate past period between the inhabitants of the first village communities. In these communities, it was believed, democratic power exercised by everyone gathered together and the strictest equality was maintained among all the inhabitants. This myth was kept alive during the colonial period. It was treated in hundreds of pamphlets and referred to, obligatorily, in every nationalist speech. This essential element of cultural resistance to foreigners was in reality a way of establishing the inversion of a colonial society founded on French rule, a colonial society founded on racially structured hierarchies and minorities with unconstructed power. In Fokonolona, the Malagasy, in opposition to Europeans, define their distinction, their identity. All these manifestations of direct democracy, this dream of a better future, whose apotheosis would be crystallized in the National Popular Congress, were factors around which nationalist unification and a national identity were to be brought into being.

As long as the Tsiranist regime was designated as the agent of a foreign power and the struggle was defined in the same terms as during the colonial period, direct democracy was a powerful means of mobilization and incorporated the nationalist aspirations of all. However, direct democracy progressively lost its effectiveness and was rejected as a survivor from the past when Ramanantsoa and his government, by separating themselves from the former regime and manifesting their independence from the former colonial power, could no longer be described in those terms as they became the bearers of nationalism.

ZOAM

The ZOAM were present during all these events. They appeared timidly at first during the school demonstrations and participated, in a subordinate position, in the group responsible for keeping order. On May 13 and 15, ZOAM members became the principal players in direct opposition to the FRS and for several hours constituted themselves as a sort of control force which strictly watched over their neighborhoods. During the final days of May, the militants of *Ny Andry* by means of violent polemics, imposed them as the fourth component of KIM. The ZOAM rapidly strengthened their organization in the popular neighborhoods and set up headquarters in the social center of the principal popular section of Tananarive. The *Ny Andry* newspaper was placed at their disposal and became the organ in which the ZOAM expressed themselves. This organization became consolidated and membership increased at the same time as the KIM, defeated in its encounter with the government, grew weaker. In July, the ZOAM center sent numerous militants to the provincial towns to organize the young unemployed along lines similar to those in the Tananarive ZOAM. All these attempts at intervention in rural districts failed. The ZOAM soon became the principal, if not the sole, supporters of the former line.

In August the ZOAM were the target of an offensive launched by the entire press of Tananarive. They were systematically accused of being delinquent and criminal. After the ransacking of two or three luxury stores in the city center, the ZOAM asserted that these acts were in reply to the behavior of the foreign owners toward their employees. The newpapers attacked these actions as mere robbery and called for the punishment of those guilty. In fact, a certain number of young people received severe prison sentences. The ZOAM were presented as proponents of violence, empty of any political significance. The Rotaka (untranslatable) and every street demonstration was attributed to the ZOAM. They were accused of being manipulated by either the politicians of the old regime or by *Ny Andry* militants. The proclamation of a state of siege was directed against them on August 29. This anti-ZOAM campaign did not diminish in intensity during the entire period we have studied. It was a matter of isolating them as delinquents and destroying any claim they had of playing a political role.

The fact that at the end of this period the ZOAM constitued the only remaining political force holding to the political line we have examined, shows to what extent this line had been blocked. In the city ZOAM militants were a marginal group. They were young and they had very early been eliminated from the schools and excluded from the salaried bureaucracy. In this urban universe, characterized by highly differentiated hierarchical levels, they occupied the lowest level. Their passionate adhesion to an equalitarian utopia and the "state of little people" celebrated through songs and poems were exalted in meeting of 500 to 600 participants held in ZOAM headquarters in the cultural center, and reflected the place that had been assigned to them in the city. Finding themselves at the lowest level of the hierarchical ladder, they adopted all the more intensely the utopia which rejected this social scale.

NOTES

1. For further information on the events in Madagascar in 1947 and 1972, the two following books have been recommended by Jean Copans: R. Archer, *Madagascar depuis 1972: la marche d'une révolution,* L'Harmattan, 1977, and J. Tronchon, *L'insurrection malgache de 1947,* F, Maspéro, 1974.

2. At the beginning of 1972 the total population of the country was around 7.9 million (5.2 million in 1966). More than half the population was under 20 years of age. Included in this figure were 100,000 foreigners; among them were 31,000 French, of whom 20,000 lived in Tananarive.

3. Tananarive was the capital of a very centralized state (in the French tradition). The division into regions introduced by the colonial authority at the end of the 19th century made Imerina and Tananarive the centers where minor agents of the colonial and commercial administration were trained. The coastal regions specialized in agricultural

production for export. Tananarive was a city dominated by bureaucrats; out of 70,000 people, two-thirds were employed by the state. The only university in Madagascar with more than 5,000 students was also in Tananarive. Students and bureaucrats were the major participants in the events we are going to describe. No factories were located in Tananarive; they were dispersed throughout distant provincial towns. The approximately 10,000 workers employed in small plants played no autonomous role. They were under the influence of the bureaucrats.

4. During the night of March 29,1947, administrative offices and military camps were attacked by large armed groups. It was the beginning of a peasant insurrection which affected all the eastern and central regions of the island. More than one and a half million peasants took part in these events. Although no links were discerned between this insurrectional movement and the nationalist movement of the MDRM, the colonial authority immediately considered the two as amalgamated and smashed the nationalist movement by means of thousands of arrests.

5. MONIMA (Madagascar held in the arms of the Malagasy) was a nationalist party created in 1958 which had only a regional influence in the southern provinces. This party remained outside of the regrouping which had become the AKFM. After 1960 it was able to avoid being eliminated thanks to its solid roots in the village. It was essentially a peasant movement.

6. This school had been the center of the secret society, the VVS, dismantled in 1915-1916, and considered the origin of the nationalist movement. The most important leaders had been, moreover, doctors trained in this school. The glorious past of this school strengthened the repercussions the strike was going to have in the city.

7. The university campus, called the Charles de Gaulle campus, was finished in 1960. It is at the periphery of the city, about three miles from the center. The barracks of the FRS (Republican Security Forces—2,000 men who were the praetorian guard of the regime) were located at the entrance of the throughway which is the only access to the campus.

8. This equality was an illusion, because the teaching was in French and given by French teachers. The children of the most highly frenchified families would naturally eliminate the others.

9. One may ask why the Tsiranist government until the very last insisted on identifying the school system with that of the former colonial power. These politicians were victims of their own cultural colonization. They adhered to the hierarchy of two cultures, two languages. Tsiranana and his ministers made repeated declarations of this nature. If they adapted the school system to Madagascar's needs, they were afaid they would create a second-rate ruling class in the coastal region, inferior to the Tananarive middle class. On the other hand, they feared that this change to a Madagascar-inspired system would give the Tananarive middle class the possibility of controlling the school system. The written and codified language was that spoken in Imerina and the majority of teachers came from Tananarive.

10. Independence Avenue is the center of Tananarive. It is nearly a mile long and begins at Ambohijatovo Park (Children's Park), which is on a slight rise. The avenue passes through the square where, until 1967, a monumental equestrian statue stood of General Gallieni, founder of the colony. The French embassy had the statue removed in spite of Tsiranana's protests. The avenue then descends toward the immense square of Zoma (Friday) Market and finally ends at the station building at a statue of Jeanne d'Arc placed there in 1948. The demonstrators did not knock down the statue but transformed it into a Malagasy and ridiculed it by dressing it up in a hat and robe similar to those worn by the Imerina peasants with a celluloid doll placed in its arms. The city hall is located on one side of the avenue toward the middle. This avenue was the setting of the big demonstrations of 1945-1947. It was there that the French troops marched on their way to suppress the insurrection in the east. It was there too that the Tsiranist regime organized its big parades—those of the army and especially those of its party, the PSD.

11. *Le Courrier de Madagascar,* a French language daily entirely controlled by Frenchmen, was founded in 1962. It was the mouthpiece of both government and the French embassy.

12. The main hill of Tananarive, the sacred site of the founding of the city, is surmounted by two palaces: the Queen's palace transformed into a museum of history of the monarchy, and the palace of the prime minister which contains the services of the presidency of the republic. These two palaces were concrete symbols of the political system set up in 1863 after a coup d'etat. The prime minister held the real power and was the husband of the queen who was reduced to playing an ideological role. The colonial authority utilized the palace of the prime minister for the important trials (1916 and 1948) whose purpose was the repression of the nationalist movement.

13. Mahamasina (that which renders sacred) is a stadium built on the plain at the foot of the hill of the queen's palace. During the last decades of the 19th century, the royal army organized its parades here. The sovereign took her oath there on a sacred stone during the enthroning. The choice of this place for a Christian service centered around Ramanantsoa was not accidental.

14. The army numbered 7,000 men and the police about 4,000. The approximately 2,000 FRS were trained by the French and Israelis.

15. The term ZOAM was used by the young unemployed (most of whom had had some schooling) who organized into groups in the popular neighborhoods. They lived outside the law (by robbery) and existed in a permanent state of guerrilla warfare with the police. They referred to themselves with the initials ZWAM (Zatovo—young, Western, Andevo—slave, Malagasy). The term Western underlined the importance they attached to Western films where they often found their inspiration for the internal organization of their bands. They penetrated school demonstrations and were the heroes of the conflicts of May 13 and 15. They marked their accession to the political struggle by changing their name to ZOAM (Zatovo Ory Asa eto Madagasikara—the young unemployed of Madagascar), thus defining themselves quite simply as the unemployed. They maintained their organization on the basis of neighborhoods in the seminar.

16. This duality of power was illustrated in the type of rites which followed the liberation of three waves of political prisoners. They went to thank Ramanantsoa in his palace office, and then presented themselves at the Ampefiloha School Center and the university campus to express their thanks for their liberation. Moreover, negotiations between the KIM and the government were followed by written communiques signed by both parties and read over the radio.

9

THE STATE, MINEWORKERS AND MULTINATIONALS:
The Selebi Phikwe Strike, Botswana, 1975

DAVID COOPER
University of Birmingham

THE STRIKE EVENT

In 1959, seven years before Botswana's independence, the Chief of the Bamangwato Tribal Territory negotiated a concession agreement with the Rhodesian (now "Roan") Selection Trust to prospect for minerals in that area. From the early stages of the development of the Zambian copperbelt, RST and the Anglo American Corporation have been the major controllers of copper production there. In Botswana, by 1967, the copper and nickel deposits at the two adjacent cattle posts of Selebi and Phikwe seemed the most promising of numerous other mineral finds.

In 1971 construction began and the mine came on stream in 1974. The initial estimated capital costs in 1970 were P107 million for the *private* mine complex and P53 million for the *government* controlled infrastructure.[1] By 1972 production was being undertaken by the locally incorporated company, Bamangwato Concessions Limited (BCL). The latter's share capital is owned 85% by Botswana RST Limited (BRST), with the remaining 15% being the Botswana government's free shareholding, as provided for in the original 1959 concession agreement (Master Agreement, 1972:1). BRST is itself owned: (a) 30% by American Metal Climax (Amax), which has held the major shareholding in RST in Zambia ever since the 1930s, and is today listed as one of the nine largest U.S.A. multinationals engaged in nonpetroleum mineral extraction (Sklar, 1975:47-52); (b) 30% by the Anglo American Corporation/Charter Consolidated Group based in South Africa and London, which also controls De Beers (Botswana) which has undertaken extremely profitable diamond mining in Orapa in the 1970s; and (c) 40% by small shareholders, mostly in the U.S.A.[2]

Besides the actual private mining complex, the general infrastructure, financed by the Botswana government by means of foreign loans (see below), included: (a) new road, rail and water supply networks; (b) a power station adjacent to the mine, which burns coal from the Morupule mine in Botswana, specifically developed by an Anglo American Corporation subsidiary for this project; and (c) township and supportive municipal services. The town was designed for an initially estimated population of 12,000 in the township and adjacent site and service areas. By 1975 the township had a population of around 11,000. However, people had also spontaneously formed a village-style residence in Botshabelo ("a place of refuge") near the mine site, and this population had swollen to over 8,000 (Botswana Central Statistics Office, 1976a: preface).

On July 29, 1975, Botswana experienced the most serious strike in its labor history.[3] Discontent, which focused on the annual wage increments expected at the end of that month (July), culminated in the adjournment of negotiations between a delegation of mine workers and BCL management on the afternoon of the 28th. Early the next morning when the day shift was to take over, some of the workers closed the main gates of the mine. Others entered the mine to request workers there to join the strike. At the same time they evicted expatriate staff from the smelter plant and other sectors and caused minor damage to some buildings by breaking windows. Outside the mine, many groups of workers went into the township and Botshabelo to notify others of the strike. Some groups, carrying sticks, also attempted to round up all the BCL marked cars, used by many of the expatriate staff, and to drive them to be left just outside the mine gates. In the process some cars were damaged and a number of unpopular expatriates assaulted. Some of the doctors and nurses were evicted from the BCL clinic and an Alsation dog was used to prevent strikers breaking into the BCL financed primary school.

A unit of the paramilitary Police Mobile Unit arrived from Francistown. At noon the vice president arrived from Gaborone, with two other ministers, and attempted to address a crowd of over 2,000 assembled at the gates. When he almost immediately raised the issue of the smelter—that if technicians had not managed to shut it down, operation of the mine could have been halted for over a year—frustrated workers shouted him down with comments like "you are talking about the smelter when we want our money" (Botswana Daily News, 1975b). The chairman of the Mine Workers Union was also shouted down and the PMU moved in and dispersed the crowd with teargas.

PMU reinforcements were airlifted into the area, which came under heavy police security for some days. On July 30, most of the expatriate workers resumed maintenance work, while all the 2,800 Batswana workers in BCL were selectively reinstated on the basis of lists drawn up by the various (expatriate) heads of the department; 622 lost their jobs. One hundred and eighty people were detained by the police and later released on bail. Eventually, two months after the strike, 60 male and 2 female former BCL workers went on trial, "charged alternatively with rioting, intimidation and malicious damage to property." In December, 34 were convicted and received jail sentences from 3 to 12 months (Botswana Daily News, 1975b).

In President Khama's broadcast to the nation the day after the strike he stated that "the Company is not obliged to reemploy any of the workers" (Botswana Daily News, 1975a). Much of the ensuing debate during the following 12 months focused on this local issue. The President, himself, when he came to address workers in Phikwe in December after the trial had ended, stated he had never intended to give the Company an excuse "economic or otherwise . . . to weed out the people they did not like prior to the disturbances" (Speech, December 19, 1975:5). Although the opposition political parties called for a commission of inquiry, the government adopted an approach of informal discussions which eventually led to half of those originally sacked being reinstated.[4] By the time of the annual Botswana Mine Workers Union Conference at the end of 1976 in Phikwe, the atmosphere was one of letting matters rest.

METHOD OF ANALYSIS

In analyzing the strike, it is easy to become sidetracked into immediate issues and details, e.g., wage disputes. Yet what is really important in terms of labor history in Africa is the context of this strike, rather than the strike itself. This contextual analysis seeks to locate the underlying causes of the strike in terms of the structural transformations and distortions taking place in the Botswana social formation. One important historical element to be considered is Botswana's "Protectorate" status during British rule between 1885 and 1966, and its emergence as a labor reserve for South African capital. Another element is the penetration of U.S.A., Western European and South African-based capital since independence, which itself is linked to the movement of workers to Botswana's towns. For instance, in 1963 the new capital was constructed at Gaborone, colonial headquarters moving from Mafeking (20 miles south of the border, in South Africa!). By 1976 Gaborone's population was 37,000. Francistown, the old northeastern center, had more than doubled its population since 1964, and had Lobatse, center of the beef export industry. Including Selebi, Phikwe and Orapa, this "urban population," as the 1971 Census defines it, had grown from around 20,000 to 100,000 in 1976, i.e., 15% of the total Botswana population (Society and Economy Tables, 1976:272).

Moreover, the Phikwe strike was in certain respects similar to other earlier strikes in Botswana. The first trade union in Botswana was formed in 1949 in Francistown, and represented workers in the retail trade sector. By 1975 there were eight registered unions, all based in the different employment sectors existing in these five towns.[5] In the 1970s some of these unions were involved in a series of strikes, particularly over issues of wages, racialism and localization (Simkins, 1975:34-35). In Phikwe as well, during the construction phase there had been a number of what could better be termed "work stoppages" of nonunionized workers that lasted a few days each over similar issues (Puisano, 1973b). Seen in this light, the Phikwe strike is not primarily important in terms of its limited subsequent impact on the society, because in effect it was largely a dramatic strike which resulted in the temporary defeat of a section of the labor movement and the destruction of some of the life chances of the dismissed workers. Rather, it can better be viewed as a barometer or indicator of the underlying distortions and tensions produced by the dependent "development" being created in Botswana through linkages primarily with monopoly capital of the Metropoles, and secondarily with South African-based capital. It is useful to quote extensively from the President's broadcast to the nation, because it captures clearly these issues around which this chapter will interpret the strike (Botswana Daily News, 1975a):

[Issue one, Multinational "development"]
The mine has been running at a lost of R3 million a month and just when it appeared that the various technical problems were nearly solved, the irresponsible action of a handful of Botswana caused a complete closedown . . . it is essential for Botswana's development that we should retain foreign investment. It is also necessary for us to import expatriate skills to aid us in our development. This can only be done if the companies who invest here obtain a reasonable return on their investments and if skilled expatriates feel that their lives and property are safe . . . illegal and unnecessary strikes have continued to such an extent that Botswana will lose its reputation as a stable and safe country in which to invest money.
[Issue two, "privileged" workers]
The number of Botswana employed in mining and industry constitutes a very small part of our total labor force. For every Botswana who is employed in these sectors, there are at least five others who would like to be similarly employed but are forced to eke out a living in the rural areas or seek employment outside Botswana. My Government is committed to sharing out the revenue derived from mining and industry among all Botswana. A strike at Selebi Phikwe, Orapa, Morupule or elsewhere, therefore, does not only harm the companies, who own the undertaking, but Botswana as a whole.

[Issue three, trade unions and "agitators"]
The procedure for settling disputes is clearly laid down in our laws. . . . I am aware
that the large majority of workers do not wish to participate in these strikes but are
intimidated into doing so by a hard core of politically motivated individuals . . .
[who] hope to reap political rewards from the chaos which could result.

The analysis to follow will assign the major causal elements in the
situation to the external economic linkages mentioned above. Before
showing how this has come about in the postindependence era, it will be
necessary, however, to (a) review earlier social formations and transformations during colonial rule. Only then can (b) the details of the net of
external linkages be described using Phikwe as a case study for what has
been occurring, albeit in a less dramatic fashion, throughout Botswana. It
will be shown that while the subimperialism of South African-based
capital is important, this is playing an increasingly junior role vis-à-vis
capital based in Western Metropoles. Then will follow (c) an analysis
showing clearly how these external networks have been transforming the
earlier social formations and generating a classical neocolonial structure
in Phikwe and elsewhere in Botswana. A detailed analysis of the
emergence of a working class in Botswana is also relevant to labor
histories elsewhere in Southern Africa. The Zambian Copperelt has long
been the focus of attention (cf. Sklar, 1975:96-133), as has mining in
Zimbabwe (Van Onselen, 1976). Some recent analyses of the development of South African capitalism have also been focusing on its
relationship to the labor history of the Bantustans (cf. Legassick and
Wolpe, 1976). This perspective of Botswana will thus help to isolate
certain common features of the Southern African political economy in
relation to the strike, as well as being out certain factors situationally
specific to Botswana. Only when this macroperspective is accomplished
will the analysis focus on more immediate causes (though these themselves are not unrelated to the macrostructure). Here (d) the trade union
bargaining framework and the relevance of the South African miners'
wages will be dealt with in terms of the events leading up to the strike.
Finally (e) the role played by the state in the strike in relation to the
various internal classes will be examined.

HISTORICAL STRUCTURES

This discussion involves an interpretation of 19th century Tswana
chiefdoms or "states" as tributary (semifeudal) modes of production
containing "nesting units" from previously dominant lineage-based
modes of production.[6] An understanding of earlier class structures and
residential patterns is essential in interpreting the rural class situations of
Phikwe workers, most of whom are "absentee farmers."

When the British declared the Protectorate in 1885, much of the territory was under the hegemony, established in the 19th century, of four ruling Tswana aristocracies—the Kwena, Ngwaketse, Ngwato and Tawana.[7] Within each of the chiefdoms was a class structure involving relative differences in power in controlling and appropriating the economic product, comprised of (1) "royals," of the ruling patrilineal lineage; (2) "commoners" (e.g., Ngwato), people distantly related to the royals or strangers long absorbed into the lineage cluster; and (3) "strangers." The latters' status depended partly on their origins, i.e., as segments of lineages originating from Tswana-speaking groups (e.g., Rolong) or other Sotho-speaking groups (e.g., Tswapong), or non-Sotho-speaking groups (e.g., Talaote, Kalanga, Herero) who are unrelated to the Sotho cultural complex of which Tswana speakers are part. It also depended on their relative, changing negotiating positions, which resulted in, for instance, semislaves (e.g., Basarwa or "Bushmen"), subject peoples (e.g., Tswapong) or subordinate allies/rivals (e.g., Talaot, Kalanga).

In the Ngwato chiefdom, for example, only one fifth of the population were Ngwato and, as in the other chiefdoms, the established residential pattern reflected this class structure. There existed in each chiefdom a capital, with sometimes over 10,000 people. It was divided into wards headed by royals, commoners or strangers, though the latter were often incorporated into the wards of the other two. Outside this capital base were smaller villages, inhabited usually by strangers, and they sometimes had their own regional subcapital. They were incorporated into this tribute network linked to the capital and treated basically as external wards.

The core of each ward was the patrilineal "family group," a set of households of headman, *some* of his sons, grandsons, brothers and brothers' sons. The organization of the ward thus enabled the amalgamation within the chiefdom of (incomplete) lineage segments of the earlier totem-based lineages (cf. Schapera, 1952). The family group was fluid enough to include other kin, dependents and servants; and wards often had a subward structure, i.e., a set of family groups.

Underpinning this politicocultural superstructure were relations of production whose core unit was the household, consisting of a married man, his wife(s), children and usually some other dependents. Many of these productive relations still play a fundamental role in enabling Phikwe workers to operate as "absentee farmers," hence some elaboration is necessary. Arable land was allocated to the households, usually by ward headman, though land was "owned" by the people of the chiefdom with the chief having ultimate veto over its allocation. Tswana custom involves arable zones, "the lands" beyond the residential centers: here wives, usually assisted by other female kin still undertake most of the subsistence crop production, though men have been increasingly needed during the ploughing season around December, ever since ox drawn ploughs were introduced.

In a country frequented by periods of drought and irregular rain, pastoralism has been much more significant than arable farming. The chief appointed overseers over areas of pasture, generally beyond the lands, wherein grazing and water rights for a limited number of households existed. At these cattle posts, cattle were cared for often by the younger boys of the family group, with married men supervising and coordinating lands and cattle activities. There was also an institutionalized "mafisa" system whereby cattle of richer households would be placed in the care of servants or commoners (in the case of royals), which allowed the herdsmen to use the cattle for ploughing and milk.

Unlike elsewhere in southern Africa, non-Africans only made up 1.4% of the total population in 1964 (Smit, 1970:47). Only 4% of the land was alienated to white farmers. Instead, Tribal Territories (49% of the land) for the above four chiefdoms were recognized by the British and three other southeastern chiefdoms were similarly designated. The rest of the country (mostly the Kalahari) was declared Crown Lands. Only in 1968 did the Tribal Land Act transfer allocation of land to Lands Boards of the Districts (previously Tribal Territories). Although the chief and one of his appointees are in a minority on these boards, the system of customary possession for use has been retained. There was never been an arable land shortage anyway, except for some small areas in the southeast and northeast. Much more problematic is good grazing land and, in particular, water sources (traditionally rivers and wells). There was thus much intermingling of herds of cattle in search of water. The new Tribal Grazing Land policy initiated late in 1975 proposes to fence such land, which will fundamentally alter the rural mode of production (see below). However, for the historical period up to the strike, many features of the mode of production described above were intact to a degree seldom found elsewhere in southern Africa.[8]

In the latter half of the 19th century, the southern and eastern chiefdoms increased the economic linkages with, and largely held their own against, the mercantile capitalism of the Cape and the farmers of the Boer Republics. The higher levels of the class structure, particularly the chiefs, were able to extend their mechanisms of appropriating surplus (e.g., rights to stray cattle) by increasing reliance on hunting and trading tribute, etc.; yet even broad strata of peasant households gained from the increasing markets for their agricultural and hunting produce and employment in building the railway in 1896 (cf. Parsons, 1974). The new, imperialist phase of Western European capitalism after 1870 (Legassick and Wolpe, 1976:93) eventually led to the establishment of a new balance of power in Southern Africa after the Boer War, the destruction of this relative boom period and the emergence of the "Protectorate" as a labor reserve for South African capital.

Internal factors such as the Rinderpest of 1896 and the periodic droughts played their part. So did the form of colonial rule: until the mid 1950s, the system of "dual rule" enabled the chiefs and their subordinates to have largely unrestricted powers within the chiefdoms outlined above while the colonial administration, anticipating the territory's formal incorporation into South Africa, until the 1950s spent up to 80% of its funds on law and order expenses (Hermans, 1974:91). Even more important was the Customs Union, prevailing from 1910 to 1969 between South Africa and the three High Commission Territories, and the 1924-1942 minimum weight restrictions of cattle exports from these territories to South Africa. Thereby, the terms of trade were turned in favor of white settler agriculture; the Protectorate even became a net importer of maize.

In 1899, to raise internal revenue for law and order costs, the administration imposed a tax on all adult males. This simultaneously suited the mining capitalists—the only way peasants could pay this tax and satisfy primary and new household reproduction requirements within their increasingly impoverished situation caused by the above factors, was by selling their labor. The chiefs, too, obtained a percentage commission from the tax collected (Schapera, 1947:152). Although Botswana had begun selling their labor earlier, the process really thus emerged significantly after 1900, and between 1930 and 1940 the figures trebled (1947:70), due primarily to the depression years and the emergence of South African manufacturing capital. By 1938, Schapera's study showed 80% of the men of eastern Botswana had had experience working as migrants (1947:71), mostly on the Witwatersrand and there predominantly on the gold mines (1947:140). The dominant pattern was for target workers between 15 and 44 years of age to spend, on average, a total of eight years in South Africa. During this time a married man would leave his wife behind in the care of the family group, where she worked the lands while he attempted to arrange contracts so as to be home for the ploughing season (1947:53-60). Kin and sons would also care for his cattle. Interviews in 1976 with Phikwe workers confirmed this life history pattern time and again, and as will be shown, most of them are treating Phikwe as "another mine contract."

During the first half of the 20th century, Botswana was therefore essentially like any other Reserve in South Africa, wherein Africans could retain possession of 13% of the land (1913 Land Act), and outside of which they were subject to the Pass Laws restricting their employment (1923 Native Urban Areas Act). In point of fact, Botswana living south of latitude 22°S (the vast majority) were subject to exactly the same laws as Africans in South Africa in terms of migratory movements to the urban areas (Schapera, 1947:87). Nonetheless, only after 1945 did the South African state rigorously begin to control the "floating and latent surplus population" (Legassick and Wolpe, 1976:102). For Botswana, however, this occurred at a time when (a) a new phase of international monopoly capitalism, which had been under way since the 1930s (1976:93), began to make inroads, while (b) interrelated decolonization struggles made it increasingly difficult for Britain to justify transfer of the High Commission Territories to South Africa. Thus the foundation was laid for the direct penetration of U.S.A. and Western European capital in all its political and ideological ramifications of late 20th century, multinational capitalism. But because of the nature of Botswana as simultaneously incorporated within South African subimperialism, and because at this point in time the economy has primarily cattle and mineral exports available, a complex system of external networks exists—a system dependent on "foreign confidence" which a Phikwe strike threatens to upset.

By 1971 in Botswana, 10% of the total population of 630,000 were estimated to be absentee migrant workers, 90% being in South Africa (50% on the mines, 8% on the farms). Most of them were males aged 15 to 54 years—25% of all such men in Botswana are estimated as absentees (Botswana Central Statistics Office, 1972:111-113). Yet when one considers the dramatic expansion of the town where, as mentioned, 14% of the population are now found, the shift is considerable. Moreover, in 1960 wage employment in Botswana was only around 13,000 more or less evenly distributed between government, white farms, trade, industry and domestic service (Halpern, 1965:307). By 1975 these numbers had risen to 58,000 Batswana (Society and Economy Tables, 1976:283), i.e., roughly 24% of all persons aged 15 to 54 (Botswna Central Statistics Office, 1972: 135).

Simultaneously, the six large capitals of the former chiefdoms have increased their role as centers of trade and local government. Including the populations of two other large centers emerging along the railway line, these eight large villages of over 5,000 persons each, made up only 15% of the total village plus lands plus cattle post population in 1971.[9] Yet the Rural Income Distribution Survey in 1975 found the median rural income per month of households in these eight centers to be P73 as against P50 for the rest of the rural population.[10] Moreover, this differentiation becomes even greater when one considers that as many as 72% of the rural population actually live in settlements of under 1,000 persons, generally the poorest sector of Botswana (using Botswana Central Statistics Office, 1972:98). Thus, besides the problem of workers being absentee farmers, consideration has to be taken of this rural population whose stratification is being reproduced by these "developments," and which itself reflects aspects of the earlier ethnic-politico chiefdom structure discussed.

THE STATE, MULTINATIONALS AND THE EXTERNAL ECONOMIC NETWORKS

Before trying to conceptualize the rural and urban classes emerging from this mass of employment figures and their relevance for the Phikwe strike, it is necessary to consider the external linkages involved in the structuration of these internal classes—and to see why the President, in the first issue of his speech after the strike, was fearful of upsetting foreign investors.

When moves toward independence began to take shape in the early 1960s, the British administration became favorably inclined to the Botswana Democratic Party (BDP), which has had a parliamentary majority since independence. This was in preference to some of the less educated chiefs and subordinates on the one hand, and what the administration perceived as the increasingly threatening "Pan African-ist" parties on the other (cf. Stevens, 1976).[11] In terms of foreign policy, a main thrust of the BDP has been to try to extricate itself as much as possible from the economic and political networks of South Africa. The Phikwe mine financial structure established after 1968 is an excellent example of the tendencies that have been taking place throughout Botswana.

Firstly, there was the private mining complex. Amax, Anglo American Corporation/Charter Consolidated, and the smaller shareholders provided around P35 million as share capital for its initial financing (Ostrander, 1974:538). The two multinationals have since had to provide massive additional funding because of recurrent technical problems concerning ore extraction and engineering design, exacerbated by world inflation and poor metal prices of the 1970s.

P52 million was loaned at a low rate of interest by an investment bank owned by the West German government and an associated consortium of German commercial banks (Ostrander, 1974:544). In return, BCL has signed a 15-year contract to sell 55% of the nickel and all the copper to Metallgesellschaft, a West German firm, which also stood as guarantee for that part of the West German bank loan not guaranteed by the Bonn Government (Master Agreement, 1972:5). The remaining nickel is also to be sold in West Germany by BCL. However, before being sold in West Germany, all the ore is first shipped (via Johannesburg and Maputo) to the Amax refinery in the U.S. for processing. This was of interest to Amax, who preferred this arrangement to utilizing Zambian or South African refining facilities because their Port Nickel plant was operating below capacity (Lewis, 1974:210). At the same time, this ore contains ½% cobalt content and because the U.S. has no domestic supply of this metal (externally obtained from Zaire, however), it is said the U.S. Government was favorably disposed to the World Bank coordinating these agreements and overcoming the often complex difficulties (interviews).

The remaining P13.5 million for the mining complex was provided at a low interest rate by the Industrial Development Corporation, an official investment bank of South Africa, on the condition that mine construction contracts totalled at least P13.5 million of South African goods and services (Ostrander, 1974:541). Triomf Fertiliser (South Africa) also contracted to purchase much of the sulphur by product.

Secondly, there was the general infrastructure, for which the Botswana Government wished to be responsible through receipt of loans, rather than it being developed by the mining companies (as in Orapa). The U.S. Agency for International Development (USAID) and the Canadian International Development Agency (CIDA) gave loans of P24 and P4.9 millions respectively at little or no interest. Because the CIDA loan was tied to purchasing Canadian equipment for the power station, the costs were higher than would have arisen in a free market situation (Lewis, 1974:216). However, the Botswana Government did insist on the development of the local colliery at Morupule as opposed to the cheaper options of importing electrical power from South Africa or coal from South Africa or Rhodesia. The World Bank loaned P24 million, with repayment guaranteed by the multinationals. BCL has also agreed to pay water and power minimum rates, railway surcharges and an annual Township Contribution, which fully services the government's debt commitments on these loans. Finally, small grants also came from the U.K. and Danish Governments.

Few workers in Phikwe in 1976, including the trade union leadership, were found to make clear conceptual distinctions between either the multinationals and foreign governments, or the foreign shareholders of BCL and the local expatriate technocracy. The dominant model current in people's minds was of *"Whites* ["Makgoa"] sent by their *countries* to steal the copper of Botswana," with their own government seen as a passive or ineffectual bystander. While this model might capture some of the strikers' immediate situation, an effective long term strategy would have to take into account a much more complex picture of the maze of networks in which they are caught—including a knowledge that an antinationalization clause has been included in the Master Agreement (1972:49). If the workers did not fully manipulate these complex networks, some of the principal foreign actors did. In a paper given to a Southern African conference, a leading Amax official stated (Ostrander, 1974:543):

> It has become an axiom of US Government and international development agencies that projects involving investment from several national sources are to be preferred to projects having a single national source of finance. . . . The finger of nationalistic anger or political animosity is not as apt to be pointed in several directions at once. . . . [This safeguard] has been built into the structure of the Selebi Phikwe deal. . . . [Moreover] Botswana has agreed [in the Master Agreement, 1972:43] to submit any major disputes with the investor to arbitration by the new World Bank sponsored International Centre for the Settlement of Investment Disputes (I.C.S.I.D.). Any serious contravention of such arbitration, or any unjustified tampering with the underlying security of the World Bank loan, would certainly jeopardize a government's access to further World Bank credit.

There are in effect three penetrating stands embodied in these external networks. Firstly, there are the multinationals. Amax, after the Zambian 51% nationalization in 1970, gained 100% control of RST (Sklar, 1975:49)—which reflects the increasing U.S. capitalist penetration into Africa. However, Selection Trust of London has been a substantial shareholder of Amax in the Zambian venture since 1933; and the RST British chairman, Sir Ronald Prain, was an important coordinator of negotiations between RST, the British Commonwealth Relations Office and the Ngwato Tribal Authority after 1959 (Ostrander, 1974:537). Anglo American was initially an 11% shareholder in Botswana RST (established 1967), but because of the increasing cost of the project, eventually became an equal partner. Anglo's vast South African industrial holdings are additionally useful, because the Amax official put it "BCL will particularly benefit from what has been described as, in effect, a single regional market for technically skilled manpower and specialised services" (Ostrander, 1974:547). Metallgesellschaft itself has long standing links, having been financially associated with the initial formation of Amax in 1889 (Sklar, 1975:48); while Charter Consolidated of London, of the Anglo Group, actually holds the largest shareholding in Selection Trust (1975:50). One thus perceives one aspect of the situation: three interlinked multinationals, a fraction of international mining capital, entering the market for Botswana's potentially rich supply of minerals ahead of their competitors.

The second strand is the backing given for these respective private capitals by the state apparatuses of the *national* social formations (U.S.A., West Germany, South Africa) on which these capitals are still based.[12] While fractions of capital form the dominant "power bloc" operating through these state apparatuses, the fact that sections of the working classes of these social formations are able to exert secondary pressure on these apparatuses for both jobs and cheap copper/nickel goods, further complicates these networks.

The third prong is the growing role of the World Bank in coordinating these various monopoly interests.

These Phikwe networks are not an isolated case. Throughout Botswana the predominant British colonial influence has slowly been augmented by influences from North America, the European Economic Community and Scandinavia. Admittedly large retail stores and construction and engineering firms are often still South African based and imorts from the South African Customs Union comprised 80% of the total value of imports in 1975 (Botswana Central Statistics Office, 1976d:11). However, the major new Gaborone brewery has German company participation, and in 1977 it is a leading German firm of consultants assisting in the Ministry of Commerce's industrial study. Lobatse, too, became the center of the beef export industry in 1954, and in 1975 meat products made up 35% of the value of Botswana's exports (minerals were 51% (1976d:10)—of which value 61% goes to the U.K. (26% goes to South Africa (1976d:7)). The operation of the Lome Convention and the way in which the EEC reduced the import levy on Botswana beef in 1975 by 90% "because it threatened to harm the country's economy" are replications of the copper nickel story, this time with cattle. Thus the fact that the Phikwe strike had the potential to upset "foreign confidence" over a wide spectrum is one crucial reason for the state's strong arm reaction. Another is related to the internal class forces and the state, which is dealt with below.

The transformation from the 1950s of Botswana from its labor reserve status has thus been different from the Transkei, for instance, which ever since 1951 (Bantu Authorities Act) has been set in a Bantustan direction. Significantly the latter's economic linkages are entirely centered around South African state investment corporations, themselves closely allied with Afrikaner capital (Innes and O'Meara, 1976:75). Nor has this initially led in Botswana to *underdevelopment* in the sense of an actual falling of real income, because the transformation of the stagnant labor reserve has made available increased income for many strata in the postindependence decade. The state has received revenues from royalties, customs duties on mining imports, wage income taxation, and interest payments from surcharges—though the enormous losses sustained so far (and hence no dividend payments) makes Phikwe nothing like the bonanza originally hoped for. While material interests dominated the financial network structure, it is admitted that some negotiators, particularly the local representatives of aid organizations and some Botswana government officials, operate with the paradigm of "developing a poor Third World country dominated by Apartheid South Africa." However, the very fact that this ideology is in part genuinely held serves to mystify the long term problems: the generation of a highly polarized capitalist internal class structure and the locking of Botswana into the network of monopoly capitalist exploitation. Despite early losses, however, the mine is at a competitive advantage against any other world copper mine which might be started at the much higher capital costs of the late 1970s. With the Selebi and two other possible nearly ore deposits still to be mined and with the world copper price potentially still to rise, enormous profits are likely to be shipped out of Botswana. It is also likely this form of *distorted development* will then generate even more conflict than the Phikwe strike did.

THE CLASS STRUCTURE IN PHIKWE

It is difficult for Botswana workers to conceive of themselves as "privileged" within the atmosphere of the expatriate situation in Phikwe. This situation will first be examined before turning to the structuration of classes and strata among the Batswana.

Of the population of 18,000 in 1975 in Selebi Phikwe around 1,200 were non-Africans, 52% holding U.K. citizenship, 31% South African and 17% from places such as the U.S.A., Greece and Scandinavia.[13] A small number were employed by the Water and Power Corporations, or worked for or owned construction/engineering firms, while a few had retail stores. Of the 350 employed by BCL (as against 2,800 Botswana), many of the artisans were flown in on short term contracts from South Africa; middle and upper level management were predominantly U.K. citizens, some with South African or Rhodesian residence, while many others had spent years on the Zambian Copperbelt. The government, as mentioned, is responsible for the general infrastructure, and local government administration controls the town affairs, i.e., Botswana's independence makes matters different on a *formal* level from the Copperbelt at its inception. Issues of discrimination are therefore refracted into more informal struggles.

For instance, the only sports club in town was not registered by the government until it was satisfied there was no racial discrimination in its constitution (because of trouble over an earlier club). Yet the constitution allowed for two clubhouses, each under its own subcommittee, though payment of subscription fees entitles membership of both. One has evolved largely as a bar frequented by Africans, though even here the subscription fee is beyond the means of the average worker. The other itself has various sports subdivisions, and the gold division, which only golfers can join, has its own clubhouse, where the majority of middle and upper level expatriate management prefers to attend.

The issue in the strike of the BCL cars, and the assaulting of some expatriates while trying to assemble these cars at the mine, must be interpreted as simply the focal point around which a whole set of these frustrations crystallized. Only heads of departments (all expatriates except two Botswana senior personnel officers) were allocated the use of these cars, but a considerable number of other expatriates had also acquired them. A story, repeated time and time again among the workers, was that "the drivers of these cars pass by mine workers of their own departments walking and hitching a lift on the mile or so stretch to work and then book them for their late arrival at the mine." In some ways neither this extreme conflict generated by the expatriate technocracy is entirely in the interests of foreign shareholders, nor is their lack of long term career commitment to BCL, which has surely influenced the degree of technical problems experienced by the mine. But it is an inevitable consequence of this form of multinational development, and the new manager sent in by the companies as a troubleshooter in 1976 can have little impact on these underlying structures and their accompanying racialism.

While the strike spilled over into these issues, the basic problem was a wage dispute. One aspect of this was the "expatriate"/"local" differentiation, as it was termed by BCL, but which was also seen as a racial divide by the strikers. In BCL the lowest grade of expatriate artisan had a basic wage of around P500 per month, while no Botswana employee earned over P330.[14] Although Botswana employees have largely subsidised housing, expatriates also have this, and in addition the "usual" inducement allowances (gratuities, etc.) and even free flights for each family four times a year for a weekend in Johannesburg. There is also one English medium primary school in the town, almost entirely financed by BCL, two thirds of whose pupils were expatriate. A BCL clinic exists for all employees, though only those earning above P200 are eligible to join the medical scheme for private patients, i.e., this only includes what will be described below as "Stratum C" BCL Batswana employees.

In the negotiations prior to the strike, it will be shown below that South African miners' wages formed an immediate point of reference for a leading group in the strike. However, the above situation was even more important in developing workers' feelings of exploitation and raising the general level of what was argued to be a fair wage during these negotiations. Although mediated by numerous categories such as race and nation, it also brought Batswana of the Third World face to face with aspects of the class position which the expatriate technocracy occupy in the international political economy as a whole, in Botswana and in their home countries. The school and clinic, mentioned earlier as targets in the strike, were symbols of this frustration.

What is perhaps as significant in the long term is how this structure of privilege is penetrating the internal class structure itself. In analyzing the Phikwe class structure, it is useful to view it in terms of the approximately 58,000 Batswana in wage employment throughout the country. They were employed as follows: state sectors, 31%; commerce, transport, services, 21%; domestic servants, 18%; manufacturing and construction, 15%; mining, 6%; agriculture, 5%; and parastatals, 4%.[15] The massive number of domestic servants points to the distorted nature of some of this development. A polarization of income levels is shown by the fact that for the private capitalist sectors, 89% of the 29,000 employees fell in the P1-P100 per month range, 9% in the P101-P200 range, and only 2% fell above P200. For the 19,000 state and parastatal employees, the ratio was 77%:17%:6%. This shows that in addition to the postindependence incorporation of large numbers into the state apparatuses, the bureaucratic bourgeoisie of middle and upper level income is relatively more numerous than those in similar levels in the private sector.

Phikwe is in many ways a microcosm of this development. A rough estimate of Batswana workers in April 1975, gave a total of 6,400 distributed as follows: mining, 44%; construction and engineering, 19%; domestic servants and gardeners, 16%; commerce, transport, services, 11%; state sectors, 8%; parastatals (water and power), 4%.[16] In addition, 4,500 Batswana (two thirds of them women) between 15 and 54 years of age stated they were not employed at all (Botswana Central Statistics Office, 1976a: Table 10).

BCL itself divides all Batswana employees into grades one to eight, and a breakdown gave 78% earning P40-P80 (grades 1-3); 20% earning P85-P200 (grades 4-6); and 2% earning above P200 (grades 6-8).[17]

The second point in the President's speech considered *all* the miners as a labor aristocracy. At first glance it is true the BCL income distribution follows closely that of the state and parastatals rather than the smaller capitalist sector. However, a deeper class analysis is necessary to evaluate this claim, as well as to evolve categories in which one can locate the class positions of the principal groups participating in the strike. What

Table 1. THE URBAN "CLASS SITUATION" OF PHIKWE

	Workers	Bureaucratic Bourgeoisie	Petty Bourgeoisie
Stratum A.1	Unemployed. Domestic servants, unskilled construction/engineering workers. Unskilled workers (P40-44): BLC grade 1, state industrial class group 4.		Small scale beer brewers, hawkers, shoe repairers, etc.
Stratum A.2	Semiskilled workers (P45-120): BCL grades 2-4 (underground span-nermen, drivers, etc.), state industrial class groups 3-1.		
Stratum B	Skilled workers: less educated BCL grades 5-6 (heavy equipment drivers, shift bosses, etc., P100-200); state and BCL (grades 2-6) technical trainees and artisans (J.C. certif. P60-200).	BCL educated grades 2-5, state staff grades (clerks, nurses, labora-tory assistants, etc., J.C. certif. P60-200).	Few self-employed (around P100-200).
Stratum C.1		Educated BCL grades 6-8 (senior shift foremen, accountants, personnel officers, etc. P200-330); senior civil servants (above P200).	Small capitalists, especially shopowners.

	Workers	Bureaucratic Bourgeoisie	Petty Bourgeoisie
Stratum C.2		Expatriate artisans, middle and upper level management (all above P500).	Expatriate and Asian retail store owners; engineering/ construction firm owners.

this analysis will be looking for, ultimately, is a clarification of which groups are tending to emerge as well as form alliances with other groups, in order to pursue their *material interests* in the struggle over the *total economic product* (created by labor time)—in a struggle ranging generally from informal economistic exchanges to fully fledged political organization. On the basis of this theoretical paradigm, the analysis will hypothesize Table 1 as a relevant conceptual map of the urban "class situation" of Phikwe workers. As can be seen from this table, the vertical axis of wage levels is mediated by the different positions of the various groups in the production/distribution process. It will be argued that education/cultural factors, residential area and the rural "class situation" of these groups are additional mediators/reinforcers, resulting in significant "breakpoints" or strata.

All state employees in Botswana are termed either "Industrial Class" or "Staff."[18] Only the latter are eligible for housing and a pension and normally a Junior Certificate (J.C., three years secondary schooling) is needed to enter the lowest clerical level (around P60 per month). A breakpoint occurred around P200, the level where higher r supervisory roles are performed and where a university degree is often needed. Unskilled industrial class workers ("Group 4") started at P40 and various semiskilled workers ranged from P45 to P120.

The definitive Botswana Government Paper (1972:5) on incomes stated: "Basic local wage and salary levels, in the private and parastatal sectors should generally conform to, and on no account significantly exceed, those paid by Government to comparable grades of public employees." BCL has been happy to follow this closely within their grades one to eight, though all employees are eligible for housing, and a grade 2 J.C. educated clerk has the same wage and conditions of service as a grade 2 semiskilled worker. However, the Table 1 divisions can be most clearly seen in the residential patterns of Selebi Phikwe.

The planned township (i.e., excluding Botshabelo, Site and Service) is cut in two by the main road which runs from west to east, and the shopping mall is in the center. The north side contains low cost houses; closer to the mall on the north and south sides are medium cost houses (which have electricity and are better finished on the outside); and further south of the mall are high cost houses. Housing is almost entirely allocated to BCL, state and parastatal expatriate and Batswana employees. No expatriates at all lived on the north side; their area was nicknamed "tshaba ntsa" (beware of the dog) by workers because of these signs on the gates. Although on the north side there are some BCL hostels and houses shared by three workers, the majority are allocated to married workers and their families. BCL management policy is for all grades 1-3 to be eligible for low cost housing, and grades 4-6 for medium cost, the latter area itself being nicknamed "Orlando" after an "upgraded" African township in Johannesburg. However, in the informal bargaining over housing (allo-cated by a Batswana-staffed department), of which there is a shortage, one finds many of the semiskilled grade fours (e.g., drivers) in low cost housing, but seldom clerical grade fours. At the same time, many of the BCL grades 5-6 are relatively uneducated, often having been "boss boys" or other semiskilled workers in the South African mines. BCL has been able to utilize this, and some have become heavy equipment drivers, shift bosses, etc., in Phikwe. They tend to cluster in certain roads of the medium cost housing area, away from the educated grades 4-6, while some of the educated grade sixes are tending to move south of the mall to join grades 7-8. There also tends to be some social separation between educated and less educated Batswana in Phikwe (e.g., public bars versus shebeens), which is complex, but if one wants a crude cut off point, it is the completion of some, usually three, years of secondary schooling.

In 1968, after the township plans were drawn up, there was some discussion about creating a more integrated system. BCL management was against this and the Cabinet decision eventually opted for relatively minor adjustments. The effect of the external networks in shaping sharply drawn class structures is thus direct.[19]

Moreover, it can be seen that in both consciousness and their role in the production process, what is termed here the lower level (Stratum B) bureaucratic bourgeoisie of BCL and state sectors is separated off from the skilled workers. Their actual productive role is important: there is a group of J.C. and above workers who are being trained by BCL and the state sectors to become skilled artisans, and their close relations with other workers in production makes them better conceived as part of the latter. However, higher level technical supervisors, e.g., senior shift foremen, are postulated as part of the higher level (Stratum C.1) Batswana bureaucratic bourgeoisie.[20]

In Botshabelo and the site and service area (a "Planned" Botshabelo) nearly half of the Selebi Phikwe population live, building their own

mud/brick houses, with water stand pipes provided (similar developments are reflected in such "periurban" areas in Gaborone and Francistown). Twenty percent of the BCL workers, nearly all of them from
grades 1-3, live here, primarily to avoid the P4 low cost housing rent;
unless they live with a relative in town, the state "industrial class" and
other Stratum A.1 workers of Table 1 also live here. For some
construction/engineering workers, there is a government-regulated minimum wage of around P27, but domestic servants and shop assistants fall
even below P20. For, as the Botswana Government Paper (1972:5)
decided (based on Ghai's recommendations):

> Government considers that the only fair and objective basis for a legal minimum
> wage for unskilled workers is that it should equal the average rural income of farmers
> with an allowance for any differential in the overall costs of urban living . . . on the
> other hand, small enterprises, which tend to be paying the lowest wages, would be hit
> particularly hard if a minimum wage were set.

The large "floating surplus population" of unemployed in Phikwe and the
"latent surplus population" in the rural areas (Legassick and Wolpe,
1976:100) provide the cutting edge to this policy which yields enormous
profits for small capitalists. Concerning the latter, besides the expatriate
construction/engineering firms, there is the retail trade dominated in
Phikwe (but not the rual areas) by expatriates and some local Asians. A
few large Batswana traders are emerging, though interviewing revealed at
least some of their profits are being invested in cattle rather than
additional stock. There are also the self-employed hawkers, vendors and
taximen. Women—single, widowed or wives of workers (including those
in the township)— are heavily involved in beer brewing. In 1976 at least
P30 could be made, and the really enterprising even penetrated into
Stratum B. Petty commodity producers exist,[21] but are not numerous
because the economic and cultural domination of South Africa results in
the importation of tinned food, household utensils, etc.

In summary then, Table 1 designates a Stratum A.1 of lumpenproletariat and reserve army *outside* both the monopoly capital and state
sectors and a Stratum A.2 of monopoly capital and state sectors
semiskilled workers. The unskilled BCL grade 1 and state group 4
workers and the small scale entrepreneurs straddle between these two.

Besides the above factors discussed in differentiating Stratum A as a
whole from Stratum B, the most important is actually their articulation
with the rural mode of production. Crucially, most workers in Botswana
are still objectively and subjectively migrant peasants who own their own
means of production and accumulation. Factors discussed relating to
land possession, cattle care and the wife's role at the lands are
fundamental. For the 80% of Botswana's population who straddle the

railway line, weekend rail plus bus trips are easily possible to any eastern rural home from the five towns mentioned—and even more so for Botswana in Phikwe, 96% of whose population comes from these areas (cf. Botswana Sua Project, 1975:162). The fact that the village remains the base is much more due to economic reasons than to the culture of migrant labor generated over decades. For people in the low cost housing and periurban areas, rural agriculture is a major way of making ends meet for their family and a security (food supply) if they lose their jobs.[22] Many of Stratum B, particularly, were employing tractor owners to plough for them and hiring people to assist in the harvest, their wives being general supervisors. This was even more so with cattle: although the Rural Income Distribution Survey (1976:110) found that 45% of the rural households owned no cattle at all, it was hard to find in Phikwe a married worker of Stratum B who had no cattle, or who was not at least in the process of buying some.

Thus Table 1 only refers to workers' urban "class situations." Most are also *simultaneously* in rural "class situations," i.e., they are part of two modes of production.

Serious problems for an analysis of workers' class consciousness in terms of strike action would occur if, for instance, groups of Stratum A were simultaneously rich peasants, and vice versa for Stratum B. However, three hypotheses based on the wider study of Phikwe workers, the results of which are not yet published, can tentatively be stated, because they tend to show that the multinational development is reinforcing earlier rural divisions:

(1) That Stratum A.1 in the Phikwe periurban areas tends to come from the smaller villages *outside the eight capitals*, i.e., predominantly from the poor peasantry.[23]

(2) That there is a tendency for the bureaucratic bourgeoisie to come from the middle or rich peasantry, because their father or other close kin needed cattle to finance their secondary education. The one case of unusual mobility is that of the shift boss group (grades 5-6) now in Phikwe after the South African mines, whose children are obtaining a much higher education level than they did.

(3) That even Stratum A.2 BCL workers (P45-P100), with the high cost of living in the towns and numerous rural dependents, find it difficult to accumulate significant cattle to become anything more than middle peasants. Moreover, the Rural Income Distribution Survey found 20% of all rural households had a gross available income of less than P27 per month and 75% had less than P90 (Botswana Central Statistics Office, 1976c:76:77). Despite problems of comparibility, even this group of BCL workers can thus in no way be seen as radically privileged: "Take off" in cattle really only begins in Stratum B, which illustrates the fact that the *actual* level of wages is a significant variable in defining the urban "class situation."

Rather than stressing privileged workers, a parallel derived from Van Onselen's study is more relevant. He showed clearly how the industrial violence of the "Compound System" crystallized at a certain stage of capitalist development in Rhodesian and South African mines. It provided the institutional setting for the maximization of output and minimization of costs by means of social, political and economic controls, and was sanctioned by the white settler state apparatuses (1976:156-157). Phikwe, in its own way too, reflects systems of control, divisions of the working class, racialism and elitism at this historical conjuncture of multinational capitalism and the neocolonial state, against which the strikers reacted by finally taking to the streets of the town.

THE BARGAINING FRAMEWORK AND EVENTS LEADING TO THE STRIKE

Within the context of the macrostructure already analyzed, it is now possible to consider the third point of the President's speech, concerning the legal framework existing for trade union bargaining and the actual strike participants.

Although there is no general federation encompassing the eight unions mentioned earlier, after the Phikwe strike government ministers encouraged workers to form such a federation. The Trade Unions Act, 1969, provides for such formations and this provision, like all the trade union legislation of 1969, is designed to promote "orderly" bargaining within specified, narrow limits. For instance, a "trade union" is defined as (Laws of Botswana, 1969a: Section 2.1):

Any combination of more than thirty persons other than an employees' association not deemed to be a trade union under the provisions of [other clauses], associated together primarily for the purpose of regulating relations between employees and employers or between employees and employees in any industry, trade or occupation.

A registrar of trade unions must refuse to register a trade union whose constitution is not in accordance with this provision (Section 8.1). These levels were framed with considerable assistance from British advisors, and links have been maintained with Britain's Department of Employment. In many ways these laws served to institutionalize the employer/employee dichotomy on a legal level in an almost anticipatory sense, before the massive urbanization had got under way and at a time when the noncapitalist mode of production was still prevalent throughout much of the rural society.

Legal provision is also made for the state to be an employer and the industrial class to form trade unions (local and central government);

associations have been formed by staff grades.[24] The former, as trade unions, have the legal right to strike and picket (peacefully), but only in relation to a "trade dispute," defined specifically in relation to matters encompassing only wages and conditions of service in that sector for which that trade union is responsible, i.e., "sympathetic strikes" are illegal (Laws of Botswana, 1969: Section 19), as well as any strikes over the pursuance of a closed shop agreement. A set of other structures have also been set up in order to rationalize labor relations: a Ministry of Home Affairs, wages councils for various sectors of industry and a Trade Union Education Center. The latter is funded almost wholly by the African-American Labor Center, and primarily it has undertaken education programs for trade unionists in relation to collective bargaining procedures (Simkins, 1975:30).

The Botswana Mine Workers Union (BMWU) was first formed in Orapa, and the Selebi Phikwe branch (henceforth, "the Union") was formed in 1972. In July 1973, a Memorandum of Agreement was signed between the Union and BCL, in which the company agreed to recognize the Union as the only organization with which to negotiate provided 25% of all employees were Union members (1973:1-2).[25] The memorandum was negotiated, however, by expatriate personnel officers who had had considerable experience on the Zambian Copperbelt in the type of bargaining situations they might have to face in Phikwe. In Zambia in the mid-1950s, the companies had successfully fostered a Mines' African Staff Association of higher income workers which was bitterly resented by the then Northern Rhodesian Mineworkers' Union (Sklar, 1975:106). The Phikwe memorandum agreed to exclude from Union membership senior staff and others, particularly (personnel) workers "who have access to confidential information." Yet senior staff were defined to include even underground junior shift bosses of grade 6, i.e., potentially further splitting the group defined earlier as skilled workers, grades 5-6, who reside together in the same areas of "Orlando." The chairman of BMWU also stated in his address to the Annual General Meeting in December 1976 in Phikwe that this ruling also excludes many of the educated grades 7 and 8, (e.g., accountants) best able to understand the complex legalities of the trade union acts, and it could enable the company to promote a militant member into a post that would deny him union membership.

The 1969 Trade Disputes Act provided a set of options, such as Industrial Arbitration Tribunals, etc., in order to facilitate strikes as a last resort; and the minister can declare a strike illegal if the existing machinery of negotiation for voluntary agreement has not been exhausted. The memorandum makes use of this potential, laying down clear stages that have to be followed before calling a strike, including notifying the labor officer of the ministry and the Union head office. In addition, an option for the minister to invoke is made obligatory by the memorandum: a two-thirds majority in a secret ballot is required before a strike can be called.

It is not surprising that, because of these complicated procedures, none of the strikes mentioned earliers that had occurred in the 1970s in Botswana had been legal, strictly speaking. Prior to 1975 in Phikwe, except for various work stoppages mentioned, there was only one serious event. This occurred in 1972 when 600 BCL workers went on strike for three days and called for the dismissal of a local personnel officer who was accused of giving jobs to "home boys" and relations. There was marching and singing through the town, confiscation of some BCL cars, the rumor of government troops being brought in and the eventual mediation by the Commissioner of Labor. The Union chairman at the time stated later that BCL, which had been dragging its feet over recognition of the Union, presented union negotiators with a rought draft of the memorandum soon after the strike (Puisano, 1973a, 1973b).

This strike could partly be interpreted as involving ethnic issues. Yet workers in Phikwe must be seen as using their "ethnic situation" instead of their class situation *if* the former proves a better power resource for pursuing their material interests than the latter. It is true that ethnic definitions are not simply instrumental, though except perhaps relationships between the Tswana-speaking majority and Kalanga (Shona speakers from Zimbabwe) or Basarwa hunter gatherers, Botswana is particularly devoid of serious ethnic conflict. "Home boy" networks among Tswana speakers themselves do, of course, exist; yet an outline of the events leading up to the 1975 strike will illustrate even further than the previous discussions have that the new class situations are becoming increasingly relevant.

The Wages Council for the Mining Industry (1973:7) established by the government, which included equal numbers of mining company personnel officers, BMWU officials and government representatives, took as its central principle the establishment of parity of mining and state sector wages, i.e., there was a displacement of BCL-Phikwe Branch Union negotiations to a higher level. In September 1974, the Phikwe Union managed to negotiate an overall percentage increase on this wage structure for BCL employees backdated to July. Issues of racial insults, use of BCL cars, medical facilities and other expatriate privileges were also raised by the Union, illustrating the fact that these grievances did not simply appear in July 1975. Still, the Union Bargaining Committee focused on wages, and despite minority disagreement, the majority of the committee eventually opted for accepting these terms rather than getting no increase at all.[26] The Union also referred the memorandum to some lawyers because it felt the terms negotiated therein were biased against it.

In May 1975, the underground workers walked out on a strike for higher wages. The chairman and a few other Union officials, called in by the personnel superintendent, spoke to a mass meeting of these workers, who agreed to elect six representatives to negotiate over underground wages. A few days later they again walked out because there had been no results from representations to management. Union officials once again mediated, and it was finally agreed their case would be considered in relation to the expected annual general wages review at the end of July. It seems the Union officials also gave tacit support for a strike if no results materialized.

The majority of the branch committee at the time were educated grades 4-6 and predominantly under 35 years of age, i.e., part of the lower level emergent bureaucratic bourgeoisie. Still, during this period, the Union cannot be seen either as a passive bystander or as simply working to neutralize workers' demands. On the other hand, very few of the underground workers were Union members, though at the time of the strike about half the potential membership of BCL employees were unionized. The thrust of the discontent came from underground machine-men and spannermen, i.e., semiskilled workers, Stratum A.2. The leaders of this group were predominantly young and, significantly, had had some primary school education, but had not completed it. Research into BCL employment records also showed most of the underground workers had previously worked on the South African mines. During these May stoppages these underground workers specifically referred to the level of wages paid on these mines, and also compared their heavy and dangerous work with that of other BCL surface workers, who were earning the same wages as they were.

The structure of wages on the South African Gold Mines is relevant.[27] This structure also divides workers into grades one to eight, but it has a two-tier system of surface and underground workers. In 1975 the lowest grade of the former earned a basic P36 per month, the latter earned P57. Analysis showed that while BCL tried to correlate its classifications with South Africa, its levels were simultaneously related to Botswana state sectors, which began at P40. In 1975 various categories of underground workers were roughly 20% worse off in BCL than their South African counterparts. However, interviewed Phikwe workers often gave as the main reason for working in BCL the fact that they could better supervise their village home, lands and cattle, i.e., they were calculating the net advantages accruing to their urban *and* rural class situations taken as a whole. On the other hand, miners in South Africa receive free food and accommodation and about 80% of their earnings after repatriation. This is a forced saving which can be used for purchasing agricultural capital, though of course they have to suffer the more oppressive life in the compounds and apartheid.

A comparison of these two wage structures showed a further problem for semiskilled underground workers of Stratum A.2. In the South African mines, many of the skilled worker jobs (grades 5-6) and those of the educated bureaucratic bourgeoisie (grades 2-8), available in BCL in Phikwe, are reserved for whites. At the same time an uneducated worker of Stratum A.2 can move into grades 5-7 in South Africa and into jobs such as "team leaders," while in Phikwe stress is laid on education for such promotion. The emergence of Stratum B in postindependent Botswana has thus served to generate feelings of relative deprivation, particularly among Stratum A.2. It is not surprising that BCL had the incredibly high annual turnover rates for 1976 of 32% Botswana surface workers and 60% underground workers—itself a reflection of the continuous circulation of persons in Stratum A as a whole between BCL, construction companies, unemployement or self-employment, lands, cattle, and South African mines.[28]

The discontent between May-July 1975 was not only felt by the underground workers, because in mid-July at a mass meeting held outside the mine by the Union there was massive pressure from the ranks for a strike at the end of the month if there were no wage increases. Although the company had claimed this could not be possible because the mine was still running at a loss, workers argued at the meeting that, if BCL could afford to pay the existing expatriate salaries, they too could obtain an increase. Management also referred to government wage levels in negotations with the Union, though as the president was to remark (Dec. 19, 1975:6):

> I am particularly concerned about the assertion that it is Government which is prohibiting parity with South African miners' wages. . . . To create such an impression is to suggest to the workers that their Government is against wage increases of any kind while the Company is prepared to reach for the sky.

The Labor Office thereafter informed the Union a strike would be illegal because stage procedures, including a secret ballot had not been followed, and that Union officials were themselves liable for prosecution unless they could prove they "had exercised all reasonable diligence to prevent the commission of the offence" (Laws of Botswana, 1969b, section 26.4). When workers were paid on July 25, they found increases had been awarded only on a selective basis for workers who had been recommended by their heads of department. Although the Union officials were due to meet on July 29 to consider the situation, on the 28th the six underground representatives again met management, later conferred in town with underground and other general workers and some Union officials and decided to strike. These six closed the mine gates early the next morning and arriving workers later formed groups, predominantly of Stratum A, carrying sticks and undertook the various acts described earlier.

THE STRIKE AND THE BALANCE OF CLASS FORCES WITHIN BOTSWANA

From the discussion it can be seen the Union did not play a leadership role in the strike. While by no means playing a reactionary role, the laws governing their bargaining situation placed Union officials in an ambivalent position: "no Union here, you're always quoting the labor laws to us" was the frequent response with which workers at the gates responded to the arrival there of the leading Union officials (interviews). Actually, all except one of the Union Branch Committee were members of the ruling BDP party at the time; yet in later recriminations the role of the opposition parties and other "known political subversives and social misfits" was raised (Speech, Dec. 19, 1975:2). An hypothesis will be put forward that the accusations reflect government perceptions that these strike eruptions have the potential to threaten the delicate balance of class forces in the society, and hence the hegemony exercised by the dominant classes through the state apparatus. This is the one side of the same coin, which has so far been neglected, the other side being the earlier issue of "foreign confidence."

The stagnant colonial economy greatly reduced the potential for the emergence of a capitalist class broadly based on cattle and, for instance, the colonial administration refused trading licenses to Batswana, even chiefs' relatives, until after 1945 (Best,1970:603). Meager savings of migrants from their low South African wages gave little basis for the emergence of even a rich peasantry. Nonetheless, the ossification and centralization of the chiefdom structures did retain and often increase the correlation between precolonial class situation, wealth based on cattle, and modern education. Chiefs and their subordinates, in particular, were able to increase their relative position through manipulation of the colonial structures, with struggles often being between included/ excluded royal factions (cf. Parsons, 1974:125). Some borehole syndicates also began to emerge by the 1930s; but the degree to which BDP receptiveness to Western aid in the early 1960s was influenced by the objective economic interests of factions supporting it—as against influences such as political realities (e.g., Verwoerd wishing to incorporate the High Commission Territories) or ideological factors (e.g., antiapartheid attitudes, mission education)—needs further research.

However, it has been argued throughout that postindependence "development" has dramatically reproduced and increased stratification. This is notwithstanding the fact that some "new men" from commoner or "stranger" backgrounds have emerged within the bureaucratic bourgeoisie, or among the rising rural trader class where prior urban experience in South Africa and/or accummulation of savings from wage provided some capital (cf. Kuper, 1970:49-60). While more evidence is needed, Holm's study is a guide. In the 1969 elections, BDP members made up 24 out of the 31 M.P.s and 113 out of the 165 elected district councilors (BDP gains slightly increased in the 1974 elections). Of the 51 interviewed councilors of three southern districts, 60% had paternal kinship links with the local chief or headman, 57% had over 25 cattle and almost 30% had rural enterprises. Higher percentages pertained for the M.P.s (Holm, 1976:457). Thus, it can be argued from this and from Phikwe data that dominant interconnected groups in the society have emerged, consisting of (1) the bureaucratic bourgeoisie of Stratum C.1 as defined, (2) the emergent traders, particularly in the rural areas, and (3) the upper levels of the rich peasantry who are merging into capitalist farmers.

In the early 1960s, western-educated activitists of the BDP had a strong "modernizing" approach to the country's problems, and there was also pressure for the new Botswana political institutions to replicate similar structures stablished elsewhere in newly independent African countries. This resulted in the sudden diminishing of chieftainship powers: a House of Chiefs (1965) with only advisory powers, elected District Councils (1965), and Land Boards (1968). Some of the chiefs were particularly disaffected by this, and in 1965 the new Botswana National Front (BNF) party under a Marxist leader tried to forge an alliance between (1) urban groups of unionized workers, (2) civil servants, and (3) disaffected traditional leaders (Vengroff, 1976:210).

The BDP has skillfully tried to incorporate some of these groups. The last group is particularly important, because support by poor and middle peasants for the party which their chief and headman support is still strong (as evidenced by the votes for the BNF in the Ngwaketse District) when it gained the support of that chief. It seems that many of the District Councils and Land Boards have come firmly under the control of the rural elite of traders and cattlemen, so that while the chiefs' power has diminished, they now simply have to share it with other people of traditionally, and sometimes newly, based wealth (cf. Vengroff, 1976;

interviews). Over the past decade, there has been a rush by the emerging elite to sink boreholes for their cattle. The new grazing policy proposes to rationalize this by providing a threefold scheme of *fenced* ranches for (a) individuals owning over 400 or so cattle, (b) syndicates of rich peasants pooling their cattle, and (c) communal organizations for poorer cattle owners (Botswana Government Paper, 1975). With only an estimated 16% of all rural households owning over 25 head of cattle (i.e., above middle peasant level), and yet with their ownership comprising around 75% of the national herd of Botswana (Botswana Central Statistics Office, 1976c:111), the chiefs and the rest of the elite will successfully be able to adapt to this new "modernization." This is not to deny the attempts being made by various government ministries to promote "rural development" for the poorer strata, though it is difficult to see how they will hold their own against the elite in the actual bargaining that goes on at the local level.

The government has not been unmindful of the second group of civil servants who predominate the bureaucratic bourgeoisie either. Professor Ghai's recommendations that civil servant salaries be reduced (1971:10) was not accepted by the government's income policy in 1972, though most of the other recommendations were.

Thus unionized urban workers, mainly of Stratum A, have been considerably isolated. However, unlike the poor and middle peasant situations, theirs has organizational and vocal power through the unions. Thus the strikes are seen by the state as having the potential for mobilizing general, antigovernmental feeling throughout the country among other groups who feel relatively deprived by the rapid and distorted development over the past decade. This is thus the real significance of the debate about the "political" nature of the Phikwe strike.

It is necessary to conclude with some considerations about the future relationship of Stratum A workers with Stratum B workers and bureaucrats. This is even more relevant after 1976, when Amax declined to take up its option to develop what was to be Botswana's next major (Sua Pan salt) mining project, both for economic reasons and because of the political uncertainty prevailing in Southern Africa now (Budget Speech, 1977: item 22). Thus the decline of this boom period is highly likely, given further political developments in neighboring countries.

BCL and state sector unskilled and semiskilled workers have had some wage increases in the 1970s, whereby the government has tried to keep them at least abreast with the rising cost of living. Admittedly, they are slightly better off than Stratum A.1 and some rural households, particularly those which have no target workers in the towns (e.g., rural households headed by divorced or unmarried women). Yet in the total political economy of Botswana, when Phikwe erupted, it was Stratum A.2 and in particular some of the young less educated workers, who have grown up in an independent country, who had the consciousness and organization to make their feelings of exploitation most felt—not the lumpenproletariat or poor and middle peasants located in the rural areas. Thus, any contradictions between Stratum A.2 and the rest of the "Third World poor" in Botswana are surely secondary contradictions at this point in time, and all have an objective interest in the radical transformation of the status quo.

Nonetheless, Stratum A.2's thrust in Phikwe was basically economistic, and generally it is in a paradoxical situation. For even at an economistic level, its goals can only be really effectively pursued by a leadership which has enough education to be able to bargain successfully over a document like the memorandum. And if it is to proceed beyond this with a more long term political strategy of extricating itself from the complex external and internal networks within which it is trapped, a leadership would probably have to have at least some secondary school education, i.e., any leadership is immediately thrust into Stratum B.

Stratum B is not a homogeneous "comprador" character, however. The less educated skilled workers, despite their upward mobility, have close cultural ties with the other workers, and they themselves experience exploitative conditions at their work place; as do the trainee artisans who, because of both their youth and their relatively higher education, were often found to be extremely politically conscious (like their Soweto student counterparts) of current ideological debate following the impact of Mozambique and Zimbabwe. The lower level bureaucratic bourgeoisie in the state apparatus does have considerable security and career mobility. However, in BCL this group experiences daily racialism and blocked promotion from expatriates, which makes them have a high sense of relative deprivation—though their demands usually center around localization of jobs rather than any fundamental changes. Still, most of the Union leadership came from this group, whose leadership was seen not to have been reactionary; rather, opinion was divided between those who wished to support the mass demand by organizing a strike soon after it actually occurred, and those who favored pursuing wage demands with the help of Labor Office mediation. In addition, nearly all this Union leadership lost their jobs after the strike.

The Phikwe strike has thus shown that the central contradiction in the international political economy today involves monopoly capital and the "Third World poor." In Botswana's case this is all of Stratum A and the poor and middle peasants. But it has also illustrated that to overcome this in the long term, it is both necessary and possible for the latter to form an alliance with (1) the skilled workers, albeit they are a labor aristocracy, and (2) at least some segments of the lower level bureaucratic bourgeoisie.

NOTES

1. One Pula equaled One Rand, which equaled 1.16 U.S. dollars when Botswana acquired her own currency in August 1976. Pula (P) replaces Rand (R) throughout the paper. In 1969, Botswana's GDP was P48 million, and total exports in 1970 were only P16 million (Ostrander, 1974:535).

2. Cf. Lewis (1974) and Silitshena (1976) for much of the empirical data of the financial networks described later.

3. This account draws on participant observation and interviews in 1976, when the author was engaged in another research project concerning Phikwe workers migration from and economic linkages with the rural areas (160 life histories were collected). For the strike, *Botswana Daily News* reports in July-August 1975 were used, as were unpublished notes by Diane Cooper who interviewed some of the strikers.

4. Dismissal figures, etc., are from the Labor Officer, Phikwe.

5. These eight registered unions were (1) Central Government, (2) Local Government, (3) General Commerce, (4) Construction, (5) Mining, (6) Meat Industry, (7) Railways, and (8) Banks (Simkins, 1975:30).

6. The empirical data is derived from, in particular, works by Schapera, Kuper, Comaroff, Legassick, Parsons, Tlou (cf. Schapera, 1976: Select Bibliography).

7. Only the Tawana (northwest) are not in the east of the country (straddling the railway line) where over 80% of Botswana's population live. Kalahari Desert spans much of the west and center.

8. Certain significant changes, e.g, some permanent settlement of the lands, emergence of matrifocal households, etc., cannot be discussed here.

9. That is, 77,658 out of 501,328, computed from Botswana Central Statistics Office (1972:97,113).

10. Botswana Central Statistics Office (1976c:88). Despite problems (e.g., response error), this survey was rigorous, covering 1,800 out of the 93,000 rural households each month for one year. The income is "Gross Available Income" to the household after deducting "running expenses" (e.g., cost of seed, taxes). It includes among other items income in kind, livestock income in terms of a "weight gained" concept and imputed rental benefit from own hut.

11. Sir Seretse Khama, BDP leader, had actually been deposed from the Ngwato chieftainship by the administration in 1949, after South African pressure, because of his marriage to a white woman.

12. Cf. Bienefeld and Innes (1976) for a useful discussion of "national" versus "international" capital.

13. In line with Botswana's nonracial policies, the census only enumerated "citizenship" (Botswana Central Statistics Office, 1976a: Table 01). The 1,200 is a rough estimate based on the simplifying assumption that all "Rhodesian" citizens in Table 01 were African refugees and all "South Africans" were whites.

14. Government proclaimed policy derives from consultant Professor Ghai (1971) and Botswana Government Paper (1972), and is embodied in the National Development Plan 1973-1978. The paradigm seeks to maintain government/private sector wage parity and prevent urban/rural disparity, thereby hoping to stem migration and unemployment and also release state revenues for rural development instead of into urban wages. Price control policy on certain consumer goods exist. Incomes policy exempts contract expatriates, though localization/training policies nominally exist.

15. This information is derived from Botswana Central Statistics Office (1976b:2). Agriculture equals 189 commercial farms only; state sectors equal central and local government and education. Parastatals equal electricity, water, plus 1,500 meat industry workers (subtracted from manufacturing). Domestic servants figure is taken from Society and Economy Tables (1976:283). For P1-P100: P101-200: above P200, ratios dealt with later, see Botswana Central Statistics Office (1976b:4), but parastatals excludes meat industry.

16. Based on figures from Botswana Central Statistics Office (1976a: Table 13); Phikwe Labor Office Survey, August 1976; and interviews of nearly every employing organization, September 1976.

17. Obtained from a breakdown of 2,432 BCL workers' employment cards, Personnel Department records, February 1976.

18. All BCL and state sector wage structures are from Bamangwato Concessions Limited (1975) and Botswana Ministry of Local Government and Lands (1974). Both sectors raised all levels about 20% in 1976.

19. See Botswana Shashe Project Management Unit (1969) correspondence from September 24, 1969, to March 18, 1970. However, the new government policy (e.g., next Sua Pan mining project) stresses much more the interspersing of site and service, low, medium and high cost housing.

20. "Bureaucratic bourgeoisie" is not an entirely satisfactory term, but it is preferred to "new petty bourgeoisie" because (1) the latter usage involves concepts of "productive labor" (Poulantzas, 1975:207-223) not accepted here, and (2) "class situation" throughout this chapter refers to appropriation of the economic product (irrespective of "surplus" existing or not) by different laboring and/or nonlaboring groups, with "surplus value" appropriation by nonlaboring owners of capital treated as a special case of this more general paradigm.

21. In Phikwe, they are chiefly dressmakers, skin curers, builders, thatchers, carpenters, watch, shoe, bicycle, and car repairers, metal workers, and traditional doctors.

22. For the nature and composition of the membership of this "extended economic household unit" straddling the urban and rural areas, see Cooper (1977).

23. Detailed rural class analysis is not possible here. *Rough* estimates concerning cattle, which are the crucial element, are that five cattle are needed for ploughing and, according to agricultural department estimates (Holm, 1976:457), around 25 cattle are needed to sustain an average household without other income sources, i.e., 25 cattle equal middle peasants. Botswana Central Statistics Office (1976c:90) treats a household owning 80 cattle as equivalent to a P200 per monthly salary (i.e., Stratum C.1), i.e., 25-80 cattle equal rich peasants, after which capitalist farmers emerge. This survey (1976c:111) estimated 45% of rural households owned no cattle at all and 39% owned 1-25 head, though it admits (1976c:303) these estimates are possibly 5-10% high because people are reluctant to admit their cattle holdings.

24. For example, staff grades left the Botswana Local Government Workers Union and formed the Botswana Local Government Workers Union and formed the Botswana Unified Local Government Service Association after they, but not the industrial class, were transferred to employment by the Unified Local Government Service rather than by local councils.

25. While this might have been a "concession" on the Copperbelt, preindependence, the memorandum does not make it clear that this is obligatory for BCL in terms of the (1969a) Trade Unions Act.

26. The Phikwe section fo the BMWU consists of a Branch Committee (10), all full time BCL employees elected at the annual AGM by a show of hands of paid up union members. Some of this committee and other union members representing various departments are coopted onto a Bargaining Committee (10). After the strike the institutionalization of shop stewards and works committees has been speeded up by the new BCL manager.

27. This data is from the BCL Personnel Department, which had received it from the Anglo American Johannesburg office, i.e., close comparisons are kept. South African daily

rates have been converted here to monthly (26 day) rates, and these 1975 rates are considerably higher than those of a few years earlier on the South African mines.

28. The figures and information on circulation of jobs are taken from the BCL Personnel Department, November 1976, and interviews.

REFERENCES

Bamangwato Concessions Limited (1975). Local employees wage schedule, 1st July. Selebi Phikwe: Personnel Department, mimeo.

BEST, A.C.G. (1970). "General trading in Botswana, 1890-1968." Economic Geography, 46(4):598-611.

BIENEFELD, M., and INNES, D. (1976). "Capital accumulation and South Africa." Review of African Political Economy, 7:31-55.

Botswana Central Statistics Office (1972). Report of the population census 1971. Gaborone: Government Printer.

_____ (1976a). Report of the census of Selebi-Pikwe. Gaborone: Government Printer.

_____ (1976b). Employment survey (August 1975). Gaborone: Government Printer.

_____ (1976c). The rural income distribution survey in Botswana 1974/75. Gaborone: Government Printer.

_____ (1976d). Statistical bulletin. September,1(2).

Botswana Daily News (1975a). "Illegal strikes in Botswana. President's worry." July 31.

_____ (1975b). "Strike trial leaves 53 in jail." December 10.

Botswana Government Paper (1972). National policy on incomes, employment, prices and profits. No.2. Gaborone: Government Printer.

_____ (1975). National policy on tribal grazing land. No.2. Gaborone: Government Printer.

Botswana Ministry of Local Government and Lands (1974). Circulr to councils No. 4. Ref. L.G. 1/4/20 I. May 21. Selebi Phikwe Town Clerk's Office.

Botswana Shashe Project Management Unit (1969). "Township 1968," File No.7. Gaborone: SPMU Office files.

Botswana Sua Project Management Unit (1975). Sociological and housing attitudes studies for planning of Dukwe township 1975. Gaborone: Government Printer.

Budget Speech (1977). Reprinted in Botswana Daily News. March 8.

COOPER, D.M. (1977). "Some initial perspectives and findings on the Selebi Phikwe mining community migration patterns and economic networks." Rural Sociology Report, No.2, Botswana Ministry of Agriculture.

GHAI, D.P. (1971). A long term wages policy for Botswana. Gaborone: Government Printer.

HALPERN, J. (1965). South Africa's hostages. Middlesex: Penguin Books.

HERMANS, Q. (1974). "Towards budgetary independence: A review of Botswana's financial history, 1930 to 1973." Botswana Notes and Records, 6:89-115.

HOLM, J.D. (1976). "Basic trends in Botswana rural development: The political dimension." Paper presented at the annual meeting of the African Studies Association (U.S.A.), November 1971. Reprinted pp.450-464 in D.L. Cohen and J. Parson (eds.), Politics and society in Botswana (vol. 2) (1976). Gaborone: U.B.S. Readings, Dept. of Political Science and Administrative Studies, University of Botswana and Swaziland.

INNES, D., and O'MEARA, D. (1976). "Class formation and ideology: The Transkei region." Review of African Political Economy, 7:69-86.

KUPER, A. (1970). Kalahari village politics. Cambridge: University Press.

Laws of Botswana (1969a). The trade unions act. No.28. Gaborone: Government Printer.

_____ (1969b). The trade disputes act No.28. Gaborone: Government Printer.

LEGASSICK, M., and WOLPE, H. (1976). "The Bantustans and capital accummulation in South Africa." Review of African Political Economy, 7:87-107.

LEWIS, D.H. (1974). "The theory and practice of direct foreign investment in less developed countries—A study of copper-nickel mining in Botswana." Unpublished M.A. thesis, University of Cape Town.

Master Agreement between the Republic of Botswana and Bamangwato Concessions Limited and Botswana RST Limited and BCL (Sales) Limited (1972). File No. Sua 10/4, Shashe Project Agreements, Sua Project Management Unit Office, Gaborone.

OSTRANDER, F.T. (1974). "Botswana nickel-copper: A case study in private investment's contribution to economic development." Pp. 534-549 in J. Barratt, S. Brandt, D.S. Collier and K. Glaser (eds.), Accelerated development in Southern Africa. London: Macmillan Press Ltd.

PARSONS, Q.N. (1974). "Economic history of Khama's country in Southern Africa." African Social Research, 18(December):643:673.

_____ (1976). "Shots for a Black Republic? Simon Ratshosa and Botswana Nationalism." Pp. 123-132 in D.L. Cohen and J. Parson (eds.), Politics and Society in Botswana (vol. 2) Gaborone: U.B.S. Readings, Dept. of Political Science and Administrative Studies, University of Botswana and Swaziland.

POULANTZAS, N. (1975). Classes in contemporary capitalism. London: New Left Books.

PUISANO (1973a). "Strike ended, Masilo out." January 19. Selebi Phikwe newspaper, publication halted. Copies, Selebi Phikwe Library.

_____ (1973b). "Comment." February 6.

_____ (1973c). "BCL and BMWU sign agreement." July 13.

SCHAPERA, I. (1947). Migrant labour and tribal life. London: Oxford University Press.

_____ (1952). The ethnic composition of Tswana tribes. London: The London School of Economics and Political Science.

_____ (1976). The Tswana. London: International African Institute.

SILITSHENA, R.M.K. (1976). Mining and the economy of Botswana. Working paper No.8. Gaborone: National Institute for Research in Development and African Studies Documentation Unit.

SIMKINS, C. (1975). "Labour in Botswana." South African Labour Bulletin, 2(5):28-35.

SKLAR, R.L. (1975). Corporate power in an African state. Berkeley: University of California Press.

SMIT, P. (1970). Botswana: Resources and development. Pretoria: Africa Institute of South Africa.

Society and Economy Tables (1976). Prepared by Central Statistics Office as part of 1976-1981 Botswana National Development Plan. Reprinted pp. 272-293 in D.L. Cohen and J. Parson (eds.), Politics and society in Botswana (vol. 2). Gaborone: U.B.S. Readings, Dept. of Political Science and Administrative Studies, University of Botswana and Swaziland.

Speech by His Excellency the President Sir Seretse Khama, Addressing Workers at Selebi-Pikwe 19th December, 1975. Gaborone: Government Printer.

STEVENS, R.P. (1976). "The establishment of the Bechwanaland Protectorate." Pp. 28-38 in D.L. Cohen and J. Parson (eds.), Politics and society in Botswana (vol. 2). Gaborone: U.B.S. Readings, Dept. of Political Science and Administrative Studies, University of Botswana and Swaziland.

ABOUT THE CONTRIBUTORS

Gerard Althabe is a former researcher in Sociology at l'Office de la Recherche Scientifique et Technique (ORSTON). He has done fieldwork in the The French Congo from 1959 to 1963 and from 1963 to 1972 in Madagascar. More recently he has been interested in workers living in the suburbs of Paris and Nates. He has published *Oppression et liberation dans l'imoginaise* (Maspero, 1969) and *Les fleurs du Congo* (Maspero, 1972).

Dianne Bolton obtained her first degree in history and politics from the University of Bradford. After teaching for three years at the Cleveland Technical College, U.K., she spent the year 1972-1973 in Kenya and Tanzania followed by graduate work at the Centre of West African Studies, University of Birmingham. She is currently completing her Ph.D. on the sisal plantation workers of Tanzania.

Robin Cohen has lectured at the Universities of Ibadan and Birmingham and held visiting appointments at Berkeley, Mauritius, and Toronto. He is presently Professor of Sociology at the University of the West Indies, Trinidad. He has long-standing interests in labor problems and has published *Labour and Politics in Nigeria* (1974) and *The Development of an African Working Class* (co-edited, 1975). While continuing his research on comparative labor questions with reference to Britain and Mexico, he has also begun work on the study of small island societies.

Jean Copans has studied and worked in Paris and has conducted fieldwork in the Ivory Coast and Senegal. He teaches at l'Ecole des Hautes Etudes en Sciences Sociales, where he has been since 1970; he has also taught at the Johns Hopkins University and at l'Universite Laval in Quebec. His main interest is in the history and criticism of anthropological theory and practice and in the nature of ideology. He published *Critique et Politique de l'Anthropologie -Anthropologie et Imperialisme,* on the Murid Brotherhood in Senegal, *Sechereses et Famines du Sahel,* on problems of the Sahel, and with N. Auge he has co-edited the collection *Dossiers Africaines.*

David Cooper is a Research Associate at the University of Birmingham. His current work concerns the emergence of a working class in Botswana.

Robert Davies is a graduate student at the University of Sussex, England, completing a thesis entitled "Capital, the State and White Wage Earners: An Historical Materialist Analysis of Class Formation and Class Relations in South Africa 1900-1960." He was brought up in South Africa where he attended Rhodes University and graduated with a degree in economics in 1969. Prior to beginning his research studies he taught development studies at a secondary school in Botswana. He has published articles on questions relating to the class structure of South Africa and paricularly the question of white labor in *New Left Review, The Journal of Southern African Studies,* and the *Review of African Political Economy.*

Myron J. Echenberg is an Associate Professor at McGill University, where he teaches African History. He was for several years co-editor of the *Canadian Journal of African Studies* and has published articles dealing with West Africa. He is preparing a full-length social history of the Francophone African soldier and veteran during the colonial period.

Peter C. W. Gutkind is Professor of Anthropology, McGill University. He obtained his M.A. at the University of Chicago and his Ph.D. at the University of Amsterdam. He has published widely and is Series Editor of the Sage Series on African Modernization and Development. His major interest is in African urban studies and labor history.

Arnold Hughes is Lecturer in Political Science at the University of Birmingham, where he is also attached to the Centre of West African Studies. His work has included research on colonial Lagos, the government and politics of the Gambia, and the influence of Garvey's ideas in Africa. He is the author of a number of articles on West African politics.

Michael Mason teaches African History at Concordia University Loyola Campus in Montreal. He has also taught at universities in Nigeria. He is presently co-editor of the *Canadian Journal of African Studies.* His major interest is in labor history in colonial Nigeria.

Sharon Stichter is Associate Professor of Sociology at the University of Massachusetts-Boston. She received her Ph.D. from Columbia University in 1972. She is the author of several articles on the history of trade unionism in Kenya, and is presently completing a monograph on the evolution of the working class movement there. Her next research project will be on women in the African labor force.

Jean Suret-Canale is often cast as the father of radical approaches to African studies in France. Agrege of Géography, he has taught in Senegal (1946-1949), in France (1949-1959), in Guinea (1959-1963) and now in Alergia (Oran). He has been a researcher at the Centre National de la Recherche Scientifique (C.N.R.S.) and for some time the Vice-Director of the Centre d'Etudes et de Recherche Marxiste (CERM). He has "introduced" African societies to the discussion of the Asiatic mode of production. His main publication is his three-volume work on West Africa which has been widely acclaimed. He is also the author of *la Republique de Guinée* (Ed. Sociales, 1970).

.